THE OPTIMIST'S GUIDE TO HISTORY

DORIS FLEXNER

AVON BOOKS ◆ NEW YORK

For Jenn and Geoff
with love
MOMOX

THE OPTIMIST'S GUIDE TO HISTORY is an original publication of Avon Books. This work has never before appeared in book form.

AVON BOOKS
A division of
The Hearst Corporation
1350 Avenue of the Americas
New York, New York 10019

Library of Congress Cataloging in Publication Data:

Flexner, Doris.
  The optimist's guide to history / Doris Flexner.
     p.   cm.
1. Chronology, Historical.   I. Title.
D11.F59   1995   94-47825
902'.02—dc20   CIP

First Avon Books Trade Printing: June 1995

ACKNOWLEDGMENTS

This book would have taken twice as long to write were it not for my crew of researchers, who spent hours in various libraries compiling the facts for the entries. My special appreciation goes to Nancy Connell for her work in the fields of medicine and science and for tracking down everything else I threw at her. My gratitude to Rosalia McKay for her expertise in the theater arts, and to Kimberly Johnson for her research in the area of education as well as the people, heroes, and legends category. A thank you, also, to Joan Jackson Hill for her contributions, and last, but not least, I would like to thank my daughter, Jennifer, my research arm in England, for her help and support. It is my fervent hope that you are still optimists.

I am also grateful to my former editor, David Highfill, who, when I somewhat facetiously suggested we do this book as a sequel to *The Pessimist's Guide to History,* took me seriously.

INTRODUCTION

The word *optimiste* appeared in a French dictionary in 1752, and was defined as someone who believes in the metaphysical principle of optimism. The principle was propounded by the German philosopher, mathematician, and world-class genius Gottfried Leibnitz, who wrote in his *Essais de théodicée* that our world is the best of all possible worlds and referred to his philosophy by the Latin word *optimum*, meaning the best. It took only a few years for *optimiste* to cross the channel where the English dropped the *e* and broadened its definition to mean someone who looks on the bright side of things and always hopes for the best. It was another eighty years or so before we lexicographically became pessimists.

Whether you agree with Leibnitz or not, our world is an astounding place. Just the fact that the earth is here and we are living on it is mind-boggling. After our planet settled into its niche in the galaxy, it bubbled and blipped and gradually cooled for about a billion years. Then when the chemical mix was right, minute creatures began to stir. Over millions of years these single-cell organisms developed into more complex life forms. Coral and horseshoe crabs, mollusks and bony fish appeared in the oceans. Tiny plants and mosses gradually formed, and eventually conifers and palms dotted the landscape. Sea creatures made their way to land and soon lizards, birds, and dinosaurs roamed the earth. Mammals evolved; hominids developed from primates, and one day we were human. Gradually our skull capacity grew to accommodate our brain and our intelligence increased until we are now known as *Homo sapiens sapiens:* wise, rational, thinking beings.

Although humans have been around for a very short period of time in the scheme of things, our accomplishments have been amazing. We invented tools for hunting and farming and developed agriculture. We learned to weave, bake, and build shelters. Small family groups banded together and became tribes, then nations, and we devised laws to govern ourselves. Commerce began so we created numbers, pictographs, and alphabets for writing the languages we spoke. We developed cultures, learned to play music, sing, dance, paint, sculpt, and build cathedrals, palaces, and great cities. Curiosity about our world turned us into astronomers, mathematicians, philosophers, and scientists. Brave men ventured forth into the unknown as we explored the Earth and discovered new worlds. Our inventions include amazing devices from simple quill pens to typewriters and computers, from thermometers to stethoscopes and CAT scanners, from the wheel to chariots and automobiles. Our engineering feats are astounding: we built pyramids, aqueducts, cathedrals, bridges, tunnels, skyscrapers, and spaceships. We conquered plagues and diseases and discovered cures for infections. Along the way we also took time out for recreation, to create games and play sports, develop the theater, devise musical instruments, and relax and enjoy ourselves. There seems to be no end to our inventiveness. And when disaster strikes—earthquakes tumble our buildings, fire ravages our cities, or floods overwhelm the land—we pick ourselves up, rise from the ashes like the mythical phoenix, reclaim the land, and rebuild our cities. We are dauntless.

As rational, thinking beings we have produced great minds and talents who have left their mark on civilization: Confucius, Plato, Leonardo da Vinci, Shakespeare, Mozart, Marie Curie, Edison, and Einstein to name but a few. They have shaped our world and our cultures, inspired us with their ideas, brought us joy and laughter, and advanced our knowledge.

Of course, we aren't perfect. We do have our faults—major and minor. We haven't quite figured out how to live together peacefully, and some among us are power hungry and greedy. There are still ill and starving people in the world and those who lack shelter. But since the first naked humans stared at fire and gaped at the heavens in wonderment, we have accomplished much. We will solve these problems. We have always done the impossible.

DORIS FLEXNER
FEARRINGTON VILLAGE, NORTH CAROLINA, 1995

DESCRIPTIONS OF EVENTS

15 Billion Years Ago, More or Less: The Beginning. A tiny particle of dense hot matter floats in a void. Suddenly, in a cataclysmic eruption that not even Hollywood wizardry could duplicate, the speck spontaneously explodes, hurtling hydrogen and helium into space. Out of this incomprehensible burst of energy, the universe, as we know it, forms and time begins. Awesome!

Instruments on the Cosmic Background Explorer satellite launched in 1989 indicate that 99.97 percent of the radiant energy in the cosmos was discharged within a year of the explosion. As these gases begin to condense, stars are created, including our sun, formed from the center of a cloud of hydrogen and particles of debris from other stars about 4.49 billion years ago. Other parts of the cloud, cooler and not as dense, broke off and formed the planets of our solar system. In 1970 Roger Penrose and Stephen Hawking, British astrophysicists, proved the Big Bang theory mathematically based on Einstein's Theory of Relativity.

In 1929 the American astronomer Edwin Hubble (who will later have the space telescope named for him) discovered the universe is expanding. The theory that it will continue to expand is called the Open Universe. On the other hand, like a yo-yo on a string, it may just be pulsating and will one day collapse in upon itself into a tiny speck again. Known as the Big Crunch, this is the Closed Universe theory.

The satellite ROSAT recently discovered in an obscure galaxy an immense cloud of gas with a mass greater than five hundred billion suns that is being held in place by an enormous gravitational force. According to astronomers, this may indicate that the universe is closed and is not going to keep expanding and that gravity will eventually grind it to a halt. It will take as long to collapse as it did to expand, and since it's still expanding, we have nothing to worry about, at least for another forty billion years or so.

Ca. 4.5 Billion Years Ago: The Earth. Our somewhat pear-shaped planet zips around the sun at sixty-seven thousand miles per hour while we settle in place, becoming the fifth largest planet; third from the sun.

For five hundred million years the earth's interior, composed of iron, silicates (the rock-forming minerals), and small quantities of elements, remained solid at about a relatively cool two thousand degrees Fahrenheit. As millions of years elapsed, energy was released by radioactive decay; the earth gradually heated up and melted some of its components. The iron melted first and sank to the center, forming a core. This forced up the silicates, and around the core a rather stable crust of solid rock arose as the earth cooled. All the while the planet quaked and shook and exploded in chaos as volcanoes spewed lava into the air and gigantic tremors rent the earth. The depressions caused by the great upheavals collected water rising from the interior through fissures, and soon there were oceans to go with the mountains. Tens of millions of years of tumult finally produced the earth as we know it today, a surface of 196,949,970 square miles, three quarters of it water. An astonishing tour de force!

Ca. 4.5 Billion Years Ago: The Moon. As our solar system was evolving, all kinds of debris left over from the original Big Bang was still spinning, crashing, and streaking around the universe like a giant fireworks display gone berserk. A huge projectile collided with the earth with such force that it ejected earthly material out into space and formed the moon. Mother Earth now had an offspring, literally.

The giant-impact hypothesis, first proposed in 1975, now seems to be the consensus among scientists based on the examination of rocks and material brought back from the moon missions. There have been a few other theories as to how the moon got where it is, such as the capture hypothesis, whereby the moon got caught up in our gravity as it came speeding by, or the fission hypothesis, which states that an extraordinarily fast-spinning earth bulged at the equator, and suddenly off shot the moon. A third theory postulates that the earth and the moon formed simultaneously from the same cloud of gas and dust.

Fortunately for us, we are bathed in moonglow every night. What would all of those poets and songwriters have done without it?

Ca. 3.5 Billion Years Ago: Life. The earth's atmosphere was nothing but a mass of gases fuming and foaming around the hot crust while the combustible planet erupted and roiled. Not a place conducive to life-forms. After a while things began to cool and calm down and the level of oxygen rose. Suddenly a blip. Something was "alive." A single-cell creature that would replicate itself until there were millions and billions of them, and then they would combine into multicelled organisms and gradually become more and more complex. The beginnings of life. A miracle.

Ca. 228 Million Years Ago: Dinosaurs: The earliest of these saurian creatures are roaming the earth at this time in what is now Argentina. Their primitive lizard ancestors had already been around for a few million years. Now they are getting bigger, and bigger, and bigger.

The word *dinosaur* comes from the Greek *deinos,* meaning "terrifying, frightful," and *sauros,* "lizard," and magnificently awesome beasts they were. If you were asked to create an imaginary monster, could you invent one more frightening than Tyrannosaurus rex, a twenty-foot-tall, forty-foot-long, eight-ton carnivore with a four-foot-long head full of enormous sharp teeth? T. rex was not the largest dinosaur; paleontologists in Utah have excavated a 140-foot-long sauropod (that's a herbivorous dinosaur) they call Seismosaurus, from the Greek word for "shake" or "quake," because that's what they figure the earth must have done with every step the creature took.

What were they like, these creatures that inhabited the earth for an astounding 165 million years and dominated it for almost as long? We now believe that some of them were warm-blooded and others may have had a variable metabolism. They were perhaps brightly colored, and may have sported spots or stripes. We think they were social creatures and traveled in groups—clusters of footprints have been found—and some of them could get up to a speed of fifteen to twenty miles an hour, faster than a human. Many of the herbivorous dinosaurs apparently cared for their young, and perhaps a few of the carnivores, too.

New dinosaur fossils and species are being found constantly, most recently in Antarctica, and we may one day know more about these spectacular creatures than we do now. They died out rather suddenly (as paleontological time goes) about sixty-five million years ago. We aren't sure why, although there are several theories. Some scientists think dinosaurs were beginning to become extinct anyway. Others believe that a huge asteroid crashed to earth, killing all vegetation, and the dinosaurs starved. A recent theory postulates that the amount of oxygen in the atmosphere depleted gradually over a few hundred thousand years and the dinosaurs couldn't adapt. It would seem likely that changes in the topography and climate of the earth that would affect the food chain hastened their extinction. Maybe it was just time for the mammals to take over. On the other hand, they may not be completely extinct. Birds and dinosaurs are related somewhere on the evolutionary chain. So just be careful around the chicken coop.

40 Million Years Ago: Cats. The ancestors of those furry independent creatures adored by ailurophiles are slinking across the terrain at this time. Fossils of a creature called a *Dinictis* have been unearthed, and they are amazingly like our modern-day cats. The *Dinictis* had a small brain, retractable claws, catlike teeth, and was about the size of a lynx. From this cat sprang the now extinct saber-toothed tigers, and along a different evolutionary line appeared the pumas, cougars, jaguars, and others, including our house cats.

Exactly when cats became domesticated is hard to say. They couldn't be trained to hunt like dogs and they aren't particularly sociable, so they must have just hung around doing nothing but silently hunting for themselves and keeping the rats out of the grain. Some early civilizations worshiped them as gods; later civilizations reviled them as the devil.

Deified or vilified, these self-reliant creatures still like to revert to their ancestral urge to prowl at night and are quite happy just to laze around during the day. They have had a lot of practice.

Ca. 4 Million Years Ago: This Thing Called Love. Cole Porter wrote a song about it imploring a couple to fall in love just like the birds, bees, fleas, goldfish, chimpanzees, and even hippopotami do. Love is, after all, what makes the world go round; it's why we are still here on earth along with all the other creatures.

On a more prosaic level, love can be defined as a rip-roaring rush of hormones that attracts two humans to each other. Nature knew what she was doing; for the species to survive, it must propagate itself. When we stood up on two feet and gazed into each other's eyes, when we began to act on reason rather than instinct, nature gave us that extra biological urge and shot us full of hormones just to make sure we would still reproduce ourselves. Love entered our lives in the form of phenylethylamine, dopamine, norepinephrine, endorphins, and oxytocin.

Whatever it is, that lovin' feelin' is here to stay. But in case the endorphins are a little sluggish, a bottle of champagne, a dozen roses, and a five-pound box of chocolates wouldn't hurt.

2 Million Years Ago: We Make Tools. Our scientific name for one of the very early humans, *Homo habilis,* means "handy or adaptable man." These ancient ancestors of ours were the first to make tools. They were very crude and made out of stone. We are thinking, inventive beings.

1.5 Million–500 thousand Years Ago: Homo Erectus. The next stage in human development brought us thinking beings who made hand axes, built dwellings of branches with stones or animal skins for floors, and crafted wooden spears and bowls. They had also learned one more important skill. They were able to control fire—not make it, but control it. They saw fire in natural gas, when lightning struck or volcanoes erupted, and one day a fearless human captured it for the first time and put it to use. Fire now kept them warm, lit their caves, and cooked their food.

1 Million Years Ago: Clothing. It's hard to date exactly when we humans starting wearing clothing or why we thought we had to. Early civilizations began in warm climates, and modesty is a cultural convention unknown at the time; therefore, some anthropologists theorize that one purpose may have been protection from insect bites. One of the main reasons, however, was probably vanity. Clothing distinguishes us from each other and can separate us into distinct classes and divisions. Throughout history, laws have been passed regarding dress in order to maintain this hierarchy of rank, class, and wealth. The chief wears the feathered hat, the admiral the most gold braid, prostitutes must wear yellow, peasants cannot wear buttons, only a knight's wife may wear ermine. However it started, the wearing of clothing eventually developed into fashion, which was brought to ridiculous heights in Europe between the sixteenth and nineteenth centuries.

The first article of clothing, if you can call it that, was probably a belt. This comes in handy because you can hang things from it, like pouches, or tuck a piece of flint in it, or later hang your sword from it, or the keys to the castle. We are still wearing belts, mostly for style, sometimes to hold up our trousers, and still to hang things from, as many workmen do. The first clothing to cover the body was undoubtedly an animal skin. We can only imagine how this came about. After a dinner of roasted meat, the animal skin may have served as a blanket until someone got the bright idea of draping it over his body and wearing it all day. Skins provided warmth and allowed humans to travel farther afield into colder climates. In other parts of the world, grasses served as body coverings when needed. When we learned how to weave, we began making cloth out of wool and flax and were soon fashioning tunics, which were the garments of choice in one form or another until the fifteenth century A.D.

Ancient Egyptian men wore a short wraparound linen skirt, which later developed into a longer style. In the eighteenth dynasty, about 1400 B.C., a triangular loincloth was sometimes worn under the skirt, which you might say was the first underwear. It was about this time that the shirt was fashioned out of a piece of folded cloth sewn up the sides with a hole cut in the fold for the head. Women wore tight linen skirts with wide suspenders and in later dynasties began wearing a draped robe similar to a toga. The peasants in the field, however, wore nothing except for the occasional loincloth. The ancient Mesopotamians wore tunic-type garb of wool or linen and had learned how to make tassels for decorations. Over their tunics they wore shawls for warmth; the wider the shawl, the higher the rank. Art from the Cretan civilization of about three thousand B.C. depicts noblewomen wearing a more complicated style of dress with long, bell-shaped skirts and sleeveless bodices. A thousand years later, this style had developed into a long fitted robe. In Greece, too, the tunic style of dress prevailed; it was called a *chiton,* and made out of linen or wool. Sometimes it was long and sometimes it was short, as fashion dictated. The later Greek women also had a garment called a *peplos,* a rectangular piece of material that could be worn over the *chiton* as a sort of cape. This clothing was later adopted by the Romans, who wore tunics and togas. Roman fashion was determined by rank and profession. Peasants, plebians, and slaves wore narrow, dark-colored coarse linen tunics while patricians were clothed in white wool. Various width stripes were worn by knights, magistrates, and senators. Throughout the history of Rome, the toga remained the dress of state for high officials and the emperor. So complicated did the draping of this garment become that the rich had special slaves to dress them.

The ancient Persians wore a coatlike garment and also breeches, the first people to do so. Trouser-type garments were worn until modern times by Persian and Turkish women, and still exist. The Japanese also wore two-piece outfits, with the men wearing trousers, and the women, skirts, while the early Chinese wore tunic garments called kimonos. In the Orient, too, rank determined style of dress.

After the fall of Rome, the toga disappeared and the tunic remained. The clothing of the Gauls and Germanic tribes melded with that of the Romans, and Europeans wore short tunics, usually of wool with trouserlike leg coverings crisscrossed with leather strips. The women wore a long, shapeless dress with long, wide sleeves and a tighter-fitting underbodice. This was the typical garment for the next thousand years until the feudal lords returned from the Crusades with silk and damask, and fashion began with a vengeance.

100 Thousand Years Ago: Homo Sapiens. The Latin name for rational man. We have developed the largest brain ever and we think abstractly as well as concretely. Of the two subspecies of *Homo sapiens,* Neanderthal man and *Homo sapiens sapiens,* it is the latter that survives and, fifty thousand years later, has expanded throughout the world.

With our intelligence we make better tools, sew clothing from animal skins using bone needles, shape clay, use spears for fishing and hunting, bury our dead, and create works of art. A nascent culture is in the making.

50 Thousand Years Ago: The Theater Begins? The origin of theater is lost in antiquity. However, it can be surmised that, based on cave wall drawings found in France, the resident

medicine man put on an animal mask and imitated the deer in a ritual designed to ensure plentiful hunting. You may not think of this as acting, but in essence it was. Primitive man probably embellished these ceremonies with dialogue, song, and dance, and expanded them to become forms of worship and myth, tragedy and comedy.

Religion and ritual played important parts in the development of Western theater. Greek tragedy can be traced back to the Dionysia, the spring festival held to worship the god of fertility and wine, Dionysus, or Bacchus as the Romans called him. The Romans later expanded on this with their Bacchanalian rites. The *thymele,* or altar to the god, was placed in the center of the dance floor known as the orchestra. The *dithyramb,* a fervently emotional hymn to Dionysus, was performed by the chorus in the orchestra area. (One might imagine that the greater the intake of wine, the more elaborate and frenetic the performance.) In the middle of the sixth century B.C., the Greek poet Thespis, credited with being the first actor and the reason all actors today are known as thespians, stepped from the chorus to assume the first role by exchanging dialogue with the leader of the chorus. Aside from giving us our word for actors, the Greeks also gave us our word for the place in which we watch the actors perform, the theater, from their word for a seeing or viewing place.

These religious rites led to broader imitations of epic poetry and heroic deeds. From these ritual plays, drama—tragedy and comedy—evolved. Playwrights such as the great tragedians Aeschylus, Sophocles, and Euripides, plus the great comedic playwrights Aristophanes and Menander, had their plays performed at the theater of Dionysus by the Acropolis. Eventually Athens sponsored great festivals, with prizes given to the best plays. Soon admission was being charged and annual prizes given, just like our Tony Awards today. The Greeks even had a form of pre-Broadway tryout in which their plays were performed in the provinces before being taken to the big time in Athens.

As the Greek civilization faded and the Romans came into power, the theater changed. While Greek theater was thought-compelling, Roman theater was sheer entertainment and quite businesslike. Troupes with actor-managers bought plays outright and produced them. Everything was very realistic to the point of holding bloody battle scenes in the theaters. Masks and costumes were worn, scenery was employed, the stage was raised, and by the first century A.D. a curtain had been added. Commercialism had taken over. The best known of the Roman playwrights are Terence and Plautus, who wrote comedies, and Seneca, the tragedian. The excesses of the theater finally became too much for the Christians, who thought, as we would say today, that the theater had no redeeming social value, and in the fifth century, after Christianity triumphed, the theaters were closed. By the end of the century the Roman Empire had fallen and the final curtain had come down on the theater. For the next thousand years it would remain down.

Ca. 12,000 B.C.: Man's Best Friend. The first dogs were probably domesticated around this time somewhere in Eurasia. Dogs are members of the genus *Canis,* which includes wolves, coyotes, and jackals. Varieties of wolves are found over most of the world, which makes the wolf the prime candidate for being the early ancestor of our dog. Early dogs no doubt crept out of the dark and scavenged around the caveman's campfire. It wasn't too long before we found out that dogs were good hunters as well as good hunting companions, and domestication for that purpose began. By this time several different breeds of dogs had already evolved, and around five thousand years ago we had hounds in the Near East such as the saluki, greyhound, and afghan. In Europe the spitz, mastiffs, and Saint Bernard developed, and another hound was the progenitor of the setters, beagles, and pointers, which hunt by scent. Terriers were trained to sneak into holes and attack foxes and badgers. Large dogs such as mastiffs were bred to protect property and to fight during war. And although it's hard to visualize a toy poodle evolving from the wolf, poodles were once used as hunters, as well as trick dogs in the circus.

Some dogs have become movie stars. Rin Tin Tin was one of them. Rescued by homebound American soldiers after World War I, the German shepherd made his debut in 1922. Whatever breed you fancy, dogs are companionable creatures and have been our loyal friends for thousands of years.

Ca. 10 Thousand Years Ago: Our Daily Bread. We don't know exactly when we started making and eating bread, but archaeologists have found the remains of breads made from barley and wheat in Swiss lake-dwelling sites from the Stone Age.

Breads can be made from many things, including wheat, corn, rye, millet, oats, barley, peas, rice, beans, and potatoes. Indians on the West Coast ground acorns, soaked the "flour" in hot water, then squeezed it into little cakes, which they dried in the sun. Ancient Sumerians made a flat bread of barley, ground sesame seeds, and onions, which is still eaten today in parts of the Middle East. Early breads were simply coarsely ground grain mixed with water, which was "baked" by placing it on hot stones and covering it with ashes. The ancient Egyptians raised barley and wheat and made flat barley cakes until they discovered, undoubtedly by accident, that if the dough is left to ferment, it would rise and form a lighter loaf. It was the first leavened bread. They were so happy about this that they built proper ovens in which to bake their new discovery. The Greeks and Romans eventually had many different kinds of bread, some of which was produced in public bakehouses and controlled by magistrates to assure purity and proper weight.

When the early colonists settled America, they ate bread made from cornmeal, water, and salt, and called it pone (from the Indian word *apan,* meaning "baked"), and when they added milk and eggs to the mixture, it became corn bread. They also had dark brown bread made from rye, cornmeal, molasses, and yeast, and when baking soda was added, they steamed the whole concoction and called it brown bread. If they used white flour rather than rye, it was called anadama bread. About 1850, baking powder was introduced to bakers, and in 1868 Charles Fleischmann began marketing his yeast cakes, which helped bakers produce a more uniform product.

Nowadays we can zip down to the market to pick up a loaf of bread and find anything from plain white, whole wheat, or sourdough, to crusty Italian and French, pita, tortillas, and everything in between. Or we can stay at home, make it ourselves, and savor the heavenly aroma of fresh-baked bread.

Ca. 8000 B.C.: We Learn to Weave. Although we don't know exactly when humans began weaving, by the end of the Stone Age they seem to have accomplished it. Perhaps some children sitting by a riverbank playing with reeds and grasses began to intertwine them and soon had formed a mat. They now had something to sleep on, to cover themselves with, to use as a wall or a door for a dwelling, and even to wear.

The earliest known looms were in existence by 4400 B.C. A depiction of a loom has been found on a bowl discovered in a woman's tomb in Egypt from that era. These were very simple devices, consisting of pegs in the ground on which the weaving was done by hand. Throughout the world different peoples had developed their own looms by this time, each differing slightly in form. It wasn't too long before these simple contrivances were made more complicated to facilitate the action of weaving and speed up the process. The Egyptians wove flax into linen, the Mesopotamians used wool, cotton was woven in India, and silk in China. Weaving cloth soon became one of our very earliest industries.

Ca. 6 Thousand Years Ago: Cosmetics. Vanity, thy name

is not just woman but man also. Archaeologists have unearthed palettes for mixing powder, vials containing oils and perfumes, and pots of unguents from tombs dating back thousands of years. The Egyptians were big on cosmetics (from the Greek word *kosmetikos,* relating to adornment; we didn't start calling it *makeup* until around 1800), and by 4000 B.C. cosmetics had become a big industry. The preferred shade of lipstick was blue-black, rouge was red, and eyeshadow usually green. Eyes were outlined, lashes darkened, and eyebrows exaggerated with black kohl, made from powdered antimony (sulfide). Henna was used to dye fingernails and palms of the hands as well as the feet, and fragrant oils were used lavishly.

The Greeks, on the other hand, went for naturalism and pre ferred their women that way, except for the courtesans, who painted their faces and lightened their hair with a compound of yellow flower petals, potassium salt, and pollen. You could say the blondes in ancient Greece definitely had more fun.

The Romans, both men and women, followed the Egyptians and painted, pomaded, and perfumed liberally once they got the knack of it. White lead and chalk were used to whiten the skin, and rouge was colored with cinnabar (red mercuric sulfide, a poisonous substance.) The Greeks and Romans also used a depilatory made with arsenic. For centuries people poisoned themselves unknowingly with their cosmetics.

The returning Crusaders brought back to Britain the toiletries of the Middle East harems, and these soon became popular among the fashionable. In the seventeenth century powder and beauty patches in various shapes adorned the faces of both men and women to distract attention from smallpox scars. When the priggish Cromwell came to power, such luxuries were dispensed with, along with the theater and other kinds of fun things, but as soon as Charles II regained the throne, things and faces brightened up again. By the 1790s, fashionable women had carried powdering their faces white to the extreme, and with red rouge on their cheeks and white wigs, they were said to resemble "skinned sheep." In 1770 an act was introduced into the British Parliament by some spoilsport providing "that all women of whatever age, rank, profession or degree, whether virgins, maids or widows, that shall, from and after such Act, impose upon, seduce, and betray into matrimony, any of his Majesty's subjects, by the scents, paints, cosmetic washes, artificial teeth, false hair, Spanish wool, iron stays, hoops, high heeled shoes, bolstered hips, shall incur the penalty of the law in force against witchcraft and like misdemeanors and that the marriage, upon conviction, shall stand null and void." It was subsequently defeated, but unfortunately the same act was passed by the Pennsylvania legislature, and the use of cosmetics was frowned upon in most of the United States except in the colonies influenced by the French. By Victorian times, the use of makeup was in disfavor and only used by those wicked women on the stage.

We can be grateful to the more liberal women in France for carrying on the practice of using makeup and to the French scientific community for developing and manufacturing the safe cosmetics we use today. By the end of World War I, attitudes towards makeup had begun to change and women once more began to enhance their appearance. Brand names like Guerlain, Coty, Lanvin, and Chanel were appearing in retail stores where one could now buy cosmetics ready-made rather than concocting them oneself. It has since developed into a billion-dollar industry.

Ca. 4000 B.C.: The Solar Calendar. The exact period when the Egyptians contrived a solar calendar is unsure, but it was probably around this time. It consisted of twelve months, each divided into three "weeks" of ten days each or thirty days in a month, for a total of 360 days a year. At the end of each year, they added on another five days. They based the first day of their calendar on the rising of the star Sirius, which corresponded with the rising of the Nile. Farmers planted and harvested their crops according to one of the three seasons noted by the calendar. The Egyptians gradually became aware that 365 days was not completely accurate, and that every four years Sirius rose a day later. They did attempt to fix this by inserting an extra day every four years, but by that time they were still somewhat off.

4000 B.C.: Beer Is Brewed. The ancient Egyptians claimed their god of agriculture, Osiris, taught them how to brew beer. This may explain why he later attained such importance among their deities. Divine or not, the process of brewing beer was also known to the Sumerians and Assyrians and may have been developed in Babylonia much earlier.

Since grains and yeast are the raw materials used in brewing, the process was frequently a baker's occupation. Barley was soaked in clay vats to allow it to germinate, during which time enzymes converted the grain's starches into sugars. The resulting mash was then ground and yeast was added. It was then formed into cakes and baked slightly, after which the cakes were crumbled into jars of water and allowed to ferment. About 1000 B.C. the Egyptians began flavoring their brew with hops.

The Greeks learned the art of brewing from the Egyptians, and the Romans from the Greeks. The people of northern Europe knew about brewing and drank a concoction of corn and honey akin to mead, an alcoholic drink made by fermenting honey and water. The Germanic and Nordic tribes of Europe as well as the Celts and Saxons of Britain were drinking beer by the early Christian era. During the early Middle Ages the brewing of beer was common in most large households and was done by women. As the monasteries grew, so did beer production, carried out by the monks, who greatly improved the process; and by the thirteenth century towns all over Britain had breweries that sold beer directly to local customers. Weak beer was drunk by everyone instead of water, which was contaminated in many areas. The Pilgrims landed where they did because they ran out of beer and were searching for water.

Brewing in America began in 1584 when the British made beer from maize in their Virginia colonies. In 1612 Dutch colonists established a brewery in lower Manhattan, and in 1683 William Penn established the first brewery in Pennsylvania. Around 1840 German immigrants began entering the country and introduced new methods of brewing lager beer, which soon became the foundation of the beer industry in the United States.

The next time you settle down with a brew to watch your favorite team on television, hoist one to Osiris.

4000 b.c.: Wine Making Established. Archaeologists have found remnants of grape seeds at ancient sites along the Mediterranean and at prehistoric settlements in Europe, suggesting that as long ago as 9000 b.c., the inhabitants of these areas gathered wild grapes. According to Genesis 9:20, Noah had planted a vineyard and then proceeded to imbibe a little too much. We do know that by 4000 b.c., *Vitis vinifera,* the best grape species for wine, was being grown in lands around the Middle East where they later developed the technique of mashing the grapes and fermenting the juice. Eventually wine became a major trading commodity among the civilizations in that area.

The Egyptians had already cultivated the species *Vinus sylvestris,* which grew along the Nile and the northern coast of Africa. Wine jars have been found in the tombs of nobles labeled by their various vintages, and some even bear the names of Syrian wine makers, who no doubt were held in high esteem.

The ancient Chinese drank wine made from millet and used it for making offerings to their ancestors. Overindulgence was discouraged, and rather than drink from a cup or bowl, they used small ladles, just to be on the safe side.

The Greeks invented the symposium, which literally means a "drinking party" (and demonstrates how meanings change over the years). It was a popular pastime in fifth century b.c. Athens among the wealthy. It usually followed a dinner and included intellectual conversation as well as drinking wine diluted by two or three parts water. It was not exactly a family affair since the only women invited were courtesans.

The Romans planted vineyards wherever they went, which was just about everywhere, and by the fifth century most of the well-known vineyards of modern-day Europe had been established, including those of Bordeaux, Burgundy, Moselle, and the Rhine. Unfortunately, after the fall of Rome, the Dark Ages descended upon Europe and the production and quality of wine fell precipitously, along with everything else, making wine an expensive luxury. Vines were still cultivated for local consumption, and with the rise of the Roman Catholic church, many of the great vineyards gradually came into its hands. Wine, of course, was used during mass, as well as for medicinal purposes and occasionally as a disinfectant. We can thank the efforts of the good monks for their tender loving care of the grapes and for the reappearance of good wine. During the twelfth century large vineyards were established and wine once again became an important commodity in international trade. Towards the end of the seventeenth century wine bottles and corks, rather than casks, became common, developed by Dom Perignon of champagne fame.

Three centuries later American marketing and packaging ingenuity developed the wine cooler.

Ca. 4000 B.C.: Fun and Games. We humans were no doubt playing games before this, but we can only speculate what they might have been. Children may have chased each other in a form of tag, drawn lines in the dirt and tossed pebbles in the squares, and thrown spherical objects at each other or up in the air.

The earliest game board, together with pieces used in its play, was found in an Egyptian tomb and dates to around 4000 B.C. In royal tombs of the ancient city of Ur in Mesopotamia, archaeologists have also found what appears to be a similar board game.

Paintings on Egyptian tombs from about 2700 B.C. depict people playing several different games. One of these is *senat* and is akin to the game found in Ur, with a game board and a drawer to hold the pieces. Variations of this game were also played by the Greeks and Romans. The modern version is what we call backgammon.

4000 B.C.: We Develop Writing. We began to write, or perhaps *print* is a better term, about six thousand years ago in Mesopotamia. It's one of our greatest achievements. Before writing we could communicate only by speech or gestures. Now we were beginning to develop a permanent method of recording our messages.

People had long been drawing abstract pictures on caves, in sand and dirt, on bones and clay. We were about to transfer this art into meaningful representation. The first writing was on clay tablets in the form of pictographs, or simple pictures, inscribed with reed "pens" and then baked. The Sumerians had a need to keep records of their business transactions and began keeping these records in ledger form. They soon devised a system of one sign for one word, and later the Babylonians advanced this wedge-shaped writing we call cuneiform, by giving it a syllabic form. Aside from record keeping, which was the main purpose of writing, we could now write down our stories and legends and our history. The Epic of Gilgamesh is the oldest story in the world and is known to have been written about 2000 B.C.

The next step in writing, at least in the Western world, was the invention of the alphabet. This system of notation seems to have arisen in various civilizations over the same period. By 1500 B.C. the Egyptians had an alphabet of twenty-four symbols, and various Semitic alphabets had their beginnings. The Phoenicians spread their version and the Greeks borrowed from them. It's from the name of the first two Greek letters, alpha and beta, that we derived the word *alphabet*. The Greek alphabet worked its way over to Italy and became Latinized. This alphabet had twenty-three letters, no *j*, *v*, or *w*. During the Middle Ages, the English alphabet divided the *i* into *i* and *j*, and the *u* into *u*, *v*, and *w*, for a total of twenty-six letters, which we use today.

There are other alphabets used throughout the world, such as the Greek, Cyrillic, and Arabic. Whatever system is used, the invention of writing has had a greater impact on advancing civilization than perhaps anything else. And it's certainly better than having to memorize everything you hear.

Ca. 3500 B.C.: The Wheel. We can only guess how or why the wheel was invented, but it may have been by a creative potter in Sumeria, for the first wheels were used in making pottery. Around this same time the Chinese had also developed and were using a wheel for the same purpose. It took another imaginative mind to figure out the wheel could be used for other functions.

Early wheels have been uncovered at archaeological sites of ancient cities in what are now Iraq and Iran. They were made from planks of wood, rounded at the edges and clamped together with clasps of copper. The axle was stationary and was attached to the wheel hub by linchpins. Later wheels were bound around the rims by metal hoops held in place by long metal clasps, which also helped to keep the wooden planks in position. It must have been a very bumpy ride.

Recent excavations in Russia and Kazakhstan have uncovered chariots, the sports cars of the ancient world, with multispoked wheels dating from about 2000 B.C. About this same time wheels with four spokes were being used in northern Mesopotamia. The new technology may have drifted from the North or it may have developed separately in each region. Five hundred years later spoked wheels were in use on chariots in Syria, Egypt, along the Mediterranean, and shortly thereafter, in China.

The idea of the wheel as a means of transportation apparently did not occur to the peoples of the Western Hemisphere or those in Southern Africa. Archaeologists have found clay figures of wheeled animals in Mexico dating back to 1000 A.D., but apparently wheels were never used as transportation until the Spaniards brought them to Western shores.

Ca. 3500 B.C.: The First Numbers. The most natural way to count is with our fingers, which is, of course, what we humans did for thousands and thousands of years whenever we had to count, which wasn't very often. When ten fingers became inadequate we began using pebbles and cutting notches on sticks. We had to call this system something, so we invented numbers. These numeral symbols seem to have appeared in Egypt about this time, and a few hundred years later in Mesopotamia. Early written numbers were short, straight lines (one line for one, two lines for two, etc.) with a special symbol for the number ten. The system was modeled on our ten fingers, which was only reasonable, and later became the basis for our decimal system. Of course, if you wanted to write fifty, you would have to write the symbol for ten five times. Since this got to be awkward after a while, the Greeks wrote a few special symbols for higher numbers, and later so did the Romans. Now five was V, ten was X, fifty was L, and one hundred was a C. It cut down on the number of strokes needed when you had to indicate a large number.

3500 B.C.: Bronze Discovered. It was probably an accidental discovery, but a fortuitous one. This combination of copper blended with tin was much more useful than just plain copper. It was easier to cast and had a better cutting edge.

Ca. 3000 B.C.: On Pins and Needles. Insignificant in the scheme of things, you might say, but the lowly pin and the needle are two of the most important household items we've ever had, especially since we started wearing clothing.

Cave people should be given credit for the invention, for it was no doubt one of them who first slung a couple of animal skins over a shoulder and stuck a piece of sharp bone through both pieces to hold it together. The idea caught on. These early people also had needles; archaeologists have found cave drawings depicting them, and artifacts of fish spines with holes for thread. About five thousand years ago, the Sumerians were using straight pins and needles created from bone and iron.

Pins were used for centuries as a means of fastening clothing together. Ancient Greeks and Romans pinned their robes at the shoulder with a *fibula,* a decorative clasp that is the precursor of our modern safety pin. Aside from their utilitarian purpose, elaborate straight pins were also used as jewelry in the hair or on the clothing, much as tie stickpins and hatpins were used in later centuries.

In medieval times in Europe, pins were made of wood, bone, ivory, brass, silver, and gold. Of course, they were all made by hand and so expensive that only the wealthy could afford them. The poor had to make do with wood. But then, their clothing wasn't as complex as the rich, who apparently used a record number of pins in their wardrobes. This sometimes created a shortage, which in turn drove up the price and caused hoarding. To remedy this, the British government, in its wisdom, passed legislation allowing pin makers to sell their goods only on certain days. Both upper- and lower-class women saved up to buy these costly items, and on the designated days rushed off to purchase them with their pin money. (And later, when pins became common and cheap, pin money began to mean money a husband gave to his wife for small expenditures.)

The French had supplied the English with pins for years, but in 1626 the Englishman John Tilsby began manufacturing them domestically, still by hand but with better equipment. With the advent of the industrial age, machine-made pins were being marketed by early in the nineteenth century. By this time, of course, the button had taken over and straight pins were used mainly by dressmakers. The modern safety pin made its appearance in America about 1849, based on the same principle as the ancient *fibula.* And it's come in handy ever since.

3000 B.C.: **Early Schools.** To children throughout America, summer is a time of fun, excitement, and most of all, no school. Take away an *m* and you have Sumer, a region in ancient Mesopotamia that was home to one of the first school systems in Western civilization. Around 3000 B.C., the Sumerians had organized schools, for boys only, with headmasters known as school fathers, teachers called big brothers, and clay tablet textbooks written in cuneiform. Imagine carrying your books home then! The subjects ranged from religion to literature and economics to administration. Classes lasted from sunrise to sunset, and boys attended school from early childhood to early adulthood. The school year was not set. The school father decided when the students would have time off, if they had any at all. This might explain why another first seems to have started in a Sumerian school. Among clay tablets unearthed in the area by archaeologists is an essay written by a Sumerian student. It is the oldest record ever discovered of a student trying to soft-soap his teacher.

Ca. 3000 B.C.: Dolls, Dolls, Dolls. Dolls have been made out of everything from wood, terra-cotta, ivory, corn husks, buckskin, china, bisque, cloth, fur, and most anything else you can think of, since time immemorial. Archaeologists haven't found any dolls in prehistoric graves, but that doesn't mean there were none, only that they were probably made out of a material that disintegrated with time. The earliest doll discovered is from ancient Babylon, is made of alabaster, and has movable arms. Egyptian graves dating to about 3000 B.C. have revealed dolls made out of painted wood with hair of clay or wooden beads. The ancient Greeks and Romans had dolls, some of them with arms and legs attached by pins so they could move or dance. Dolls are not always just toys, sometimes they are symbolic or are used in rituals, but whatever their purpose, they are found throughout the world in almost every ethnic group.

During the Middle Ages in Europe, dolls seem to have dropped out of fashion, but then it was a slow time for culture. Things picked up during the Renaissance, and soon dolls and dollhouses were again on the scene. The Germans and French were in the forefront of doll making: the Germans with their bisque and glazed porcelain heads for Dresden dolls, and the French with their fashion dolls. The golden age of dolls reached its zenith about 1890 when the bisque dolls, or china dolls, as many called them, were dressed in the ornate fashions of the day.

In the following decades cuddly baby dolls increased in popularity, and with advancing technology they became more and more lifelike to the point of being able to "wet" their diapers and "drink" out of a bottle. Given the choice, however, many a child would prefer to drag around and snuggle up to an old-fashioned rag doll than its more sophisticated counterpart.

Ca. 3000 B.C.: The Abacus.

Numerals were being used about this time, and people tended to count with stones because they were handy. The abacus probably evolved in Babylonia; some form of it was widely used by all ancient peoples. In sixth century B.C. China the abacus consisted of stones on strings similar to the beads on wires of abaci in use today. With this instrument people could add, subtract, multiply, and divide, and do it very quickly. A clever invention, it was the precursor of our modern calculators.

Ca. 5 thousand Years Ago: Egyptian Numbers.

The Egyptians based their numbers on a scale of ten, naturally. It makes one wonder how our system would have developed had humans had, say, five fingers on one hand and six on the other. The Egyptian method was very simple. A single stroke represented the number one, ten was denoted by what looks like an upside-down *u* (∩), one hundred looks like an apostrophe (૭), a lotus flower is one thousand, and so on up to one million.

As time went on these symbols became simpler and less repetitive. By about 2000 B.C. hieratic script was being used by scribes who wrote with pen and ink on papyrus. New symbols developed to note numbers. Four is no longer four vertical strokes, but a single horizontal one. Seven has evolved from seven strokes to a ૨. It takes less time to write and is more efficient.

Ca. 2600 B.C.: The Pyramids of Giza.

These wonders of the ancient world arose in the Egyptian desert to immortalize three kings, Cheops (Khufu), Khafra (Chephren), and Menkure. New technology, probably devised by the architect Imhotep, enables the Egyptian stonemasons to erect these magnificent structures without mortar and to move stones weighing up to five tons without heavy equipment. Khufu's tomb, known as the Great Pyramid, is considered by some to be the greatest building ever erected and contains over 2 million blocks of stone. It has an almost perfectly square base, covers a little over thirteen acres, and rises to a height of 481 feet. Five thousand years later the pyramids are looked upon as marvels of engineering and technology. They sure knew how to build things to last in those days.

Ca. 2600 B.C.: Weights and Balances. Commerce was developing; we needed to weigh everything from gold to livestock. We now use various-size blocks of stones as weights along with a primitive balancing system.

2500 B.C.: Higher Learning. The Sumerians had the first system for higher education. Their "Houses of Wisdom" can be called the first universities. The schools began to appear around 2500 B.C. and taught linguistics, theology, magic arts, medicine, astronomy, and mathematics. Religion played an important part in this system, and each House was associated with a temple.

Ca. 2500 B.C.: Egyptians Produce Papyrus. The manufacture of papyrus "paper" by cutting the long stems of the reedy papyrus plant, weaving the strips together, then soaking them in water, hammering them together, and drying the end result in the sun was begun about this time in Egypt. They had invented a new writing material that was used throughout the ancient world and into the medieval period in Europe. What is believed to be the oldest extant book in the world was written on papyrus during Egypt's Fifth Dynasty, about 2500 B.C. It was found in the tomb of King Neferirkare and consists of fragments of temple records listing payments in kind to priests in return for their services. Papyrus was portable, scrollable, lightweight, long lasting, and easy to store. Record keeping had become easier.

Ca. 4 Thousand Years Ago: Dice Games. Knucklebones (the anklebones of sheep) have been around since prehistory and were probably thrown in some kind of dice game, although they could have been used for religious purposes and for lotteries. Dice have been found in ancient Egyptian tombs dating from 2000 B.C. and were used by all ancient peoples in some form or other and by all societies throughout the world. During their long history, dice have been made from bone, ivory, wood, stone, metal, amber, jade, glass, and gems. Archaeologists have even discovered "crooked" dice in a few excavations. So, wherever one may be in the world, there is sure to be a game using dice, or someone shooting "craps," legally or otherwise. Before you play, be sure to check the dice.

Ca. 2000 B.C.: Ice Cream. During this era in history, the Chinese began milking farm animals, which must have been a radical idea at the time, and then had to do something with the results. They concocted a dish made from a soft paste of cooked rice and milk, added some spices, and packed it in snow to freeze it. The result was more of a milk ice, but it was the forerunner of our modern ice cream. Of course, it was only to be enjoyed by the wealthy. The Chinese also mixed fruit juices with snow, which would be akin to our sherbets, and the Greeks and later the Romans made ice cream from honey, fruit juice, and milk.

Making and eating ice cream seems to have faded into oblivion along with most things during the Dark Ages in Europe but perked up again when Marco Polo brought back recipes for milk ices from his travels in China. Once again they were only for the wealthy, and the recipes were closely guarded. When Catherine de Médicis married the future Henry II of France in 1553, her retinue included ice cream chefs who not only made fruit ices, but a semifrozen dessert made from thickened cream which was very much like our modern ice cream. It was a Spanish physician in Rome who discovered that saltpeter added to ice increased the speed of freezing, and soon the Florentines were serving solidly frozen concoctions.

Philadelphia was where ice cream began in the United States. Thomas Jefferson brought the recipe back with him from France, and Dolley Madison served it in the White House when she was the first lady. Soon ice cream houses were popping up all over Philadelphia. It was there that the ice cream soda originated in 1874. The ice cream cone came about during the 1904 World's Fair in St. Louis when an ice cream vendor ran out of paper dishes and "borrowed" a thin waffle from a neighboring Persian waffle maker's concession. The combination was a smash hit, and a decade later ice cream cones made up more than a third of all ice cream eaten in the States. We now have our choice of more flavors than there are days in the year, but the old standbys— vanilla, chocolate, and strawberry—are still the favorites.

Ca. 2000 b.c.: Glass Discovered. Give or take a few hundred years, glass was in use around this time, and once again, was probably discovered by accident. Fragments of crude pieces of glass have been found in Mesopotamia. Glass, a combination of silica, soda, and lime, was first used to make vases and beads for jewelry, and later, larger decorated balls of glass were used for trade. These glass balls reached as far as China, where the Chinese then invented leaded glass. Around the first century B.C., it was discovered, perhaps by some inventive artisan, or maybe by a playful one, that a glass bulb on the end of a tube could be blown into a shape and formed by hand. This eliminated the molds that had heretofore been used and began a whole new craft. These ancient peoples would be astonished to know that we now have enormous buildings made almost completely of glass. Of course, the vases and jewelry are still around, too.

Ca. 1750 B.C.: Code of Hammurabi. The great king of Babylon, Hammurabi, amended and codified the ancient common law of his land and had it inscribed in twenty-one columns on a stone stele. In 1901 a French archaeologist discovered the great stone, and it now resides in the Louvre in Paris. One of the oldest known legal codes and the most complete, the inscriptions detail laws affecting property, family life, social classes, business, trade, and criminals.

Ca. 1400 B.C.: Time Drips By. Early humans rose with the sunlight and went to sleep with the moonrise. The time of day was irrelevant. Around 3500 B.C., however, we know the Egyptians would plant a stick in the ground and calculate the "time" of day by the shadow it cast. It was, in essence, a primitive sundial. By 1400 B.C. they had devised a crude water clock, which the later Greeks called a *clepsydra* from the Greek words *kleptein,* "to steal," and *hydor,* "water." A bucket was filled with water, which then dripped through a small hole at the bottom. The inside of the bucket was marked to indicate the amount of time that had passed when the water had emptied to that level. These not-too-accurate first "clocks" were later improved upon by the Greeks and Romans. In Roman times they became mechanical with a wheel and ratchet system that moved a pointer over a dial. The Chinese and the Arabs perfected the accuracy of these dial water clocks, which were in use for centuries.

Ca. 1372 B.C.: The Exquisite Nefertiti. The wife of the Egyptian king Ikhnaton, Nefertiti was celebrated as the most beautiful woman in the world. The famous painted limestone sculpture of her head, now in a Berlin museum, gives credence to her legendary pulchritude. As the poet Keats wrote, "A thing of beauty is a joy forever."

Ca. 3 Thousand Years Ago: Marbles. Playing marbles is a child's game throughout the world and has been since the time of the ancient Egyptians. In seventeenth-century France, however, it was upper-class adults who devised a game in which marbles were flicked through little gates to score points. It's an idea that would appear later in pinball machines.

Ca. 850 B.C.: The *Iliad* and the *Odyssey*. It is the dawn of great literature and the two epic poems that epitomize the era and will be studied to this day are attributed to the Greek poet Homer. Although the historian Herodotus claimed Homer wrote them, they seem to be a compilation of oral history and poetry that had been repeated for centuries. We will give Homer his due, however, for the *Iliad* and the *Odyssey* rank among the superb works of world literature. (Centuries later some students will refer to them as the Idiot and the Oddity, but students can be perverse.)

The *Iliad* is the story of the siege of Ilium (Troy) by the Greeks in the twelfth century B.C. in which the Trojans are finally overcome by the infamous wooden horse which they are persuaded to let into their walled city as an offering to Athena, goddess of wisdom, the arts, fertility, and prudent warfare. Hiding inside the horse are Greek warriors who emerge at night, open the city gates, and let in the waiting Greeks, who then sack the place. From this experience comes the expression "Beware of Greeks bearing gifts." The *Iliad* is famous for its cast of characters including Priam, Paris, Menelaus, Hector, Aphrodite, Agamemnon, Achilles, Odysseus, and Helen. It was for Helen, wife of Menelaus, that the war was fought. She had been captured by Paris, son of the Trojan king Priam, and the Greeks were trying to get her back. Centuries later, the English poet Christopher Marlowe would pay tribute to her with his immortal lines:

> *Was this the face that launch'd a thousand ships,*
> *And burnt the topless towers of Ilium?*
> *Sweet Helen, make me immortal with a kiss!*

The *Odyssey* is the story of the adventures of Odysseus (Ulysses), king of Ithaca, and his companions, who left their home to fight in the Trojan war, and of Odysseus's return to his wife, Penelope, and his son, Telemachus, twenty years later. It is a tale of survival, magic, conspiracy, suspense, and revenge.

The two famous poems will inspire many in future centuries. Rembrandt will paint his *Aristotle Contemplating the Bust of Homer*; James Joyce will write his own *Ulysses*; and the *Iliad* will fire the imagination of the archaeologist Heinrich Schliemann to discover the ancient cities of Troy.

Ca. 800 B.C.: Phoenicians, the Great Traders.

By this time the Phoenicians had established themselves as a great sea-trading empire. Their routes included Cádiz on Spain's Atlantic coast, as well as Cornwall in Britain. Their journeys brought back knowledge of other civilizations as well as goods and material.

776 B.C.: The Olympic Games.

The ancient Greeks were a sports-minded people and would race, wrestle, or jump wherever and whenever they could. The competitive games they held were called *agones* (originally meaning "assemblies"—the agony of defeat came later), and the events were known as *athla* (from which we get *athlete*). Some *agones* awarded victory wreaths to the athletes and some gave prizes such as olive oil or cloaks. These contests of skill were held in several areas of Greece in honor of various gods, but the event that we emulate today was first held about 776 B.C. at Olympia in honor of Zeus and continued for nearly twelve hundred years until abolished by the Romans.

At first the Olympics lasted only one day and consisted of one race. The remainder of the day was spent in festivities celebrating Zeus. Gradually more races were added, then the discus throw, the javelin toss, the broad jump, boxing, wrestling, the pentathlon, and so on until there were so many events, the Olympics went on for seven days, including time to honor Zeus. Women were not allowed to participate, nor were they allowed to be spectators, except for the priestess of Demeter.

The athletes trained rigorously for these events, and at the beginning of each Olympic competition, the athletes, their trainers, families, and judges took a solemn oath to play fair and give just decisions. Sportsmanship was equally as important as winning. To wear the wild olive garland awarded the victor was a great honor, not just for the athlete but for his hometown. The winners were national heroes, feted by their cities, and celebrated in song, verse, and sculpture.

Ca. 772 B.C.: Temple of Artemis. This temple to the Greek goddess Artemis (known as Diana to the Romans) was begun at Ephesus on the coast of Asia Minor (now Turkey). After being burned in 356 B.C., it was rebuilt, but little is now left. It is considered one of the Seven Wonders of the World and was famous for its size as well as the sculptures adorning it. Fragments of the temple can be seen in the British museum.

Ca. 600 B.C.: Africa Circumnavigated. The Egyptian Pharaoh Necho II sends Phoenician sailors on a voyage from the Red Sea around Africa and back through the Straits of Gibraltar, according to the Greek historian Herodotus.

Necho II also attempted to join the Red Sea and the Nile Delta by a canal, restoring the route of a canal previously dug about 1900 B.C. under Sesostris I. It was finally completed by the Persian Darius I about 500 B.C.

6th Century B.C.: Greek Numbers. At this time two systems of numerals are in use by the Greeks, who are great traders and businessmen and need a way to keep their accounts. One system is called Attic notation and is very simple. The numbers one through four are indicated by single strokes—1, 11, 111, 1111—and five is represented by the first letter of the word for five, *pente,* Π. From six through nine, Π was used plus the single strokes. The number eight is therefore Π 111. For ten, *deka,* the letter symbol is Δ, for one hundred, *hekaton,* H. One thousand is X, and M is ten thousand.

The other Greek system is known as the Ionian, which uses alphabetic numerals, as did many Semitic peoples at various times. In this method, each number is given a letter of the alphabet. One is represented by A, two by B, three is Γ, four is Δ, and so on down the alphabet. After I (iota), symbolizing the number ten, the letters represent numbers by tens to one hundred, then by hundreds to nine hundred. The classical Greek alphabet only had twenty-four letters, so in order to have enough letters to represent their number needs, they dredged up some old letters. Instead of omega, Ω, being the last letter, sampi, Λ, was resurrected to indicate nine hundred. So once you knew the alphabet, you could do your arithmetic.

6th Century B.C.: Hanging Gardens of Babylon. One of the Seven Wonders of the World, the so-called hanging gardens are built during the reign of Nebuchadnezzar, and must have been a magnificent sight. Babylon itself, situated in southern Mesopotamia between the Tigris and Euphrates rivers, was composed of vast parklands of trees supported by a great irrigation system, which lasted until the thirteenth-century Tatar invasion. The legendary Garden of Eden was supposedly sited just north of the city. The gardens did not actually hang but were built on a series of large terraces with full-size trees, waterfalls, walkways, and small palaces all enclosed within an enormous wall. It was the earliest form of landscape architecture and a brilliant beginning.

Ca. 590 B.C.: The Reforms of Solon. Solon was elected chief magistrate of Athens at a time when strife between rich and poor, aristocrats and commoners, was rampant. In an effort to give hope to the farmers, he canceled all debts on land and abolished the policy of enslavement for future nonpayment of debts. He did away with old laws regarding wills and contracts and reformed the currency. He encouraged farmers to produce olive oil and wine for export, which increased trade. His constitutional reforms enabled freemen for the first time to participate in the assembly. He encouraged artisans and intellectuals to settle in Athens and offered them citizenship. Solon recognized the worth of the individual and gave him respect. The foundations of democracy had been established.

551–479 B.C.: Confucius. His name was K'ung Fu-tzu, Master K'ung, and he was one of the world's great teachers and philosophers. One of his basic tenets is "What you do not like when done to yourself, do not do unto others." Confucius believed that government should have as its objective the happiness of its people. To govern thusly, one must be virtuous and understanding of others. He stressed the importance of education and believed everyone had a right to make decisions for himself. Confucius accepted students from all walks of life as long as they were intelligent, hardworking, and sincere, taught them ethics and human relations, and the importance of family harmony. His theories and moral reforms had a profound influence upon Chinese culture and what is today called Confucianism.

510 B.C.: The Roman Republic. An aristocratic conspiracy and an army of the people overthrow the Etruscan tyrant Tarquinius and establish the Roman republic presided over by two magistrates. It is the beginning of an empire that will eventually rule most of the ancient world for a thousand years and whose language and influences remain today.

Rome was founded 250 years before by the twin brothers Romulus and Remus, who as infants were suckled by a she-wolf who rescued them from the Tiber, where they had been thrown by their wicked uncle. If you believe this, you will also believe that their mother was raped by the god Mars and subsequently gave birth to the twins.

Such is the stuff of legends.

Ca. 500 B.C.: Carthaginians Explore West Coast of Africa.
Hanno, a Carthaginian leader, sets sail with thirty thousand men and women through the Straits of Gibraltar and down the African coast, establishing new colonies along the route.

Ca. 2,500 Years Ago: Spinning Tops.
One of the oldest toys for children everywhere in the world is the top. This simple device was probably around in prehistoric times. It was recommended to parents of children in ancient Rome as better than dice, played with by children in South Pacific islands, and spun deliriously in medieval Europe. Tops come in all shapes, sizes, and designs, and games played with tops still amuse children in all parts of the world today.

5th Century B.C.: Aspasia.
A woman known for both her brains and her beauty, Aspasia is a central and controversial figure in Athens. She is best known as the mistress of the ruler Pericles. Many prominent Athenians, including Aristophanes, the dramatist, ridicule and attack her, for being a non-Athenian citizen, and for her relationship with Pericles. However, another segment of Athenians views her as part of an intellectual center of society, a center to which even women throng, and her home is the hub for the literary and philosophical figures of this Golden Era in Athenian history.

Did this woman write any of the speeches that Pericles delivered or coach Socrates in rhetoric, as some of the rumors of her day claimed? Since she had one of the great minds of the period, one can only wonder.

5th Century B.C.: Herodotus. We call him the father of history, mostly for his nine-volume *History,* which details the events of the Greco-Persian war as well as describing the history and cultures of the time. Herodotus traveled widely and his curiosity led him to observe many things about the people and places he visited, all of which he wrote about in prose, the first European writer to compose such a large narrative in that form. He includes anecdotes, dialogues between characters, and legends in his narrations and is not without a sense of humor. His great masterpiece, although not always completely accurate, is our leading source for Greek history of the period as well as that of Egypt and the eastern Mediterranean. A true scholar, genius, and a bit of a philosopher, Herodotus remains one of the great historians of all time.

Ca. 518-438 B.C.: Pindar. The greatest of the Greek lyric poets, Pindar wrote poems commemorating victories in the Olympic games, honoring famous men, and celebrating festivals. He wrote hymns, paeans, dithyrambs (wild choral chants), processional songs, dirges, and odes, and is known for his imagery and wonderful use of language.

Ca. 460-404 B.C.: Thucydides. The intellectually brilliant Greek historian is known for his *History of the Peloponnesian War,* which is divided into eight books. Unlike his predecessor Herodotus, Thucydides was interested in just the facts and is much more authoritative, although perhaps not as much fun to read. His descriptions are precise, his accounts accurate and impartial, and his feelings about situations are intense. It is from Thucydides that we have learned so much about Athens's Golden Age under Pericles. His fame as a great historian lives on.

Ca. 460-377 B.C.: Hippocrates. The man who is considered the father of modern medicine, Hippocrates, lived during the Golden Age of Greece, although not too much is actually known about his life. The practice of medicine had long been based upon primitive superstitions and ridding the body of demons. To effect a cure, the demons and bad spirits had to be driven out by prayer, purging, and puncturing. Hippocrates contradicted these theories and methods and taught that curing the patient himself would be more effective than attempting to expel the spirits, which he denied were the cause of illness. It was a revolutionary turning point in the history of medicine. He wrote of the need to sterilize (heat) water, recognized the cause of lockjaw, knew that surgeons infected patients with their hands and instruments, and that nutrition affected the body. The group of writings known as the *Hippocratic Collection* describes symptoms, diseases, cures, surgical procedures, and of course, contains the famous Hippocratic Oath in which doctors are admonished to do no harm.

458 B.C.: Cincinnatus. Rome is in danger of attack from the Aequi, one of the hostile tribes to the east. What to do? The Senate sends for their general, Lucius Quinctius Cincinnatus, who leaves his farm, is named dictator, assembles his troops, and defeats the Aequians in one day. He then relinquishes his dictatorship and returns to his farming.

Some people want to be king for a day. Cincinnatus was happy with being dictator for two weeks. He has a city in Ohio named after him.

458 B.C.: The Oresteia Trilogy. The Greek playwright and poet Aeschylus, completes his trio of dramas, which includes *Agamemnon, The Libation Bearers,* and *The Eumenides*. The stories are full of murder, matricide, sin, illicit love affairs, jealousy, passion, and revenge, and provide enough material for generations of dramatists. Similar dramas are acted out today on our soap operas, although not on such a grand scale.

438 B.C.: The Parthenon Completed. Pericles was determined to build Athens into a glorious city, and as part of this project, work was begun in 448 B.C. on the Temple of Athena atop the Acropolis. The architects Ictinus and Callicrates supervised the construction, and the sculptor Phidias was responsible for the frieze that decorated the four sides as well as the statue of Athena that once stood inside the building.

The Parthenon remained as it was built for eight hundred years and then was transformed into a church. In 1458 the Turks turned it into a mosque, after they overran Athens. In 1687 a powder magazine inside the building blew up while Athens was being bombarded by the Venetians and destroyed the middle of the temple. In 1801–03, the British Lord Elgin removed the frieze and sold it to the British Museum, where it can be seen today.

Currently under reconstruction by archaeologists, the Parthenon remains today a monument to the architectural and artistic genius of those who designed and built it.

Ca. 430 B.C.: Statue of Zeus. One of the Seven Wonders of the ancient World is completed by the Greek sculptor Phidias. The majestic statue of Zeus sitting on his throne is thirty feet high and plated with gold and ivory. Unfortunately, the temple and statue at Olympia were destroyed in 426 A.D.

411 B.C.: Aristophanes Presents *Lysistrata*. The famous Greek writer of comedies writes an antiwar play in which the women of Greece, led by Lysistrata, seize the Acropolis and treasury of Athens and declare they will withhold sex until the men make peace. There's food for thought in this farce.

Ca. 400 B.C.: Atomic Theory of Democritus. The great Greek philosopher Democritus of Abdera in Thrace reportedly traveled to more places than any of his contemporaries, having been to Athens, Egypt, Mesopotamia, and perhaps even India. Along the way he developed his theory of atoms in which he stated that all matter is composed of small particles that cannot be reduced. He called these particles *atonom,* which means "indivisible." Democritus then explained that the universe formed when these atoms, vibrating in a void, collided to form larger bodies and thus the universe. Sort of like an early Big Bang theory.

Ca. 300 B.C.: Tales of India. Although Alexander the Great had invaded the northwestern part of India, not much was known about the land. Alexander himself thought the Indus River was part of the Nile and that more of Ethiopia lay beyond it. Geography was not his strong point. About this time the Greek ambassador, scholar, and traveler Megasthenes was sent from Macedonia to record what he saw there. Although some of his stories seem incredible, he did bring back knowledge of this strange land and its inhabitants, including their two religions, Hinduism and Buddhism. We are gleaning information about cultures outside the Mediterranean shores.

Ca. 300 B.C.: Explorations of Pytheas. The Greek navigator and geographer Pytheas sails along the Atlantic coast of Europe to the British Isles and possibly Norway. He notes that the Pole

Star is not at the true pole and observes that tides are affected by
the moon. From some of his measurements, later scholars calculated parallels of latitude. He was, however, way off when he
calculated that the circumference of Britain was four thousand
miles. Maybe it was just a misplaced comma.

280 B.C.: The Colossus of Rhodes. One of the Seven Wonders of the World, the statue of the sun god, Helios, stood at the
harbor on the island of Rhodes. It was made of bronze reinforced
with iron, was over one hundred feet high, and took twelve years
to build. It must have been either an intimidating or welcome
sight to see as your ship entered the port. In 225 B.C. it broke
off at the knees during an earthquake but remained where it fell
until A.D. 653 when Arabs raided the city and carried the bronze
off piece by piece to sell for scrap.

214 B.C.: Great Wall of China Begins. Shih Huang-Ti, the
first emperor of Ch'in (the dynasty that gave its name to China),
having united the territories under one rule, sought to defend his
frontiers and keep out the marauding Mongolian tribesmen. Some
existing walls between former kingdoms were connected and new
sections were built to form a fortification of fifteen hundred miles
from the Yellow Sea to Mongolia. Built of earth and stone, the
wall later was reinforced with brick. In the fifteenth and sixteenth
centuries newly built sections reached a height of thirty feet. The
wall is wide enough across the top to accommodate marching
troops. It is so large, it is the one man–made object that can be
seen from outer space.

Ca. 200 B.C.: No More Two Left Feet. The earliest known
footwear ever discovered is a sandal of woven papyrus from an
Egyptian tomb of 2000 B.C. The Babylonians wore moccasins
around 1600 B.C., and five hundred years later Assyrian soldiers
were wearing calf–length laced leather boots with heavy soles. It
wasn't until about 200 B.C., however, that the guilds of Roman
shoemakers began making shoes specifically for the right and left
foot. After the fall of Rome, however, we couldn't tell our right
foot from our left until the fourteenth century in England when
the shoemaking trade started up again. Cobblers also began making
shoes in standard sizes at that time after King Edward I decreed
that one inch was the length of three barleycorns.

Ca. 2 Thousand Years Ago: Hopscotch: A hopscotch diagram has been found on the floor of the ancient Forum in Rome, making it one of the earliest children's games that we know about. As their empire expanded, the Roman soldiers taught the game to the children of France, Germany, and Britain, scratching diagrams on the stone roads for which the Romans were famous.

70 B.C. to A.D. 18: Three Giants of Poetry. Three of the greatest and most celebrated poets in history live during Rome's most tumultuous and triumphant era. The first is Virgil, considered the greatest Roman poet, who is born in 70 B.C. of peasant stock in Mantua. His *Eclogues* are pastoral poems inspired by his love for the countryside and the people who live there. His *Georgics* concerns farming, and his third and most famous is the *Aeneid,* the story of Aeneas, a Trojan who leaves Troy and with divine guidance travels west to found a new city which will rise to glory. The Romans consider it their national epic. The *Aeneid* expresses Virgil's feelings of sorrow for the suffering of man's life on earth and the soldiers who die during battles. It contains the phrase "Arms, and the man I sing . . ." which the twentieth-century playwright George Bernard Shaw will use as the title for one of his dramas.

Horace, Virgil's friend and contemporary, is perhaps the best-loved Roman poet. He is born in 65 B.C., the son of a freed slave, and writes 41 verse essays (*Satires, Epistles,* and *Ars Poetica*) and 121 extant lyric poems (*Epodes, Odes*). He describes himself in middle age as "a little baldish man, easygoing though quick-tempered, fond of the sun." His poems cover topics such as love, morality, ethics, philosophy, and literary criticism. In his *Satires* he writes, "He prepares to go mad with fixed rule and method," which a future English playwright will later paraphrase in his play *Hamlet* as "Though this be madness, yet there is method in it."

The youngest of the trio, Ovid, is born in 43 B.C. and is a friend of Horace, but as he writes in his biographical poem, *Tristia,* "I had but a glimpse of Virgil." Ovid is born into a middle-class family and moves in a sophisticated, pleasure-seeking circle about which he often writes. He is the author of *Metamorphoses,* which tells the story of the creation and history of the world up to his time and includes Greek and Roman legends which he vividly describes. He is, however, most notable for his love poems such as *Amores (Loves)* and *Remedia amoris (Remedies of Love).* His

Ars amatoria, a guide to seduction and intrigue for men, was originally two books, but by popular demand he wrote a third book,
this one for women. The emperor Augustus, who was attempting
to put the Romans on the straight and narrow path as far as
morals are concerned, finally banned Ovid's books from the public
libraries. Then he banished Ovid himself, at the age of fifty-one,
for reasons not quite clear to historians. It may have had something
to do with Ovid's alleged complicity in the adultery of Julia, the
granddaughter of Augustus. Needless to say, being exiled from
Rome and its culture to a provincial outpost on the Black Sea
did not make Ovid too happy. For obvious reasons, of the three
poets, Ovid was the most popular.

52 B.C.: Vercingetorix. The chief of the Arverni tribe of Gaul
leads a rebellion against the armies of Julius Caesar. When the
revolt fails, Vercingetorix heroically surrenders himself to Caesar
to save the lives of his people.

Vercingetorix tried to unite the different tribes of Gaul into
one unified force to protect their homeland and way of life from
the encroaching Romans. Despite the fact that he led a disorga-
nized and sometimes disjointed army, Vercingetorix fought well
against Caesar, but strategy and will are not enough. Caesar laid
siege to the city of Alesia (northwest of present-day Dijon), where
the majority of Vercingetorix's forces were encamped. After a long
battle, the Gallic army was dispersed and Vercingetorix then had
to choose whether to surrender himself to Caesar or risk having
his men slaughtered. He made a brave choice. Gaul soon came
under Roman influence and was absorbed into the empire.

19 B.C.: The Pont du Gard. Built by the Roman Marcus
Agrippa, the aqueduct in Nîmes, France, is six hundred yards long
with a series of arches in three tiers rising to a height of 155 feet.
It is still standing and is a monument to the engineering ingenuity
of the Romans, who constructed many aqueducts throughout the
empire to bring water into cities and towns.

1st Century A.D.: Celsus. Aulus Cornelius Celsus, although he
didn't write an oath that would make his name a household word
like Hippocrates, was the greatest of the Roman medical writers.
His *De Medicina,* ignored by his contemporaries, gives elaborate
explanations of surgical operations and instruments as well as clear

and detailed descriptions of Greek medicine and pill preparation. In his work, the first mention of the word *insanity* (*insania*) occurs, as well as *heart disease* (*cardiacus*). Because of his excellent writing style, his work was widely read during the Renaissance when it was one of the first medical books printed and thereafter became one of the best medical textbooks of the period. His books are among the oldest existing medical records and are a wonderful look into ancient Greek medicine.

43: Londinium Founded. The Roman emperor Claudius sought the road to glory by expanding the empire. His troops invade Britain and on the banks of the Thames establish a settlement they call Londinium.

There had been a few prehistoric villages along the river, but the essential history of the city begins with the Roman colony. A wall eight feet thick is constructed around the town and the Romans occupy Britain until the year 407 when the legions are recalled to protect the empire closer to home.

Eventually the Saxons took over the town, and as the centuries ensued, it grew into a magnificent city, becoming the capital of England and the center of the British Empire. We now call it London; you can still see part of the Roman wall in various sections of the old city.

Ca. 50: De Materia Medica. The Greek pharmacologist Pedanius Dioscorides compiles a five-book treatise on the characteristics and effects of over six hundred plants as well as descriptions of animal products useful in nutrition and medicine.

Dioscorides, regarded as the father of pharmacology (from the Greek meaning "the study of drugs"), was for many years an army surgeon, and while following the Roman armies, learned of rare drugs and remedies chiefly derived from plants. One of the items in his work describes making a paste of willow ash to safely remove corns. Willow is a natural source of salicylic acid (aspirin)— check the foot-care books today; this method is still being recommended. The writing in the ancient books, which have survived intact, is straightforward and methodical and covers almost all the drugs used in the ancient world. It was our first *Physicians' Desk Reference,* the book today's doctors consult to check on prescription drugs.

60: Queen Boudica Strikes. Standing tall in her chariot, red
hair flying in the wind, a golden torque gleaming on her neck,
with her bright cloak flapping around her, Queen Boudica leads
her Iceni tribespeople in a rebellion against the Roman settlers of
Camulodunum and sacks the town.

Boudica—variously spelled Boadicea, Boodicia,. or Bunduica—
was outraged, and rightfully so. The Romans had invaded Britain
one hundred years before and were slowly colonizing the island.
The Celtic tribes were restless and resentful of the intrusion, having been for the most part subjugated by the Romans into client-
kingdoms. Prasutagus, Boudica's husband and king of the Iceni,
had died, having willed part of his lands and personal possessions
to his wife and two daughters, and part to the Roman emperor,
hoping to keep the kingdom peaceful. The Roman administrators
ignored the will, grabbed everything, humiliated the Iceni, flogged
Boudica, and raped her daughters. It was a Roman belief that a
woman was incapable of ruling because a woman, as Cato allegedly said, "is a violent uncontrolled animal" and not able to be
disciplined. Boudica rebelled. It was a serious revolt against the
Romans and it was led by a woman. After Camulodunum (present-day Colchester), the Iceni, now joined by other tribes and
still led by Boudica, attacked a group of Roman legionaries, then
swept on to destroy Roman Londinium (London) and Verulam-
ium (Saint Albans).

As another battle approached on the plains, the Roman historian
Tacitus has Boudica fighting "as an ordinary person for my lost
freedom, my bruised body, and my outraged daughters,' a woman
who would rather perish than live in slavery. Alas, the loose array
of Celts, though more numerous than the Romans, were no
match for the highly trained and well-equipped troops they faced,
and the tribes were routed. Boudica was gone, either dead on the
battlefield or poisoned by her own hand.

A bronze statue in London depicts the heroic Boudica in her
chariot with her two daughters. Inscribed on the base are the
words of the poet William Cowper: "Regions Caesar never
knew/Thy Posterity shall sway."

105: The Art of Making Paper. It was a Chinese court
official, Ts'ai Lun, who conceived of the idea of making paper
from softened tree bark, hemp waste, rags, and old fishnets. Maybe
he was just trying to figure out how to recycle these things; at

any rate, it worked. Before the invention of paper, the Chinese had been using woven cloth on which to write their characters with a camel-hair brush they had invented about 250 B.C. They now had a less expensive material, and that's what they alone used for the next five hundred years. In the seventh century the process spread to Japan, where it was introduced by Buddhist monks. One hundred years later Arabs occupied Samarkand in Asia and purposely held captive the many Chinese who knew the art of paper making. Flax and hemp were in abundance in the area, and soon Samarkand became the center of the industry, taught to the Arabs by the Chinese. From there it spread west to Damascus and Baghdad, which soon set up state-owned mills. A thousand years after Ts'ai Lin produced his first paper, the process reached the continent of Europe. What would we do without it?

121: The Pantheon. Completed under the reign of Hadrian, the Pantheon in Rome was one of the great engineering feats of the time. The building is circular with a dome that measures 141 feet in diameter, the largest ever built until the modern era. Although the bronze girders and trusses and the gilt bronze tiles covering the dome have all been stripped off, the interior remains as it was two thousand years ago. The building itself, once a place to worship all the gods together, was dedicated as the church of Santa Maria Rotunda in 609 and still serves its first purpose, that of worship.

130–200: Galen. Doctor, pharmacist, researcher, writer, and, for a time, official physician to the gladiators, Galen was the son of a wealthy and educated Greek farmer who dreamed that his son should study medicine. By the age of fourteen, Galen had been trained in theology, biology, literature, and many other skills. While still a student, he started writing and researching and became an expert in Hippocratic medicine, gradually believing he was the best interpreter of this knowledge. By all accounts he was brilliant. He was also vain, impatient, and jealous. He dissected animals and apes and twice dissected human corpses, which was against Roman law. His anatomical findings were correct for the most part and he was the first to pronounce that arteries contained blood and not air and accurately described the valves of the heart and the heartbeat. He knew that the expansion of the chest by diaphragm and muscles filled the lungs, and that the kidneys, not the bladder, make urine. He wrote complicated prescriptions based on extracts of plant juices, and the term *galenical* is still used today to describe prescriptions not chemical in nature. He wrote books on diet, hygiene, and exercise as well as medical treatises and gave the world what was desperately needed at the time, a solidified code of medical knowledge. After Hippocrates, Galen was the greatest physician in ancient times.

Ca. 200: Ptolemy's Geography. Ptolemy of Alexandria, astronomer, geographer, and mathematician, compiles his *Guide to Geography,* which would exert great influence over future generations of explorers. There were inaccuracies. Ptolemy thought the Indian Ocean was completely surrounded by land, determined the circumference of the earth to be thirty percent smaller than it is, and put the equator too far north. His placement of Asia as extending much farther east than it does helped confirm Columbus's opinion that he could sail west to reach it. Perhaps we should thank him for this little error.

Ca. 250: Algebraic Notation. The Greek mathematician Diophantus of Alexandria compiles thirteen books known as *Arithmetica,* of which six survive. Known somewhat inaccurately as the Father of Algebra, Diophantus introduces symbols and abbreviations in his calculations. Unlike previous Babylonian mathematicians who were content with approximate solutions to problems, Diophantus worked on exact solutions to equations. By the way, he did not use X for unknown, as we learn in school, he used a symbol somewhat like the Greek letter $S,$ which he may have taken from the last letter of the Greek word *arithmos*.

313: Edict of Milan. The Roman emperor of the Western Empire, Constantine, and Licinius, ruler of the Eastern provinces, agree to religious tolerance for all during a meeting in Milan. On June 15, 313, an edict is issued at Nicomedia announcing the policy of religious freedom and the restitution of property previously confiscated from Christians.

6th Century: The Noble Game of Chess. The origins of chess are a little hazy, its invention having variously been ascribed to almost all ancient peoples from the Greeks and Babylonians to the Chinese and Egyptians. It can most accurately be attributed to the Hindus, who evidently played it since the beginning of time and called it *chaturanga,* which, loosely translated, means four arms of an army: elephants, horses, chariots, and foot soldiers. The army, of course, was depicted by the chess pieces. Sometime during the sixth century the game appeared in Persia, and later the Arabs called it *shatranj.* By the eleventh century it seems to have been known in Europe. Along the way the pieces evolved into the king, queen, knights, bishops, rooks, and pawns we use today, and some of the pieces can now move in directions originally denied them. It is interesting to note that by the fifteenth century the queen, once a weak player in the game, had become one of the most versatile and powerful pieces on the board. The bishops' limited sphere of action also increased. Perhaps chess, originally a war game, reflected the politics of the day.

Chess now produces masters and grand masters and the occasional child prodigy. It takes superb concentration and a great deal of skill to play it well and has had more books written about it than any other game.

Ca. 500: Grammar. About this time the Latin grammarian Priscian compiles his work for the teaching of grammar into eighteen volumes titled *Institutiones grammaticae.* His opus, along with the fourth-century grammar of Donatus, will be studied by Latin scholars in Europe through the Renaissance. Eighteen volumes of grammar! This is only mentioned so you'll know how lucky you were in English class.

7th Century: Playing Cards. Playing cards were not invented by the devil, as asserted by Saint Bernardino of Siena in the fifteenth century, although men of the cloth have condemned them at various times throughout history. We know the Chinese played cards in the seventh century, although they seem to have originated before then from fortune-telling emblems in Korea. In fact, most cards were originally used to tell fortunes, and are still used for that purpose today in the form of tarot cards, first introduced in Italy about 1320.

By the fourteenth century playing cards were in use in most of Europe and consisted of fifty-six cards in four suits. There were ten numbered cards plus a king, queen, knight, and knave. This was later reduced to a fifty-two-card deck, which eventually became standard throughout the world. In the sixteenth century the symbols we now use, hearts, spades, diamonds, and clubs, were introduced in France and England. And while Western playing cards are rectangular in shape, in India they are round.

During the middle of the nineteenth century in America, card playing began to take on more respectability and was looked upon as less sinful than the Puritans had purported it to be. Nowadays almost everyone has at least one deck of playing cards in the house, and the variety of card games, including solitaire, bridge, canasta and hearts, is endless.

Ca. 680–750: Al-Khwarizmi, Mathematician. A thirteenth-century Latin translation of this great Persian mathematician's book begins, "Dixit Algorismi . . ." ("Thus said al-Khwarizmi"), and so we have a new word, *algorithm,* which was the term used until it was changed to *arithmetic.* The translation of his works also first introduced Arabic numbers to Western culture along with the zero sign. His book on other mathematical functions gave us the term *algebra,* which we took from his title, *A Brief Account of the Methods of al-Jabr.* In Arabic the word means "transformations," which more or less describes what we do when we use algebra. Al-Khwarizmi based his writings on what he knew of Hindu mathematics, and his use of zero and numerals from one through nine made calculating much easier. But it was still the eighth century and not everyone was willing or ready to give up his abacus or counters or Roman numbers. It would take another four centuries or so for Europeans to begin to see the light.

8th Century: Scandinavians Explore and Settle. Sometime during this century and for the next two, the Vikings with their longboats equipped with oars and sails, and cargo carriers that held families, animals, and goods, began the sea voyages that would take them east to Kiev and west as far as the northeast coast of America. Along the way they settled on the islands of Orkney, Faroe, Shetland, Iceland, and Greenland and founded the colony of Dublin, which became an important trading post in Ireland. We are adventuring farther out into the vast ocean to explore the world.

731: English Chronicles. The Anglo-Saxon theologian and historian Bede, later called the Venerable Bede, and even later Saint Bede, completes his *Historia ecclesiastica gentis Anglorum.*

Known in English as *The Ecclesiastical History of the English Nation,* his work is a significant source of information about the life and times of the people and places in early Britain from the time of the Romans to his day. Aside from being of historical value, his writing is the greatest literary achievement of the time. His fame spread throughout Europe, and scholars to this day still study his books. This modest priest, brought up in a monastery from the age of seven, was one of the brilliant literary lights and teachers of the period and is revered even today. His remains are buried in Durham Cathedral in England.

Ca. 766: Baghdad on the Tigris. The ancient circular city is built for the caliph al-Mansur of the Abassid dynasty. At the center stood the new palace, and encircling the city, which was about a mile and a half in diameter, were three concentric walls with four gates. From each gate a road led to the four corners of the empire. Called the "City of Peace," Baghdad became the center of knowledge and wealth, and featured in the tales from a *Thousand and One Nights.* The original city no longer exists, but what a glorious place it must have been.

Ca. 10th Century: Fireworks. We all know the Chinese invented fireworks. Well, maybe. In the seventh century the Arabs were making a fireworks type of rocket for warfare and knew about potassium, one of the necessary ingredients. To make the explosive compound, you need sulfur, charcoal, and saltpeter (potassium nitrate). All of these were found in Chinese kitchens, and as legend has it, a cook accidentally mixed them together and created a spectacular explosion. No dinner that night. The inventive Chinese soon figured out that by packing the ingredients into bamboo and lighting a fuse at one end, the hot gases produced by the combustion rush out the other end and the bamboo rockets into the air. It was great fun and soon these fireworks were being used to celebrate everything from the New Year to weddings. Of course, this mixture was also used for gunpowder, but since guns hadn't been invented yet, nobody knew that.

Fireworks didn't reach Europe until about the seventeenth century, and by the eighteenth, no royal festivity was without a spectacular exhibition, always in shades of yellow and reddish amber. During the nineteenth century, however, newly discovered ingredients were added and soon we had more colorful displays. Now fireworks are a part of celebrations everywhere around the world. What would the Fourth of July be without them?

Ca. 11th Century: Medical School. After the fall of Rome, much of the Greek and Roman knowledge of medicine was forgotten and it seemed the study of medicine might become a lost art form. However, at Salerno, Italy, a town known as a health resort due to its mineral springs, the monks of Monte Cassino prevented this from happening. They translated Greek medical works and those of the great Persian physician Avicenna into Latin. Around 1065 Constantine of Carthage settled in Salerno and began lecturing on the very subjects the monks were translating. The growing medical studies at Salerno got what you might call free advertising from Robert, Duke of Normandy, who stopped there to have his wounds tended on the way home from the First Crusade in 1099. He spread word all over Europe of the medical knowledge to be found there. Soon students interested in medicine flocked to Salerno to study and the first European medical university was formed. It became so well known that in 1221 the Holy Roman Emperor Frederick II proclaimed that no one should practice medicine unless he had been endorsed by the masters at Salerno.

11th Century: Law School. The university at Bologna, Italy, becomes the first school to teach law as a subject.

The study of Roman law had all but ceased after the empire fell, but after a copy of Justinian's *Digest,* a book containing all the codes for Roman law, was found at Pisa, the subject was revived. It was also around this same time that the Italian city-states in the Po Valley were searching for a way to justify their independence from Germany, and one of the sources to which they turned was the old Roman law. In Bologna, Irnerius, formerly a teacher of the arts who had studied law in Rome, helped to tie these two events together into the founding of a university. Irnerius interpreted and reconstructed the *Digest,* lectured on Roman law, and became famous enough throughout Europe to attract several students. Now that the source material, need, and teacher had been provided, Europe began to realize the benefits of having law professionals again. The study of law became its own subject, and Bologna the first university to teach it. The profession of lawyer also became an accepted part of European life.

Accepted, maybe, but not loved if Shakespeare's famous line in *Henry VI,* Part II, is any indication. One of the characters says, "The first thing we do, let's kill all the lawyers." It always gets a laugh.

11th Century: Forks Introduced in Tuscany. "Don't eat with your fingers," admonishes Mom. The truth is, many people throughout the world do eat with their fingers, as we also did until very recent history. Although we stabbed food with a knife and slurped from a spoon, the fork we take for granted did not appear until the eleventh century and remained a disdained curiosity for several centuries afterward. Roman etiquette of the upper classes required that one eat politely with three fingers, while commoners used all five, a class distinction that seemed to be in effect until the nineteenth century. Forks became fashionable late in the eighteenth century as a sign of luxury and status. As manners became more popular among aristocrats, the use of forks increased and touching food was considered uncouth. By the middle of the nineteenth century, most families were eating with knives, forks, and spoons unless they were very poor.

Ca. 1000: Beowulf. The remarkable epic poem *Beowulf* is written down in Old English about this time, although it was undoubtedly composed a couple of hundred years before by a brilliant but unknown Anglo-Saxon. The poem tells the story of Beowulf, a young noble from a tribe in southern Sweden, who kills the monster Grendel, which has been ravaging the court of the Danish King Hrothgard. Beowulf is rewarded for his exploits and eventually becomes king of his people. After a wise and peaceful reign of fifty years, Beowulf once more encounters a monster and, with the aid of the young Wiglaf, kills it, although Beowulf is mortally wounded.

The poem is rich in details of armor, fighting, and politics as well as the court and social life of the times, and provides us great insight into the life and conditions of the era. The author was probably connected to the royal court, an abbot perhaps, possessed knowledge of German and Scandinavian folklore, and was certainly brilliant as well as accomplished. The poem is part of our great cultural heritage.

11th to 16th Centuries: Miracles, Mysteries, and Moralities. As the Dark Ages begin to lighten, the theater begins to return in the form of religious dramas, known as "miracle" and "mystery" plays, and "morality" dramas, which were less reli-

gious but designed to be instructive also. To affix definite times and origins is exceedingly difficult because generally they were all developing around the same time. The primary function of the three types of plays was to teach an illiterate Christian population. They were didactic in content and usually performed in conjunction with a church service or religious pageant such as a feast day.

The name "mystery" derives from the French *mystère,* which in turn comes from the Latin *mysterium,* meaning "service," and indeed these plays did grow out of the church liturgy. They contained Biblical stories from both the Old and New Testaments, often having to do with redemption and salvation. The mysteries spawned the miracle plays, which told stories of saints and martyrs and, one can presume, the miracles attributed to them.

Morality plays were popular in England in the fifteenth and sixteenth centuries. At that time, they were called "interludes" or "moral interludes." An English adaptation of the Dutch play *Everyman,* sometimes performed even today, is a prime example of the morality play. Moralities were written in allegorical terms with virtue, the seven deadly sins, good and evil, for example, personified and represented by various characters, with Mankind always the hero.

In France, *mystères* meant both mystery and miracle plays and generally dealt with redemption through salvation as represented in the New Testament. The Spanish called their dramas *autos sacramentales;* in Italy they were *sacre rappresentazioni;* in Germany, *Geistliche Spiele.*

For the most part, these early dramas were performed in the church with its blessings. When tradesmen's guilds began taking over the production in the twelfth century, plays moved outdoors to marketplaces, play wagons, and courtyards. There are various reasons given for this transformation. The church may have become discontent over the subject matter, or some of the plays may have become so opulent and elaborate with scenery that they could no longer be held inside and had to be performed outdoors. The settings varied from country to country, with ancient theaters sometimes used in France and Italy, including that scene of early Christian persecutions, the Roman Colosseum, ironically turned into an arena to further Christianity. *Corrales* or courtyards were used in Spain for performances, and play wagons were sometimes used in England. Play wagons could be moved from town to town in an early version of our modern road companies.

As interest in the classical world began to take hold as early as the fourteenth century, and as scholars began studying and performing the ancient Roman and Greek plays, new dramatists became inspired to write their own versions of these plays. Gradually they began to write more humanistic plays with real characters, imaginative plots, and relevant themes. Religious dramas of hellfire and damnation began to take a backseat and the saints and sinners of the miracles and mysteries no longer trod the boards. The theater had become secular.

1010: The Book of Kings. The Persian poet Firdausi completes the sixty-thousand-verse poem *Shah-Nama* (*Book of Kings*) the great epic of Persian history, and is considered the most distinguished of the Persian poets. The original text survives to this day.

Ca. 1057: Godiva's Guileless Gallop. Lady Godiva, wife of Leofric, Earl of Mercia, rides naked on her palfrey through the town of Coventry to protest her husband's weighty taxes.

The lord and lady had previously founded and generously endowed a monastery at Coventry, and Lady Godiva, who owned property in her own right, was a benefactor of several other monasteries. As chronicled by Roger of Wendover two hundred years after the alleged ride, Lady Godiva had constantly begged her husband to reduce Coventry's heavy tax burden. Tired of the nagging, the earl agreed to do so if Godiva would ride through the marketplace naked. So up on her horse went the lady, and with her long hair covering her body, accompanied by two soldiers, she rode into legend. True to his word, Leofric remitted all taxes except those on horses.

There are other later versions of the historic ride, whether legendary or not. Curiously enough, during the reign of Edward I (1272–1307) an investigation into Coventry's finances showed that, except for horses, no tolls were paid there.

No doubt she was beloved by all the citizens of Coventry for her daring deed.

1065: Westminster Abbey Consecrated. The Abbey, founded by Edward the Confessor in 1050, stands as one of the most magnificent examples of medieval architecture in England today. The original edifice, except for the nave, was demolished by Henry III in 1245, and replaced by the present church. Rebuilding of the nave was carried on from the fourteenth to the sixteenth centuries in keeping with the original design. The towers were completed in 1745 and rise to a height of 225 feet. The exterior length of the building is 531 feet and the transepts measure 203 feet. Adjacent to the Abbey are several other buildings, all constructed during the thirteenth and fourteenth centuries.

Since William the Conqueror, all but two British monarchs (Edward V and Edward VIII) have been crowned at Westminster. It is the burial place of many kings and queens as well as the final resting place of many famous and some infamous British subjects. Added to these are memorials to soldiers and statesmen and the celebrated "Poet's Corner" commemorating such immortals as Geoffrey Chaucer and Ben Jonson.

Today Westminster Abbey and its grounds, aside from functioning as a place of worship, is probably the most famous tourist attraction in England and a treasure trove of history.

1066: The Battle of Hastings. It is dawn on October 14. Duke William of Normandy assembles his invading army of archers and crossbowmen, heavy infantry, and knights to the left, center, and right. Across the valley on a ridge the army of the English king, Harold, is arrayed in an unbroken line, hoping to use their heavy battle-axes, slings and spears to wear down the Normans. A kingdom is at stake.

The trumpets sound; the battle begins. The Normans are repelled. Their knights on horses charge, then retreat. The Normans counterattack again; the English break ranks. There is a stillness while both armies regroup. Again the trumpets sound. Part of the English line is driven back. Exhaustion sets in and the Norman knights withdraw. The English foot soldiers follow, recovering weapons to replace those they have lost. They have blundered. The Normans turn on their horses, ride into the scattered English troops, and disperse them, grasping victory from the jaws of defeat. The duke rallies his troops and charges again. By dusk King Harold is dead and the English begin to flee. Fifty horsemen are lured into an abyss by an English detachment and plunge to their death. It is the last battle. By nightfall all is quiet.

In one day the course of history has been changed. The duke will become known as William the Conqueror, and on Christmas day in Westminster Abbey he is crowned king of England. For someone who was the illegitimate son of Duke Robert I of Nor-

mandy and the daughter of a tanner, he certainly went far. It just
shows what can be achieved with a little ambition.

1086: The Domesday Book. One of William of Normandy's
great achievements after he had conquered England and become
king was the compilation of the Domesday Book, a survey of
nearly all the counties of England, summarizing the property and
assets of the landowners. It includes the names of everyone from
the king to bishops, earls, and tenants; details the size of each
holding; records the number of villeins, mills, ponds, tools, animals, and just about everything else. It was so complete that one
Anglo-Saxon writer stated that not a cow, pig, or ox escaped
notice by the king's commissioners.

William wanted the country surveyed, of course, so he knew
what he owned and what his tenants-in-chief owned. He could
then make sure he was collecting taxes on everything that wasn't
his. The survey was a monumental task and the Domesday Book
today serves as a fascinating document of great importance to
historians. It is even occasionally quoted in courts of law in cases
of property disputes.

12th Century: Beginnings of Gothic Architecture. What
we term today the Gothic style has nothing to do with the Goths,
those so-called barbarians who overran Rome. The name was
given to the style by Giorgio Vasari, a mid-sixteenth-century Florentine painter, architect, and art historian who reviled the pinna-
cles, spires, pointed arches, ribbed vaults, and grotesque
decorations characteristic of the architecture. Vasari preferred the
simple classical style, and felt anything else must have been originated by the Goths, whom he considered an uneducated Germanic
tribe with no knowledge of the classics. Despite Vasari's prejudices,
the Gothic style inspired some of the most beautiful and famous
cathedrals and buildings in the world, culminating in the Cathedral
at Chartres, France.

1123: Omar Khayyam Dies. Omar, son of a Persian tent
maker, was an astronomer and mathematician of some note. He
was apparently also an authority on history, philosophy, and law.
Most of us know him, however, as the composer of the quatrains,
or *ruba'is,* that he wrote, which number about a thousand. In
1859 the English poet and translator Edward Fitzgerald translated

Omar's work into the *Rubaiyat of Omar Khayyam,* which catapulted them both into fame. The most often quoted lines are:

> *A book of verses underneath the bough,*
> *A jug of wine, a loaf of bread—and Thou*
> *Beside me singing in the wilderness—*
> *Oh, wilderness were paradise enow!*

1150: Angkor Wat. The Hindu funeral temple of the Khmer
king Suryavarman II is completed in this year. He was the powerful king who built Angkor Wat in Cambodia, one of the great
archaeological sites of the world. Between the ninth and thirteenth
centuries, successive kings made their capitals on the site, and each
built a new temple complex. It is estimated that the greatest of
these, Angkor Wat, is the world's largest stone monument. Its
buildings are altogether larger than the pyramids, and its sculptures
the equal to those of ancient Greece. It took thirty-seven years
to build and required millions of tons of sandstone, all transported
by rafts on the river. Adjacent to Angkor Wat is the walled city
of Angkor Thom, with another huge temple of courtyards and
corridors and enormous sculptured stone faces.

As the empire declined, the buildings fell to ruins, and by the
nineteenth century, when the French arrived, the jungle had en-
croached upon the ancient cities, and huge trees and vines now
entwine themselves among the stones of the massive temples. The
site is a marvel of art and architecture and part of the cultural
heritage of the Khmer people.

1152: The Magnificent Eleanor. On May 18, in a brief
ceremony at Poitiers in France, Eleanor of Aquitaine, the most
desired heiress in Europe, becomes the bride of Henry Planta-
genet, Duke of Normandy.

The raven-haired, green-eyed Eleanor, one of the most fascinating women in history, had recently been divorced from King
Louis VII of France on the grounds of consanguinity. Two years
hence the former queen of France will become the queen of
England when her husband succeeds to the throne as Henry II.
Between the two of them, they will control all of western France
as well as England.

Born to the Duke of Aquitaine about 1122, Eleanor became
the best catch in Europe as heir to her father's extensive lands,

which stretched from the Pyrenees to the Loire in southwest France. Louis VI, with his eye on the vast property, arranged for his son and heir to marry Eleanor in 1137, and a year later, after Louis VI's death, the two teenagers were crowned king and queen of France. When Henry became involved in the Second Crusade, Eleanor and many of her ladies accompanied him to Antioch and Jerusalem and apparently had a wild time of it if the rampant rumors about her affairs and unladylike behavior are to be believed. One must give her credit, however, for embarking on such a long and dangerous journey.

The court of Eleanor and Henry became a thriving center for the arts. Queen Eleanor was known as the patron, protectress, and guiding light of western and northern French literature, and in return the troubadours and poets not only dedicated their work to her but based some of their characters on her.

Intrigue was also part of Eleanor's life. Henry had not proven himself a competent ruler. He had trouble with his nobles and barons and in general was not well liked. When two of Henry and Eleanor's sons, Geoffrey and Henry, became involved in a plot to overthrow him, Eleanor supported them. When the plot failed, Henry kept her in confinement and used her as a pawn in his political games. When Henry died in 1189, their son Richard the Lionheart became king, and Eleanor was restored to her rightful place. She leaped into the political fray, arranged Richard's marriage, and when he was captured on his return from the Third Crusade and held for ransom by the Duke of Austria, she raised the money to free him. All the while he was away, she ably governed the realm. When Richard died of wounds a few years later, his brother John became king. At the age of seventy-seven Eleanor slogged her way across the Pyrenees in winter to bring back her granddaughter, Blanche of Castile, as the prospective bride for the son of the king of France. Three years later she retired to the nunnery at Fontevrault and quietly passed into history there in 1204.

Except for two years of her life, Eleanor, either directly, through her husband, or through her son, held control of Aquitaine. This was quite an amazing feat in a world where women had little power. But then, the beautiful and intelligent Eleanor was an amazing woman: Wife of two kings, mother of two kings and two queens, diplomat, regent, traveler, and art patron, Eleanor

seemed to know everyone who was anyone in medieval Europe.
It must have been a wonderful life.

Ca. 1170: Arthurian Romances. About this time, the French
poet and troubadour Chrétien de Troyes completes his story of
Le Chevalier de la Charette, which introduces Sir Lancelot to the
cast of legendary heroes and heroines of Arthurian romance. Chiv-
alry is in bloom, courtly love is flowering, and troubadors are
singing songs about Arthur, his wife, Guinevere, Sir Lancelot, and
Perceval, their loves and adventures. These characters and more
will be reincarnated in ensuing centuries in poems, novels, operas,
musicals, and movies, and King Arthur's home, Camelot, will
become synonymous with happy times and idyllic retreats.

1174: The Sport of Kings. Horses, noble beasts that they are,
have probably been raced since humans first domesticated them.
An ancient Hittite manual on the care, feeding, and training of
horses, written about 1500 B.C., has been uncovered in a town
near present-day Ankara. Speed and endurance were being bred
into horses even then. The first record of an actual horse race was
during the thirty-third Olympic Games in Greece, about 644 B.C.
The Romans used horses in the chariot races for which they were
famous, but when they invaded Britain, they were met with
equally skilled charioteers, and it was in Britain that modern horse
racing as we know it began.

The first true racetrack was built in 1174, at Smithfield outside
the gates of London, where horse fairs attracting the nobility were
held on Fridays. The thoroughbred horses, ridden by jockeys,
were raced over the track so that the would-be buyers could judge
them before they bought. Sometime during the reign of Richard I
(1189–99), the first race for a money purse was run, with the
horses ridden by knights. About 1500, horse racing was established
at Chester, England, and has existed there ever since.

It was the monarchy's interest in racing and the establishment
of breeding farms and racetracks that spurred on the sport. Charles
II, frequently called the "father of the British turf," was a consummate horseman, and occasionally rode his own horse to win a
race. His friends, to whom he parceled out land in America,
brought the sport with them to the New World. The first track
was established about 1665 near what is now Hempstead, Long
Island, and called Newmarket, after the racecourse in England.

The name of the track was changed to the Union Racecourse after the Revolutionary War, and racing continued there for about one hundred years. Virginia, Maryland, and the Carolinas were popular states for horse breeding and racing, and the sport continued to spread. Betting on races was only between owners or among spectators until bookmakers from England introduced their method here in about 1871. Pari-mutuel betting, although not as popular, was begun about the same time, and after the reform movement in the United States, which shut down many racetracks, pari-mutuel betting was the only kind allowed and is what we use today when we make a bet to win, place, or show. And at the finish line, when you're standing there with the winning ticket at twenty to one, the joy is uncontrollable.

1174: Leaning Tower of Pisa. Under the direction of the architect Bonanno Pisa, the now infamous round bell tower is begun. It is built of white marble inlaid with colored marbles, with walls thirteen feet thick at the base. The interior stairway has 296 steps. The foundation of the tower is only about ten feet deep, and its circumference is the same as the tower. During construction the foundation settled slightly on one side and some of the floors were straightened to compensate for this. Apparently not enough, however, since by 1829 it was over fifteen feet off kilter, and by the middle of the twentieth century, it leaned more than seventeen feet. The foundations have since been reinforced with concrete.

It was supposedly on top of the tower that the mathematician Galileo dropped cannonballs of different weights to prove his iconoclastic theory that objects fall at the same rate of speed despite their difference in weight.

The slight error in engineering has, however, brought fame and tourists to Pisa to view the celebrated cockeyed campanile.

13th Century: Checkers. Its roots go back much further than this, to ancient Egypt and Greece and Rome. Exactly how it was played, we don't know, but checkerboards and pieces similar to ours have been uncovered by archaeologists, and Plato and Homer have mentioned it in their writings. The game as we know it today probably originated in southern France or Spain around the thirteenth century and spread from there. The British call their game draughts, which comes from an old English word meaning to "move" or "move along." The English once referred to chess moves as draughts, and the word spilled over into the checkers game. The rules of checkers are much simpler than chess, although it can be just as intriguing. As the English writer Samuel Johnson stated, "The game of draughts is peculiarly calculated to fix the attention without straining it." Perhaps that's why so many of us find it so much fun.

13th Century: The Buttonhole Devised. Buttons had been around since the dawn of history, but only for ornamental use. They were usually made of precious metals or stone, and over the centuries became symbols of rank. The button makers' guild was formed in Paris about 1250, establishing button making as a legitimate craft, and thereby assuring that only the wealthy could afford to buy them. This increased their value as status symbols even more. It may well have been one of these craftsmen who thought up the ingenious idea of putting a button on one piece of cloth through a hole on another piece of cloth and fastening the two together. Still a status symbol, but now a practical one. It would be another six hundred years before the invention of the zipper.

1202: Zero. Leonardo of Pisa, also known as Fibonacci, completes his *Liber Abaci* treatise on algebra and urges the use of Hindu-Arabic numerals. Fibonacci illustrates the first nine Hindu figures and the 0, which in Arabic is called *zephyrum*. In Italian the word was written as *zeuero* or *zepiro,* and in a contracted form, *zero,* which the French borrowed and gave to the English.

The concept of a zero had been known to the ancient Babylonians and also to Greek and Arabic astronomers. The Babylonian system of notation used the base sixty, rather than ten, and used a place-value system. They invented the zero for the empty space that occurred during their computations. It made arithmetic easier to write down. Think how you would have to write 1, 10, or 100 otherwise. Of course, if you got a zero on your last math exam, you might feel you could live without it.

1215: Magna Carta. On June 15, in the meadow of Runnymede, between Staines and Windsor, King John of England sealed the charter known as the Magna Carta. It has been a symbol against oppression ever since. When William of Normandy conquered England in 1066, he was in a position of supreme power, dominating not only the barons who had fought with him but the church as well. His son, Henry I, thought it prudent to make concessions and promises to the barons and clergy, and did so in a charter sealed with the king's great seal. The next three monarchs followed suit upon their coronations. Common law increased during this period, as well as financial liabilities, and the barons soon began to feel their power waning and the king's gaining. Richard I had increased taxes in order to pay for his Crusade, his ransom, and his war with France. The last straw was King John's excommunication by Pope Innocent III for refusing to allow the new archbishop of Canterbury entrance to England. The barons threatened civil war and John submitted. The charter reaffirmed the rights of the barons according to the feudal system and curtailed the power of the monarchy. The charter was revised several times, and the charter of Henry III, sealed in 1225, is the one future governments would remember when forming their own laws on the fundamental rights of people.

1249: Universities Begin in England. University College, the earliest college of what will become Oxford University, is founded in Oxford, England.

Scholars had lectured in the town for over a hundred years, and religious communities of monks had advanced it as a center of learning. A college itself was a communal house in which students lived and ate, similar to today's dormitories, but where they also studied with their masters. Prior to having a college in which to dwell, students boarded with townspeople, who seemed to overcharge them for everything, thereby creating great animosities.

In 1263 Balliol College was founded by the Scottish nobleman John Balliol, who had quarreled with the bishop of Durham and as penance was required to support several students in a house at the university. After he died, his wife endowed the scholars and gave their house a charter. In 1264 Merton College was established by Walter de Merton, chancellor of England and Bishop of Rochester. During the next century four more colleges were added, by which time Oxford had established itself as a prestigious university.

Cambridge University, Oxford's great rival, began with Peterhouse College, established in 1284. The story behind the university's founding is rather amusing. Back in 1209 at Oxford, there had been what one might today call a rumble between the students and the townspeople (the old town-versus-gown problem, which still occasionally flares up). Consequently some of the scholars and masters relocated in Cambridge and continued their studies there. In 1229 Henry II of England offered sanctuary at Cambridge to some restless students who had left Paris, advising the town fathers that they should be happy to have them and that the scholars would bring honor to the town. To assure safe haven to all, no scholar could stay unless supervised by a master. The students and masters lived together in boardinghouses, and when order finally became too much to maintain, a separate college was established for them by Hugh de Balsham, bishop of Ely. Within the next seventy years, seven more colleges had been founded. In 1441 Henry VI established Saint Mary and Saint Nicholas (Kings College), and in the next century several more were added, elevating Cambridge to the forefront of the scholarly world.

1253: The Sorbonne Founded. Robert de Sorbon, a chaplain, builds a school to accommodate indigent theological students, which becomes the first college of the University of Paris, the most celebrated university in western Europe.

Universities during the Middle Ages were not quite what they are today. The word *university* comes from the Latin word *universitas,* meaning "guild" or "corporation," which was exactly what universities in the Middle Ages were. They provided an established community within a feudal society which had rights separate from the church and could establish rules governing apprenticeships, licenses for teachers, and a secure place for its members in society.

From the eleventh century Paris had been the home of internationally known scholars such as William of Champeaux, Peter Abelard, and Peter the Lombard. They attracted a great number of scholars and students to the city, and in time, the University of Paris became so respected that it served as a role model for the majority of universities established in England and France in the Middle Ages.

In order to be considered a medieval university by European standards, a university had to offer the arts (philosophy, classical studies, etc.), law, medicine, and theology. Very few schools opened their doors with all four areas intact, and the University of Paris was no exception. A school of the arts had existed before 1200; by 1208 a school of theology had been added. The law school was founded in 1271, and the medical school was established in 1274, thereby making the University of Paris a full-fledged medieval university.

Among the great scholars teaching there in the thirteenth and fourteenth centuries were Saint Bonaventura, Albertus Magnus, and Saint Thomas Aquinas. Abelard almost certainly could never have imagined the growth of the school he helped to found. Archaeology, physics, literature, economics, and other areas of study now offered are certainly a far cry from the four basic subjects that allowed a school to become a university.

Ca. 1254–Ca. 1324: The Adventures of Marco Polo.

One of the world's most famous travelers, the Venetian Marco Polo accompanies his father and uncle on a journey to the Far East and spends the next twenty-four years trekking through Asia, Persia, and India, and visiting Sumatra and Malaysia. His father, Nicolo, and uncle, Matteo, merchants from a noble family, had journeyed in 1265 to the court of the great Kublai Khan in what is now Beijing and were two of the few Europeans of that era to visit China.

Three years after the trio left Venice, they arrived at Kublai Khan's summer palace, where they were received favorably once again. Marco studied the Mongol language and became a trusted envoy for the Khan. During his travels he made precise notes about the people, customs, agriculture, products, and incidents he encountered along the way and related these to the Khan, who was eager for knowledge of these vast lands.

The travelers arrived back home, where their relatives apparently did not recognize them after twenty-five years, and were said to have brought much wealth with them. Marco became a naval officer, was captured during a short war between Genoa and Venice, and imprisoned for less than a year. It was during his captivity that he dictated his adventures to a fellow prisoner, a writer of romances. His chronicles contain a wealth of information about the remarkable culture of China, its science and geography, economics and politics. Europeans, however, seemed rather apathetic towards this new knowledge, and it took another two centuries in a more enlightened era before much of the scholarship came into use. Columbus apparently drew on the material while researching his route to China.

Aside from the romantic, adventuresome figure he is portrayed as in books and movies, Marco Polo seems to have been intelli-

gent, open-minded, farsighted, and perhaps a man ahead of his
time; a man for all seasons.

1260: Chartres Cathedral Consecrated. Built mostly be-
tween 1195 and 1228, the Cathedral of Notre Dame at Chartres,
in France's Loire Valley, is finally consecrated. The cathedral is
famed as a magnificent example of Gothic architecture at its
height.

Ca. 1280–1286: Eyeglasses Invented. In ancient China
judges wore smoky-colored quartz glasses, which supposedly hid
their expressions when they were hearing legal evidence. This
gives a new twist to the "justice is blind" adage. It was the Chinese who, in the middle of the thirteenth century, began inserting
convex quartz into tortoiseshell frames to help them read more
clearly. Whether these were the first eyeglasses, or whether they
were devised in Europe about the same time, is speculative. For
a while Europeans had been wearing magnifying glasses enclosed
in frames to better their reading, also.

Roger Bacon, the English philosopher and scientist, recorded
the earliest comments on the optical use of lenses in 1268, when
he included drawings of convex lenses in his *Opus Majus*. What
would be considered true eyeglasses appeared in Italy sometime
between 1280 and 1286. They were probably made by an unknown Tuscan glassmaker, and were introduced by Alessandro di
Spina of Florence. The frames did not have a bridge, and sometimes the two eyepieces were riveted together. Obviously keeping
them on was difficult, but they did improve vision.

The first lenses were made of transparent quartz and were convex in shape, therefore only able to be used for reading. With the
invention of the printing press and the spread of reading material,
the demand for glasses increased. Optical glass was adopted for
lenses, which made the spectacles more efficient, and later led to
the invention of the microscope and the telescope. The lenses
were made of various intensities and were sold in shops or by
street peddlers. Customers merely tried on various glasses until a
suitable pair was found. Concave lenses for the nearsighted finally
appeared in the late fifteenth century and were no doubt a boon
to those who could finally see the forest as well as the trees. A
portrait of Pope Leo X painted by Raphael in 1517 shows him
with a pair of concave lenses.

We can thank Benjamin Franklin for inventing bifocals. Franklin was nearsighted, but as he aged he found he couldn't see the printed page as easily, either. He eventually had two pairs of glasses, one for distance, and one for reading. Exasperated by the necessity of switching back and forth, the inventive Franklin came up with the idea of cutting the lenses horizontally in two, using the top half for distance and the bottom half for reading. These lenses were held together by wire frames. Cemented bifocals were invented in 1884, the fused type in 1908, and one-piece bifocals in 1910. A short time later trifocals were introduced.

Leonardo da Vinci conceived the idea of contact lenses, but it wasn't until 1887 that they were first used. The early lenses were made of glass, covered the whole eye, and were not too popular. In the 1940s the corneal lens appeared on the market, as well as plastic lenses, which were much more comfortable and gained wide popularity. Contact lenses are invisible and give a wider field of vision than eyeglasses do. In 1958 bifocal contact lenses were developed. Today, half the people in the United States wear either contact lenses or glasses.

Aside from improving vision, over the centuries the wearing of glasses has occasionally been a fad and even a status symbol. Sometimes only the frames were worn for adornment. In 1679 a countess visiting Madrid noted that she was surprised to see so many young ladies wearing spectacles whether they needed them or not. She was told it was done to make them look serious, invalidating Dorothy Parker's famous remark, "Men don't make passes at girls who wear glasses." In this same Spanish court, the men wore glasses, too. Apparently as the man increased his wealth or rank in society, the size of his spectacles increased proportionately. Today, of course, glasses and sunglasses are worn by those in public life for a variety of reasons, not the least being to call attention to oneself.

1307: The Divine Comedy. One of the most famous poems in literature is begun by Dante Alighieri, the greatest of the Italian poets. Written in three sections, *Inferno, Purgatorio, Paradiso,* it relates the story of Dante's imaginary journey through hell, purgatory, and paradise. Appearing in the poem are such characters as Virgil, Saint Bernard, citizens of his hometown of Florence, historical philosophers, kings, and popes, as well as Beatrice, the love of his life.

1345: Notre Dame Completed. Under construction for 182
years, the cathedral on the Ile de la Cité in the Seine at Paris is
completed. Renowned for its flying buttresses and gargoyles, the
cathedral is perhaps even more famous as the setting for the darkly
romantic 1831 novel by Victor Hugo, *Notre Dame de Paris*. Better
known as *The Hunchback of Notre Dame,* it tells the tale of the
deformed bell ringer, Quasimodo, who saves the gypsy girl, Esmeralda, by whisking her off to the bell tower and out of the
clutches of the wicked archdeacon. Unfortunately, Esmeralda is
recaptured, but Quasimodo gets his revenge as he throws the
archdeacon off the belfry. The story expanded Notre Dame's fame
and it was no longer just another great Gothic cathedral.

1354: The Alhambra. After being under construction for over
one hundred years, the beautiful Alhambra Palace in Granada,
Spain, is completed. Situated in the Alameda (park) de la Alhambra
were several buildings including the royal palace, a smaller residence for court officials, and the castle with massive ramparts and
towers. Among the structures were courtyards, fountains, and gardens. After the expulsion of the Moors from Spain in 1492, much
of the Alhambra was defaced and destroyed, and over the ensuing
years parts of it were rebuilt in different styles, then damaged again
in the 1821 earthquake. Restoration was begun in 1828 under
King Ferdinand VII and continued for the rest of the century.

The Alhambra, with its filigree walls, marble columns, colorful
tiles, domed roofs, and vaulted ceilings, is an outstanding example
of Islamic architecture.

Ca. 1378: Robin Hood. The English poet William Langland,
in his poem *Piers Plowman,* mentions "rhymes of Robin Hood,"
and a century later the printer Wynken de Worde prints *The Lytell
Geste of Robyn Hode,* the first complete ballad of the story of
Robin Hood.

We don't know who Robin Hood was, or *if* he was, but his
heroics are legendary. He may be a composite of several people
or he may have been a follower of Simon de Montfort, who led
a baronial revolt against King Henry III, a court servant of Edward
II, or just a common outlaw. Whether his name was Hood, Hod,
or Hobbehod, he seems to have done his good deeds in Yorkshire
in Barnsdale Forest, rather than Sherwood. Although celebrated
for stealing from the rich to give to the poor, Robin Hood was

probably more of a rebel against authority, a Saxon still fighting the Norman takeover of Britain. His derring-do is the stuff of legends, and for over six hundred years he and his band of merry men have fought injustice and championed the cause of the downtrodden in poems, dramas, books, and movies. Maid Marian, by the way, didn't hook up with Robin until 1601, although she had originally appeared in a thirteenth-century French pastoral ballad with another gentleman named Robin. They seem to have been a good match.

1384: The Flourishing of No Theater. Motokiyo Zeami, the Shakespeare of Japan, is twenty-one when his father dies. A brilliant actor since the age of eleven, when he attracted the shogun's attention and gained his patronage, Zeami is now the leading force in the No theater, which he and his father have created and which survives today. Of the 200 plays Zeami wrote in his life of eighty years, 124 are still in the repertory. His subject matter deals with warriors and ghosts, insanity, historical characters, beautiful women, demons, gods, and prosperity. Originally the dramas lasted all day, with comic performances during intermissions, but in the last few decades the performance time has been greatly reduced. In the realm of Japanese literature Zeami and his father, Kanami Kiyotsugu, are celebrated for their beautiful poetry and for raising the drama to high art.

1394–1460: Prince Henry of Portugal. The brother of the King of Portugal, Henry the Navigator, certainly a misnomer since he never navigated a thing, underwrites and directs explorations along the western coast of Africa for forty years—not for altruistic reasons, but to search for sources of gold and other commercial ventures, as well as for diplomatic reasons and the glory of God. Henry subsidized scholarly research into cartography and hydrography and the development of new navigational techniques and shipbuilding.

Not renowned for his own exploits, Henry is remembered for accelerating the great age of discovery, which expanded European explorations and created a whole new world.

1400: The Canterbury Tales. England's celebrated storyteller and poet Geoffrey Chaucer is writing his most famous work when he dies at the age of about sixty. *The Canterbury Tales* make him

immortal and give us some of England's first great poetry. The
original plan was for 120 stories, two for each pilgrim to narrate
on the way to Canterbury and two on the way back, but only
twenty-two were completed. The tales are told by such characters
as a miller, a friar, a summoner, a knight, and a wife of Bath. The
stories are full of comedy, satire, farce, realism, and insight into
human nature. The characters are culled from the society of the
day, and some are said to be based upon people Chaucer knew.
The poet enjoyed life, and it is reflected in his work. He was
buried in Westminster Abbey, at the time quite an honor for
a commoner.

1436: The Duomo Is Consecrated. The great Cathedral of
Santa Maria del Fiore in Florence, Italy, is finished after being
under construction for 140 years. Among its features is the 350-
foot-high dome, measuring 138 feet across, designed by Filippo
Brunelleschi, one of the great architects and inventors of the Renaissance. Among the sculptors who worked on the cathedral are
Donatello and Luca della Robbia.

Ca. 1440: The Gutenberg Press. The acknowledged inventor of the printing press using movable type is Johann Gensfleisch,
a printer from Mainz, Germany. We know him as Johann Gutenberg, the name of his family estate. Although other printers were
experimenting with the same procedure elsewhere in Europe, Johann seems to have been the first to assemble all the necessary
materials together to accomplish his feat. He made the molds from
which to cast individual letters of the same length, developed an
alloy of lead, tin, and antimony for the type, and improved the
consistency of the ink he used. Paper had also become abundant
in Europe by this time.

The first large book printed with movable type was the Bible,
now known as the Gutenberg Bible, several copies of which are
still extant. The printing press was an invention whose time had
come. During this period in history, the number of university
students was increasing, expanding the need for books, and the
rising middle class was becoming more literate. The printing press
had a tremendous impact on civilization. By 1500 it is estimated
that thirty-five thousand different editions of books had been published, with a total of somewhere between fifteen and twenty
million books in print. The Renaissance was upon Europe, and

books would soon spread new ideas, art, and technology throughout the land.

1446: Blarney Castle Completed. Built by Cormac Laidliv McCarthy, lord of Muskerry, with walls eighteen feet thick, the fortress in County Cork, Ireland, is renowned mainly for one reason. In a turret below the battlements on the southern wall is a limestone rock, the Blarney Stone. Eloquence of speech, or as some call it, the gift of gab, will be conferred upon anyone brave enough to hang downward to kiss it. The legend appeared about two centuries ago, perhaps made up by some enterprising public relations man to stir up the tourist business in nearby Cork.

Ca. 1457: The Game of Golf. Humans have probably been swatting at stones with a stick since prehistory. They didn't know it would eventually lead to that most frustrating of games we call golf. The Romans played *paganica* in which they drove a feather-stuffed ball with a club, and may have introduced this throughout Europe. By medieval times Europeans were playing similar games, and in Britain they played *cammock* or *cambuc*, a word that originally meant a "bent stick."

Golf as we know it first appeared in Scotland and was so popular that King James II banned it because it interfered with archery practice for the troops. In 1754 the Society of Saint Andrews was formed, which developed the rules and traditions of the game we play today. The ball these Scots used was made by hand out of bull's hide filled with boiled goose feathers, which was then hammered into a rounded shape and painted. It could only be hit about 150 yards. In 1845, however, a ball made from gutta-percha, the latex of several varieties of trees in Malaysia, was devised. These were longer-lasting, cheaper to make, and improved the game. They were used until about 1900, when the rubber ball that we use today was invented.

The game came over to America in the late nineteenth century, but never attained the popularity of football and baseball until about 1920. After World War II, golf became more accessible to the average person, and with the advent of televised tournaments, more and more of us began taking a swat at the ball.

Ca. 1483: A Shropshire Lad. The small memorial stone in the floor of the south transept of Westminster Abbey reads:

Tho. Parr of Y County of Sallop born in AD 1483. He lived
in Y Reignes of Ten Princes viz: K. Edw 4; K. Ed. V; Rich.
3; K. Hen 7; K. Hen. 8; Edw. 6; Q. Ma; Q. Eliz; K. Ja. &
K. Charles, Aged 152 years & was buryed here Novemb.
15, 1635.

He might have lived longer, but it seems the excesses of life at the
court of Charles I finally did him in.

"Olde, olde, very olde" Thomas Parr, as he was called, was born
in Winnington in Shropshire, England, the son of an agricultural
laborer. Although the exact date of his birth cannot be verified, it
is documented that in 1563, at the age of eighty, he married for the
first time and sired two children. The marriage lasted thirty-two
years, during which time Thomas's dillydallying with another
woman obliged him to do penance in a white sheet at the parish
church. Eight years after his first wife died, he married again, and
it was rumored he took another mistress. By the time he was 130,
he was still leading the simple but rigorous life of a farmer, with
diet consisting mainly of cheese, coarse bread and onions, milk, and
occasionally ale.

King Charles I heard about him through the earl of Arundel and
invited him to court. The earl sent a litter to carry him to London,
and for his amusement along the way, supplied him with a jester.
Alas, court life and rich food and wine took its toll and Thomas
succumbed at the earl's home on November 14, 1635. The great
physician William Harvey performed an autopsy, found his organs
to be in a very healthy condition, and concluded that the change
of diet and bad London air had contributed to his death. He was
buried in Westminster Abbey.

The secret to longevity may be a simple diet, fresh air, and hard
work. On the other hand, it may be to marry very late in life and
then sow your wild oats.

1492: Columbus Discovers the New World. On October
12, Christopher Columbus lands in the Bahamas and is convinced
he is in Asia.

Until his dying day, Columbus refused to admit he had discovered a whole new continent. He was, after all, en route to Asia,
and to admit otherwise was to admit failure.

After the Portuguese refused Columbus's proposal to sail to
China by a westward route, Columbus proposed his scheme to

Ferdinand and Isabella of Spain in 1486. Six years later, on August 3, with a crew of ninety and three ships, the Genoese mariner set sail for China, carrying letters from the Spanish royals to the rulers of the Orient. After a brief stop in the Canary Islands, the trio of ships departed on September 6 and headed westward into the unknown. We can only conjecture what went on in the minds of these brave souls as they sailed into that great expanse of ocean. When they could no longer see land, fear and trepidation overcame the crew and they accused Columbus of risking their lives. The relief they felt when land was finally sighted must have been enormous as shouts of gladness and thanks to God filled the air. The journey proved the indomitable spirit of humankind.

Columbus named the island he landed on San Salvador and truly believed he was off the coast of China. He continued sailing, discovered Española (Haiti), and in January returned to Spain, where he was honored by Ferdinand and Isabella. On his second voyage with seventeen ships and over one thousand passengers, Columbus founded the settlement he named Isabella, on the island of Española, as a base to explore the Orient. He was either determined or stubborn. During this voyage he also discovered Puerto Rico, Guadeloupe, Jamaica, and Cuba, which he makes his crew swear is the mainland of Asia. On his third voyage he discovered Trinidad, Venezuela, and the mouth of the Orinoco River, and on his fourth and last expedition, which was also his fastest crossing, twenty-one days, he discovered Martinique and sailed along the coasts of Honduras and Panama, believing he was nearing the Ganges River. Obviously it was wishful thinking.

Whatever his original motives were (for God, king, and riches), Columbus and his valiant men had changed the course of history and reached a whole new world that would, in centuries to come, bring forth wealth beyond their imagination.

1489: Plus or Minus.
The Germans loved algebra and any books on the subject. In fact, the Germanic word *coss,* meaning "unknown," nearly replaced the Arabic word *algebra,* so we narrowly escaped having to do cossic equations for homework. The Germans did triumph, however, when the symbols for addition and subtraction, p and m, were displaced by + and − in our notation. These two signs had been used commercially when reckoning warehouse inventory. An arithmetic book published in 1489

by Johann Widman, who taught at Leipzig University in Germany, is the oldest book in which these symbols appear.

1493–1541: Paracelsus. Philippus Aureolus Theophrastus Bombast von Hohenheim, aka Paracelsus, was born in Switzerland, the son of a physician. His name was typical of the period, but Paracelsus dismissed it as he dismissed the theories of organized medicine.

Depending on the generation, Paracelsus might have been called a crackpot, flake, weirdo, or far out. He was not a certified doctor and would not take the Hippocratic oath. Medicine was, until this time, studied only by aristocrats, and their knowledge was off-limits to laymen. Paracelsus was ostracized because he brought medicine to the common man, sharing his knowledge and experience, and lecturing in German rather than the learned Latin. This reckless wanderer and mystic may have been disliked by the medical establishment, but he was just what the doctor ordered; the right man at the right time. Paracelsus opened a new era of medicine, and in spite of, or perhaps because of, his eccentric qualities, made many contributions. He was the first to propound the idea of medical chemistry, introducing nonpoisonous chemicals for medicinal use. He recognized silicosis and tuberculosis as diseases in miners, and that syphilis could be congenital. He theorized about antiseptics and introduced the idea that disease had an external cause and was not the result of some inner spiritual demons.

As the navigators of this period sailed into the unknown oceans to find new routes and new lands, and new avenues of religious thought arose, a new world of medicine began to grow after Paracelsus knocked down the old walls of science.

1497–99: Vasco da Gama Rounds Africa. A Portuguese navigator, da Gama continues the sea exploits of Portugal and is the first to sail around Africa into the Indian Ocean. He opened up the spice trade between Europe and India and established Portuguese colonies there and on the east coast of Africa.

1498: Chinese Invent the Toothbrush. Although toothbrushes in the form of a twig with one end frayed into fibers have been found in five-thousand-year-old Egyptian tombs, the toothbrush with bristles didn't appear until almost the sixteenth century. The bristle were plucked from hogs and attached to bone or bamboo handles. The toothbrush gradually found its way to Europe through trade, where the hog's hair was replaced by softer horsehair. The masses of people never bothered with cleaning their teeth, and those who did preferred toothpicks, as was the custom in ancient Rome. Our modern-day nylon toothbrush wasn't marketed until about 1938 and soon replaced hog bristles as the brush of choice, much to the relief of the world's hog population. In 1961 the electric toothbrush was invented, and a year later the cordless electric appeared. Don't forget to floss!

16th Century: Native Tongues Begin to Babble. Schol-
ars, philosophers, theologians, statesmen, and other learned men spoke and wrote Latin and were taught in Latin. (Every university town had its Latin Quarter where the students hung out *salve*ing each other and going off *imbibere* if they had any *pecunia*.) Along came the Protestant Reformation and the printing press and out went Latin. In came a new form of elementary school (formerly called a *ludus litterarius*) in Germany in the sixteenth century designed to teach in the "common man's" or vernacular language.

The idea of writing in one's native tongue was not unheard of, but for the most part, it was held that education should take place in Latin. The vernacular was fine for business and trade, since the average trader or merchant had little use for reading or writing skills. Latin was the language of the educated; most scholarship was international, and the common language of Latin bridged that cultural barrier. The printing press provided the means for challenging this. Written material could be copied much more easily than by hand, so books or bulletins could now be mass-produced, gradually making the written word available to the average man both in terms of number and price.

This might not have come to much if it had not been for the work of men like Martin Luther, who found the printing press useful in spreading his ideas to the masses. As part of his role in the Protestant Reformation, he preached that the common man should be able to read the Bible. Not only did this mean translating it into the vernacular and distributing it, but also increasing literacy. The printing press could help with the former, but the education system had to be revised to improve the latter. And that's what happened. With the help of advisers and colleagues of Luther, many Protestant communities set up vernacular elementary schools to teach the basic skills of reading and writing, plus practical instruction in trades. Secondary schools taught Latin, Greek, and Hebrew as well as such scholarly pursuits as history, science, and mathematics. A basic education was now available to many more individuals than before.

As Protestantism spread, so did the vernacular schools. Although education was still tied to religion, people demanded more and more schools for their children where they could learn their catechism in their native tongue. By the time the Pilgrims arrived on our shores, teaching children in their own language was the accepted method. *Deo gratias!*

16th Century: Pencils and Pens. In 1564 in Borrowdale, England, a raging storm uproots a huge oak tree. This fortuitous happening uncovers a deposit of exceptionally pure graphite, which will be mined and made into pencils.

We refer to these instruments as lead pencils (from the Latin *penicillus,* "little tail") because graphite was originally thought to have been a type of lead, called black lead, or plumbago. In 1779 the Swedish chemist Carl Wilhelm Scheele identified it as a carbon, and ten years later the German geologist Abraham Werner gave it the name graphite from the Greek *graphein,* "to write."

And write, we did. First we used chunks of graphite cut into stick shapes, which, of course, left as much residue on our hands as words on the paper. So someone had the bright idea of wrapping the graphite with string, which worked fairly well. Pieces of graphite were also inserted into tubes or held by metal claws. The real breakthrough came when Kaspar Faber opened his pencil factory in Nuremberg, Germany, in 1761 and produced pencils made of one part sulfur and two parts graphite encased in wood. In 1858 the first erasers appeared on the ends of pencils and replaced the bread crumbs that had been used for centuries to remove lead marks. That was not only a vast improvement but kept the pesky birds away.

In 1828 in Birmingham, England, John Mitchell began manufacturing pens with steel nibs, although handmade steel pens had been made in the middle of the eighteenth century. The new process brought joy to the avian world, which no longer had to contribute its fine feathers for use as writing instruments. Quill pens had been used for centuries (archaeologists have, however, discovered bronze pen points in the ashes of Pompeii), and it gives one pause to think of all the famous documents that have been written with quills.

The next step in the evolution of pens was the fountain pen, which could hold a supply of ink, making it unnecessary to continually dip the nib in the inkwell. The first practical fountain pen was introduced in 1884 by L. E. Waterman, and quickly caught on. A few years later the ballpoint pen was patented by an American inventor and was used mainly for writing on irregular surfaces. The first really practical ballpoint pen was patented in 1937 by the Hungarian Lazlo Biro, who was living in Argentina. It first became popular in Great Britain and owes its acceptance here to the Army Quartermaster Corps, who found it fit their requirements: It didn't leak at high altitudes, contained an ink supply that lasted a long time, and used a fast-drying ink that wasn't affected by changes in climate. What was good enough for the army was good enough for the rest of us. Inexpensive and disposable ballpoint pens began to sell like the proverbial hotcakes. They have been improved since the first ones were manufactured and continue to sell in the millions in various sizes, shapes, and colors.

Pens and pencils, two little items we don't think much about except when we are looking for one.

16th Century: High Heels. Oddly enough, heels were first worn by men. They discovered that a slight heel on their riding boots helped keep their feet in the stirrups. But it was Louis XIV of France, the king who brought culture and refinement to heights of excess, who spurred on this fashion. Louis was short, so he added an inch or two of heel to his shoes. Naturally, the courtiers copied the royal style. This, of course, made Louis short again, so he added another couple of inches to his shoes. This could not go on ad infinitum and it didn't. The gentlemen descended to reality, but the ladies did not. Women's shoes have had high heels ever since, including the short French heel that boosted Louis's ego.

16th Century: Doughnuts. We can thank the Dutch for these treats. They called their little fried nuts of dough *olykoek,* or "oily cake." The Pilgrims learned to like them during their stay in Holland and brought them to New England, where they were called dough nuts. When the Dutch settlers arrived in the New World, they also introduced a long, twisted pastry they called a cruller (from the Dutch *krullen,* "to curl"), which was equally as popular. The hole in the doughnut appeared courtesy of the

Pennsylvania Dutch, who were really German and called their
doughnuts *fastnachts* because they served them on Fastnacht Day—
Shrove Tuesday. With a hole in the center, the doughnut could
be fried more evenly and the soggy center was eliminated. Whatever you call them, a coffee break isn't the same without one, as
any cop on the beat will attest.

Ca. 1500: The Iroquois League. Hiawatha, a Mohawk In-
dian, along with the Huron Indian mystic Deganawida, form the
first intercommunity democracy on American soil.

These two men negotiated and campaigned for an end to tribal
fighting among the Mohawk, Oneida, Onondaga, Cayuga, and
Seneca tribes in upstate New York. The alliance formed between
these tribes became known as the Iroquois League and not only
ended the majority of the fighting among these five tribes, but
allowed for a representative form of government, with each tribe
being represented on the council by an elected member called a
sachem.

Supposedly the framers of the American Constitution kept Hia-
watha's basic framework for the League in mind when the time
came to create their own government.

We don't know much more about this imaginative Indian's life,
but Henry Wadsworth Longfellow borrowed his name for his
great poem, a fitting tribute to a man of such vision.

1500: Amazon River Discovered. Of course, the native In-
dians knew it was there, and now so did the Spanish. Vicente
Pinzón and his expedition traveled as far as fifty miles inland from
the Atlantic on the river they called Río Santa María de la Mar
Dulce. In 1541 the Spanish conquistador Pizarro and his company
of men and Indians crossed the Andes from Ecuador and discovered the Napo River, the headwater of the Amazon. It was Francisco de Orellana who reached the Amazon itself from the Napo.
He seems to have given it the name Amazon, referring to the
ancient mythological female warriors, after a battle with the local
Indians in which he thought the women fought alongside their
men, although it could be from the Indian word *amassona,* meaning "boat destroyer." Whatever its derivation, it is aptly named.
It is the largest river in the world in the volume of water it carries,

and the third longest, thirty-nine hundred miles, a little shorter than the Mississippi and not as long as the Nile.

Ca. 1507: La Gioconda. Leonardo da Vinci made a few sketches of Lisa di Anton, wife of businessman Francesco del Giocondo, and then worked on the painting for a couple of years. The *Mona Lisa* now hangs in the Louvre in Paris, arguably the most famous painting in the world. It is the enigmatic smile on her face that has catapulted her to such prominence.

Leonardo—painter, sculptor, architect, illustrator, philosopher, poet, scientist, mathematician, inventor, and world-class genius—was born in 1452 at Vinci, near Florence, the illegitimate son of a peasant girl and a public official. Fortunately, his father acknowledged him, brought him up, and apprenticed him to an artist. He was in Milan in his thirties under the patronage of the Sforza family, where he engaged in all sorts of activities, including military engineering, sculpting, and anatomical research, and painted his second most famous work, the *Last Supper,* a fresco on the refectory wall of the monastery of Santa Maria Delle Grazie. He left Milan and began work for Cesare Borgia as an engineer and architect. After a brief stay in Florence, he was invited to the French court to paint Louis XII's portrait as well as other paintings such as the king desired. He later went to Rome for a while under the patronage of the de Medicis, where he conducted scientific experiments and worked on designs for St. Peter's, along with practically every other renowned artist of the time. Returning to France in about 1517, he worked for the king as a painter, architect, and engineer until he died in 1519.

It is for his extraordinary drawings that Leonardo is greatly acclaimed as an artist. Fortunately most of them exist and are now in museums in Milan, Paris, and Windsor Castle in England. Leonardo's notebooks, which he wrote from right to left so one needs a mirror to read them, illustrate his scientific bent. His drawings include diagrams for diving bells, underground canals, military equipment, flying machines, and model city plans. His notes detail studies on anatomy, geology, geography, and studies in light and shade. His incredible curiosity could not be stilled, which frequently led him to begin new projects while leaving others incomplete. This genius of his age, and indeed of all ages, was also adept at arranging banquets and pageants, especially to impress foreign visitors to town. His patrons and the king loved him for it. He must have been a great dinner partner.

1508: Michelangelo Tackles the Sistine Chapel. Michelangelo Buonarroti considers himself first and foremost a sculptor and is more than a little perturbed when Pope Julius II calls him to Rome to paint the ceiling of his private chapel. Michelangelo had already created the exquisite marble *Pietà* for St. Peter's (the only sculpture he signed) and the magnificent statue of David in Florence. Now he must hoist himself up on a scaffold and repaint the barrel-vaulted ceiling. It is a monumental task, and when he is finished, in September 1512, the Sistine Chapel is filled with biblical figures from Genesis to the time of Noah. The Pope is very pleased.

Aside from being a sculptor and painter, the Florentine Michelangelo was also an architect and a writer and a true man of the Renaissance. Born into an ancient established family in Florence in 1475, Michelangelo flouted convention and, against the wishes of his father and his uncle, chose to pursue art as a career. During his lifetime of eighty-nine years, however, he remained true to tradition and took financial and social responsibility for his family of siblings, nieces, and nephews.

Michelangelo's patrons who commissioned works include the ruling de' Medici family of Florence and four popes, for whom he created sculptures, designed tombs, drew up architectural plans, and painted. Pope Clement VII insisted he finish decorating the Sistine Chapel, for which Michelangelo produced the *Last Judgment,* an enormous fresco on the wall behind the altar, completed in 1541 for the new pope, Paul III. Its gigantic figures depicting the damned descending into hell, the apostles and martyrs, saints and angels, with Christ as the judge, completely overawed the Pope.

Today thousands of tourists visit the Sistine Chapel in the Vatican to view Michelangelo's work, which has recently been cleaned and repaired. It is ironic that the man who considered himself a sculptor should become most famous for painting one of the world's extraordinary masterpieces.

1513: Ponce de León Discovers Florida. De León arrived in the New World with Columbus on his second voyage. A few years later he explored and settled Puerto Rico and was named

its governor. Having heard tales of a fabulous fountain or spring that had great curative powers and would make men young again, de León obtained orders from the Spanish king to sail to Bimini, in the Bahamas, to search for the Fountain of Youth and, of course, for riches. At Easter time he landed near what is now St. Augustine and promptly named the land Florida from the name of the day on the calendar, Pascua Florida. He explored the coast on both sides, but not far enough apparently, since he thought he had discovered a large island.

Four hundred years later, the great American migration to the Sunshine State began in earnest, mostly for the same reasons Ponce de León had sailed there. He may have found the fountain, after all.

1513: Balboa Discovers the Pacific Ocean. The tall, handsome, and gallant Spanish conquistador had been unsuccessfully attempting a living as a pioneer farmer on the island of Hispaniola. To escape his creditors he hid in a cask and was carried aboard a ship headed to reinforce a colony on the Colombian coast. He joined a company of explorers and founded the colony of Santa María de la Antigua on the Isthmus of Darien in what is now Panama. Convinced that another sea and great riches lay not far beyond, he set out with 190 Spaniards and 800 Indians on September 1. Two weeks later he had crossed the isthmus and from the top of a hill became the first European to view the Pacific Ocean, or South Sea as it was called. He immediately claimed it and all the land along its coast for Spain.

1517: Ninety-five Theses. On October 31, Martin Luther, an Augustinian monk, nails his ninety-five theses to the door of the church in Wittenberg, Germany, marking the beginnings of the Protestant Reformation.

1519–21: First Circumnavigation of the Globe. On September 20, 1519, Ferdinand Magellan and his fleet of five ships and 265 men leave the port of Sanlucar de Barrameda in Spain, sail south to the Canary Islands, turn westward towards South America, and on December 13, reach the Bay of Rio de Janeiro, where they head down the coast to begin the search for the waterway to the "sea of the south."

By order of a papal bull in 1493, a longitudinal line of demarcation had been drawn declaring that all territories east of the line belonged to Portugal (which included Brazil), and all those to the west belonged to Spain. Magellan (a Portuguese nobleman who had been told by his own king to go serve elsewhere) cannily suggested to King Charles I of Spain that by sailing west to reach the wealthy Moluccas (Spice Islands), he could claim them for Spain. The king thought it was a great idea.

The journey is long and harsh. After quelling a mutiny and seeing one of his ships wrecked, on October 21, 1520, Magellan and the four remaining ships enter the straits that will later bear his name. During the harrowing and dangerous journey, another ship deserts the fleet and sails back to Spain. Magellan is resolutely determined to continue his odyssey, and on November 28 the tiny fleet reaches the ocean. Magellan cries for joy.

The sea the mariners now cross is so calm that they name it the Pacific Ocean, and although there are no storms on their route, it takes much longer than expected. Ninety-nine days later, the starving, debilitated, intrepid explorers make landfall at Guam in the Marianas. Here they take on much-needed supplies, then set sail once again. Instead of heading directly towards the Moluccas, Magellan lands at the island of Cebu in the Philippines, perhaps with the thought of taking on more food and securing a base of operation. There he makes an alliance with the native king, who in turn converts to Christianity. Unfortunately, this diversion costs Magellan his life. He is killed in a battle between the king of Cebu and a neighboring kingdom on April 27, 1521.

Two of his ships do reach the Moluccas, where they take on spices, then set sail for home. En route one ship is wrecked, and only one vessel, the aptly named *Victoria,* reaches Seville, Spain, on September 8, 1522, with their captain, El Cano, seven crew members, and four Indians surviving.

It had been one hundred years since the great age of exploration had begun that altered the map of the world and changed the course of history. Magellan was the first to cross the Pacific from east to west, disproving the theory that the Spice Islands were a mere few days' journey from the New World. His daring feat did prove that all the oceans of the world are connected and confirmed absolutely what many had long known, that the world is, indeed, round.

1525: Low-Rent Housing. Jakob Fugger II was a very wealthy and prominent member of a German merchant and banking family. He was also a philanthropist concerned with social problems. In Augsburg, Germany, he built a series of houses, called the Fuggerei, which he rented at very low rates to poor Catholic laborers and artisans. The settlement, the oldest housing project for the poor, still exists, supported by the Fuggerei Foundation which Jakob so generously endowed.

1534: Act of Supremacy. The British Parliament passed the Act of Supremacy in November 1534, declaring King Henry VIII the supreme head of the Church of England. This officially removed England from the power of the Roman Catholic pope and established the new Protestant Anglican Church.

Henry VIII had been seeking an annulment of his marriage to Catherine of Aragon in order to marry Anne Boleyn (later the mother of Queen Elizabeth I), but more for political than ecclesiastical reasons, the pope refused to grant him his request. Undaunted, Henry had already forced the English clergy to recognize his authority as head of the church in England, and by financial threats and political wiles, elevated the sympathetic Thomas Cranmer to bishop of Canterbury. Parliament then passed the Great Act of Appeals, which made Cranmer's bishopric the highest ecclesiastical tribunal for English court cases. Cranmer then, of course, granted Henry his divorce and he married Anne. The Act of Supremacy followed; England was out from under the thumb of the pope for the first time in history and turned to Protestantism with a vengeance.

1540–42: Coronado Explores the Southwest. In search of gold, the Spanish explorer Francisco De Coronado and his men trek over what is now Texas, New Mexico, and Arizona. Their explorations to find the legendary Seven Cities of Cibola with their vast treasures ended in disappointment. Some members of his expedition did, however, find something equally as magnificent, the Grand Canyon. We can only imagine what they must have thought upon viewing this vast chasm.

Apparently it was not significant to them, for it wasn't until 1776 that two Spanish priests rediscovered it.

1541: De Soto Discovers the Mississippi. With a force of over five hundred men and two hundred horses in nine ships, the Spaniard Hernando de Soto leaves Havana on May 18, 1539, and

a week later arrives in Tampa Bay, intending to explore and conquer Florida, a land of indeterminate size.

The group ventures northward, spending the winter in Tallahas-
see, and in the spring reach as far as what is now Columbia, South
Carolina. From there they explore part of North Carolina, then
cross westward into Alabama. On May 21 they come to the river
the Chippewa Indians called *micisibi*, "big river." De Soto and his
band cross it and continue their explorations as far as what is now
Arkansas, then head south into Louisiana and back to the big river.
It is there, exactly a year to the day that he first set eyes on it,
that de Soto dies of a fever and is buried in the river we now
call the Mississippi.

The men are then led by Luis de Moscoso and apparently reach
the Trinity River in Texas before returning to the Mississippi.
There they build boats and follow the coastline south until they
reach Tampico on the Gulf of Mexico.

De Soto's great journey not only resulted in the discovery of
the Mississippi but developed new information about the Indians
of the southeastern part of North America and led the way towards
future colonization of the region.

1543: A Revolutionary Idea. The Polish canon, amateur
astronomer, and mathematician Nikolaus Copernicus publishes his
De Revolutionibus Orbium Coelestium in which he hypothesizes the
highly imaginary idea that the earth rotates daily on its axis and
orbits, with the other planets, around the sun. This challenges
church doctrine that maintains the earth is the center of the universe. Martin Luther calls him "an upstart astrologer" who "wishes
to reverse the entire science of astronomy." It will be a while
before he is proven right.

Ca. 1545: Artificial Limbs Designed. Historians are aware
that as far back as 500 B.C. simple artificial devices were used by
those who had lost a leg. People have been trying to build spare
parts for centuries. One of the first attempts was a peg leg, which
was just a wooden stump, and a hook for a hand is still in use,
although vastly improved. In the sixteenth century, however, the
French battlefield surgeon Ambroise Paré replaced amputated
limbs with false ones he had designed and built. He tried to make
them as functional as possible by the use of mechanics and is
considered the founder of prosthetics as a science.

1546–1601: Tycho Brahe, Astronomer. The Danish astronomer and mathematician was fortunate that Frederick II of Denmark gave him an island on which to build the world's first modern observatory. Of course, the telescope had yet to come into scientific use, so all of Brahe's work was done by the naked eye and with the most sophisticated instruments then available, most of which he designed. He discovers a new star in the constellation Cassiopeia, which he realizes is beyond the moon, contrary to popular belief. Brahe publishes his treatise on the motions of the sun and moon and fixes quite accurately the places of almost eight hundred stars. He doesn't quite agree with Copernicus, however, and although he believes the planets revolve around the sun, he maintains the earth is stationary.

Ca. 1550: The Theater Stages a Comeback. The Confrérie de la Passion, a French acting group that had been producing mystery plays since 1402, builds a theater from the ruins of the duc de Bourgogne's town house in Paris, making it the first true public theater built since the fall of the Roman Empire. Since the troupe was not allowed to perform the popular religious dramas, they turned to comedies and tragedies and the occasional farce, which did not always pay the bills. To help fill their empty coffers, the Confrérie began to lease the theater to touring companies of thespians during their stays in Paris. This proved to be a successful ploy and the Hôtel de Bourgogne, as the theater was aptly called, continued presenting plays until 1783.

1557: The Equal Sign. The Welshman Robert Recorde came up with this one. He taught mathematics at Oxford and Cambridge, then received his medical degree and became physician to Edward VI and later to Queen Mary. In his book *The Whetstone of Witte,* the first use of the equal sign, =, appears. Recorde invented it, as he states, "to auoide the tediouse repetition of these woordes: is equalle to." It will take about a century before its use becomes standard.

1561: St. Basil's Cathedral Completed. St. Basil's in Moscow's Red Square is typical of Russian medieval architecture and is similar in form and structure to the older wooden churches. The nine chapels comprising the basilica are topped by variously shaped onion domes and spires complete with colorful decorations.

1570: First World Atlas Published. Abraham Ortelius, a cartographer and dealer in maps and antiquities in Antwerp, publishes his *Theatrum orbis terrarum* to great acclaim. The atlas includes seventy maps, all in identical style.

Ortelius frequently revised his maps when new information was received and produced several more editions through 1598. So good were his maps that they were printed through the seventeenth century.

1574: Uffizi Palace Completed. The palace joins the Pitti Palace across the Arno in Florence, Italy, by means of a corridor atop the Ponte Vecchio.

The Uffizi was headquarters for government offices while the Pitti remained a ducal residence. The Uffizi and the Pitti are now among the world's most famous art museums.

1576: England's First Theater. James Burbage, a carpenter-turned-actor, leases land in a northeast section of London and builds the first English theater. He calls it simply the Theatre, which indicates both its true purpose and a serious lack of imagination on his part.

1577–80: Sir Francis Drake Sails Around the World. In his famous flagship the *Golden Hind,* the English navigator and privateer Francis Drake leads an expedition across the Atlantic, through the Straits of Magellan, and up the coast of North America as far as Oregon. He continues westward and becomes the first Englishman to circumnavigate the globe.

1581: Ballet Comique de la Reyne. The queen mother of France, Catherine de Médicis, throws a big bash on October 15 to honor her guests, and makes history by presenting the first ballet. Written and choreographed by Italian violinist and court festivals director Baldassarino de Belgiojoso, the story relates the legend of Circe and is acted and danced by the queen, her retinue, and the nobles of the court. According to Belgiojoso's accounts, ballet is "a geometrical arrangement of many persons dancing together under a diverse harmony of instruments."

The ballet as we know it grew out of these dances performed by nobles and aristocrats at the royal courts. As time went on, the simple steps grew more complicated, and by the time of the reign of Louis XIV of France, the amateur courtiers could no longer keep up with technical demands. So Louis established the Academie Royal de Danse in 1661, to make up for his nobles' ineptness. He later founded a music academy to which was added a school of dancing to train professionals. These academies of music and dance then merged to become the Paris Opera, which is still functioning today.

Pierre Beauchamp, the first choreographer of the Paris Opera, invented the five positions of the feet that are the basis of all classical ballet movement and also devised a system of dance notation. Women's movement was impeded by the heavy dresses of the day, but the men soon started jumping higher and higher and leaping farther and farther, which must have been difficult in those high-heeled shoes of the time. In 1726 Marie Camargo, a brilliant Parisian dancer, took the daring step of shortening her skirts to midcalf, the better to show off the jetés and entrechats for which she was famous. She also added underpants to her costume and invented the ballet slipper. By 1800 ballet steps included the grand jeté, or "great leap," and sustained pirouettes. It was about this time, too, that women began to dance on their toes. On March 12, 1832, Marie Taglioni danced in her father's new ballet, La Sylphide, at the Paris Opera wearing a costume that inaugurated the era of the tutu. La Sylphide also changed the themes of the earlier ballets, which were based on Greek legends and serious works, and introduced a more romantic atmosphere to dance. The Frenchman Petipa left his mark on the ballet in Russia, where he was a leading dancer and then a major choreographer until he died in 1910. It was the Russian composer Tchaikovsky who wrote some of ballet's memorable music, including scores for Swan Lake, The Sleeping Beauty, and The Nutcracker, and Prokofiev who composed the music for Romeo and Juliet and Cinderella. The famous names in Russian ballet are legendary, among them the choreographer Diaghilev and the two immortals Pavlova and Nijinsky.

Ballet appeared in America in 1735 when a dancer from London presented The Adventures of Harlequin and Scaramouch in Charleston, South Carolina, but the colonists had other things to do and ballet wasn't seen much until after the French Revolution when French dancers sought refuge on our shores. Most of the dancers audiences saw were from Europe, and it wasn't until 1940 that the Ballet Theater was established in the United States.

Ballet is now popular in many countries throughout the world. It's a far cry, however, from that October day when sixty-two-year-old Catherine de Médicis stepped regally about the stage in the part of the première danseuse.

1582: The Gregorian Calendar. By the time of Julius Caesar, the republican calendar of Rome was so out of whack with the seasons that the equinox of the calendar differed from the astronomical equinox by three months. That meant that winter was in the fall and the fall was in the summer. In 46 B.C. on the advice of the astonomer Sosigenes of Alexandria, Caesar interposed sixty-seven days between November and December to catch up. Then he abolished the lunar calendar and decreed the solar calendar should be the basis for reckoning. He was a dictator, so he could do all these things. Sosigenes then noted from his observation that the year is 365¼ days long. Since it wasn't possible to have a quarter of a day every year, it was decided there should be three years of 365 days followed by one year of 366 days. That seemed to take care of things and on January 1, 45 B.C., the new calendar was adopted. The following year the month of Quintilis (from the Latin word *quinque,* meaning "five"—the new year started in March, so Quintilis was the fifth month) was renamed July in Caesar's honor, and later the month of Sextilis (originally the sixth month) was renamed August to honor Augustus Caesar. Otherwise the months have retained their old Roman names. I might add here that Julius Caesar was assassinated on March 15, 44 B.C., but that's politics.

Sosigenes's calculations were fairly accurate, but the length of the year was overestimated by .0078 days. That may seem trivial but comes out to one whole day every 128 years. And over the centuries this miscalculation can add up. In fact, the discrepancy was pointed out several times by those in the know as centuries passed. In 1472 Pope Sixtus IV beckoned the famous mathematical genius and astronomer Regiomontanus to Rome to change the calendar, which by that time had a discrepancy of nine days between the true vernal equinox and calendar equinox of March 21. Alas, Regiomontanus died shortly after he arrived, possibly assassinated by his enemies, and calendar reform was put on hold. It wasn't until the sixteenth century that the calendar as we know it was revised under Pope Gregory XIII. Leap years remained except for turn-of-the-century years that were multiples of four hundred. By this time, too, the calendar was off by ten days, so October 5, 1582, became October 15 and we began again, at least in the Roman Catholic countries and states. The Protestant countries gradually acceded, but Great Britain did not adopt the new-style calendar, as it was called, until 1752, when the day following September 2 became September 14. This caused rioting in the streets as people demanded their days back, as well you might if you were planning to celebrate your birthday on, say, September 10. It was at this time, also, that the New Year was changed to begin on January 1 rather than March 25. The Scots had been celebrating the New Year on January 1 since 1600.

The Gregorian calendar is now correct for the next twenty thousand years, so there's no excuse for forgetting your anniversary.

1585: The Decimal System. The Chinese had been using decimal fractions in measurements for centuries, and by medieval times, had incorporated decimals into their mathematics. The Western world did not use the decimal system until 1585, when the Belgian-born Simon Stevin wrote his *The Tenth* in which all fractions were treated as whole numbers. It was John Napier, the Scottish inventor of logarithms, who thought up the decimal point, however. The system certainly made calculating those exasperating fractions easier.

1586: Kabuki Theater. A young Japanese woman, O Kuni, is credited with the beginning of Kabuki, theater for the common man, when she performs parodies of Buddhist prayers surrounded by her troupe of dancers. The females dance male parts and the males dance as females. This did not sit too well with the authorities, who banned it in 1629, claiming it was immoral for women to dance in public. Thereafter, the men took over all the roles, as they did in Elizabethan England.

The subject matter of Kabuki dramas is more realistic than No theater, frequently depicting actual or historical events of some significance. The greatest of the playwrights is considered to be Mokuami Kawatake, who lived during most of the nineteenth century and whose plays revolve around the daily lives of ordinary people. Dance is a vital part of Kabuki, and at times is very stylized, necessitating rigid training on the part of the actors. New plays have been written in the past few decades, and Kabuki, although somewhat modernized, is still being acted today. The same actors, however, can also be seen in that newer art form, motion pictures.

1587: Isfahan. Shah Abbas I succeeds to the throne of Persia and moves his capital to Isfahan (now Esfahān in central Iran). He plans and rebuilds the city, and under his rule Isfahan, with a population of over half a million, becomes one of the most beautiful cities in the world. Long, wide roads are built, mosques and pavilions erected, bridges span the waterways, artificial lakes are formed, and courtyards, gardens, and fountains dot the city. The area artisans had been celebrated for centuries for their metalwork, weavings, and mosaic and polychrome tiles, and during this period their fame spread even farther and the city prospered. To encourage trade and industry, the shah resettled six thousand Christian Armenians from northern Persia to the suburbs of Isfahan, granting them freedom of worship among many other privileges, and invited the English and Dutch East India companies to build factories.

Upon the death of the shah, his son Abbas II continued in his father's footsteps. The Frenchman Jean Chardin, who lived in Isfahan for a while, described it as having 100 mosques, almost 50 colleges, 1,802 caravansaries (inns), and 273 baths. This does not include the palaces, churches, gates, and verandas that also enhanced the city. With their lacy filigree work and brightly painted tiles and mosaics, the buildings must have been a beautiful sight among the trees, gardens, and pathways.

Unfortunately, the Afghans besieged the city in 1722, and it hasn't been quite the same since, although the modern-day Persians have rebuilt it in part. Isfahan is proof of what can be accomplished when peace and prosperity prevail under wise and forward-looking leadership.

1587: Tamburlaine. The first great English dramatist, Christopher Marlowe, completes his play *Tamburlaine the Great* and establishes blank verse as the form all playwrights will use rather than the standard rhyme form. Marlowe, celebrated for his lyrical gifts as a poet as well as a playwright, does all his writing in a five-year span and produces his immortal *Dr. Faustus* as well as some of the most beautiful poetry ever written. Unfortunately, at the age of twenty-nine, this genius of verse was accidentally killed during a squabble in a tavern. His work still thrives in lines such as these from his famous poem "The Passionate Shepherd to His Love":

> *Come live with me and be my love.*
> *And we will all life's pleasures prove*
> *That valleys, groves, hills, and fields,*
> *Woods, or steepy mountain yields.*

1590: The Microscope. The first instrument every science student becomes acquainted with was invented by a Dutch optician, Zacharias Janssen. One of the most important tools of science, the microscope shows us a world too small to be seen with the naked eye. It is, in its simplest form, a magnifying glass, with greater magnification achieved with two lenses rather than one. Although Janssen's compound microscope, with a concave and a convex lens, gave only slight magnification, it was improved upon rapidly. In 1610 Galileo used a microscope to study insects. The prototype of the modern microscope was based on an idea by the German astronomer Kepler, who suggested using only convex lenses, which gave a larger field of vision. In 1684 the Dutch scientist Huygens invented a two-lens eyepiece, which is still widely used.

The microscope was a boon to the study of what would become bacteriology. In 1680 Anton Van Leeuwenhoek, a Dutch naturalist, succeeded in grinding his own lenses to build a microscope that would magnify two hundred times. He looked at drops of water, skin, and human hair. He proved ants and fleas came from eggs. He was the first to describe red corpuscles in the blood. In 1683 he discovered living organisms in scrapings from his teeth: the beginning of the germ theory.

We owe a huge debt to those early microscope builders. Without them, science and medicine would have made slow progress. We now have much more powerful microscopes, each with different capabilities, than those pioneers could possibly have imagined. The original design, however, was used for many years by those whose success depended on seeing beyond what the naked eye could see.

Ca. 1591: Shakespeare Treads the Boards. The poet and playwright began his theatrical career as an actor, and according to the few accounts available, was fairly good at it, although he apparently played only small parts. He may not have had time for anything more since it was about this time that his first play, *Henry VI,* was produced, starting him on a career that would make him the most famous dramatist in the history of the world. His works have been translated into more languages than any other writer's, and his plays have been performed in almost every country on the globe. Although his plots were not all original, he certainly had a way with words.

He wrote for the company of players who were the best and most popular in London and for Richard Burbage, their leading actor. Shakespeare never became rich during his twenty years of writing, receiving only six or eight pounds for each play, as was the custom. He was financially secure, however, since as an actor in the company, he received a salary and a share of the profits, and later owned one tenth of the prosperous Globe theater. About 1610 he retired to Stratford, where he was born, and with his wife, Anne, lived the life of a gentleman, enjoying the company of his two daughters and their families.

As he is England's most famous and quoted personage, and gave the world much of its magnificent poetry, one would expect to find Shakespeare ceremoniously entombed in Westminster Abbey. Instead, he is buried in his parish church in Stratford under a gravestone engraved with a verse he wrote:

> *Good frend for Jesus sake forbeare,*
> *To digg the dust encloased heare!*
> *Blest be ye man yt spares thes stones,*
> *And curst be he yt moves my bones.*

No one has dared move him yet.

1596–1650: René Descartes. The Frenchman was a man of many disciplines: mathematician, scholar, traveler, physicist, philosopher, and thinker. We know he was the latter from his famous statement *Cogito ergo sum,* "I think, therefore I am." And think, he did, about practically everything. In fact, he used to loll in bed until late in the morning just thinking. He is called the father of modern philosophy as well as analytic geometry. His most famous work is *Discourse on the Method of Reasoning Well and Seeking Truth in the Sciences.* According to Descartes, the guide to reason is first to doubt everything systematically until one arrives at a clear idea beyond doubt. To him, the physical world was made up of invisible particles of matter in ether which interacted with each other.

His fame became so great that Queen Christina of Sweden invited
him to tutor her. He was reluctant to head for the "land of rocks
and ice," as he termed it, but was persuaded to do so. You can
imagine how he must have felt when he found that he had to
begin teaching at five in the morning. The climate took its toll
on his fragile health; he caught a chill and died. He should have
stayed in bed.

1596: Thermometer Invented. Galileo invented the first
thermometer. It was a long glass tube at the top of which was a
small sphere filled with air. The other end of the tube was dipped
in colored fluid. The change in temperature was indicated by the
rise of the fluid into the tube. It was somewhat unreliable since
the thermometer also reacted to changes in barometric pressure.
Of course, this type of thermometer couldn't be used for medical
purposes, but it was a beginning.

How high a fever you have is an important clue for a doctor
in diagnosing your illness. Before the thermometer, doctors could
only guess at temperatures. If a patient was flushed, perspiring,
and felt hot, these symptoms indicated illness, but an accurate
measure of body temperature was needed. In 1626 an Italian physician, Santorio, devised his own thermometer, based on Galileo's,
a twisted tube of glass with a globe on top and an open bottom.
The patient held the globe in his mouth, and the other end of
the tube was placed in water. As the air in the tube was warmed
by the patient's body heat, it moved through the tube and created bubbles in the water. The more bubbles, the higher the
temperature. Not exactly accurate, but a good indication when
compared to the number of bubbles created by a healthy person.
Santorio's invention caught on and soon other physicians took up
the challenge, the device was improved upon, and by 1654, there
were thermometers similar to modern ones. In 1717 the German
physicist Daniel Gabriel Fahrenheit produced dependable instruments containing mercury, rather than water or alcohol, and developed the standard for measurement.

Now we have digital thermometers. The device is stuck in an
ear and immediately registers a reading. Santorio might have found
this device hilarious as well as amazing.

1596: The Water Closet. Odd as it may seem, the first practical flush toilet was invented by an English poet, Sir John Haring-

ton, and installed in the palace at Richmond for Queen Elizabeth I, who also happened to be Sir John's godmother. He later wrote about his invention in a rather coarse satire for which he was banished from court for the second time, having once before offended young ladies by his translation of some sensual passages from Ariosto's *Orlando Furioso*. The water closet (or WC as it will become known in Britain) was apparently not a huge success as the chamber pot and privy continued in use for a few more centuries.

1597: Plastic Surgery Textbook. Gaspare Tagliacozzi of Bologna publishes his 298-page masterpiece *On the Surgical Restoration of Defects by Grafting*. The book, including twenty-two illustrations, describes the reconstruction of the nose and lip using a flap taken from the patient's arm. The technique is still known as the "Italian method."

The sixth-century Hindu physician Susruta had described the reconstruction of the nose using cheek tissue. In ancient India amputating the nose was a conventional form of punishment, so these nose jobs were undoubtedly a necessity. The Chinese were repairing cleft lips back in the third century B.C. Although a knowledge of this reconstructive surgery existed, especially in the Arab world, not much was performed in Europe until about the fifteenth century. Oddly enough, after Tagliacozzi's book was published, this field of surgery diminished until Karl Ferdinand von Grafe of Berlin published his *Rhinoplastik* in 1813. Nineteenth-century plastic surgery (a term coined by Edward Zeis in 1838) branched out from the nose to include eyelids, cleft palates, ears, lips, cheeks, jaws, and hands. In the 1920s a Frenchwoman, Suzanne Noel, was one of the first doctors to practice cosmetic surgery as well as to record the procedures she used.

Plastic surgery can literally be a lifesaver when skin grafts are necessary and can produce dramatic results by restoring parts of the body that have been damaged by injury or scarred by a birth defect. The "nips" and "tucks" of cosmetic surgery, while considered pure vanity by some, are no less important to those who feel their looks interfere with the quality of their lives.

After Tagliacozzi's death, the city of Bologna erected a statue of him at the university's anatomy school. It depicted him holding a nose in his hand.

1597: A New Art Form Begins. Jacopo Peri, a Florentine singer of noble birth, is a member of a learned group who attempt to perform ancient Greek plays by singing them. They experiment with recitative, a style of vocal music somewhere between speaking and singing, and present the first performance of *Dafne,* a pastoral drama set to music by Peri. The successful production is the beginning of opera (so called from *opera in musica,* "musical work"), which quickly spread to other cities. In 1637 the first opera house opened in Venice. It wasn't long before the aria crept into opera. It soon became the medium of expression for some of the world's most powerful and beautiful voices.

1598: The Edict of Nantes. Henry IV, one of the most popular kings in French history, signs the Edict of Nantes in August granting religious freedoms to the Huguenots, the French Protestants.

The Edict allowed the Protestants to continue holding public worship wherever they had previously been granted the right, enabled the great nobles to hold services in their homes and the lesser nobles to do the same for gatherings of less than thirty people. Protestants were also granted civil rights, which meant they could trade, inherit property, attend universities, and hold official appointments.

Henry himself had been brought up as a Protestant but converted to Catholicism when he became king, mostly to appease the Catholic League, which opposed him, and because he thought it was what the people wanted. Unfortunately, tolerance towards Protestants only lasted until 1685 when the edict was revoked by Louis XIV. A mass exodus of Huguenots ensued, some of whom emigrated to America, where they could practice their religion without fear of persecution.

1599: The Globe Theatre Built. The Globe is arguably the most famous name in theaters for its association with Shakespeare. When the lease on the Theatre built by James Burbage expires, as does Burbage himself, his two sons, Richard and Cuthbert, are caught up in a lawsuit with the landowner. In the landlord's absence they surreptitiously tear down the Theatre and transport the lumber across the Thames to Bankside, where, in one of history's most famous recycling jobs, they proceed to construct the Globe.

It is at the Globe that Richard Burbage will become the greatest

actor of the Elizabethan age and where he will create the roles of
Macbeth, Othello, Richard III, Henry V, Romeo, Hamlet, and
King Lear when Shakespeare's plays are first presented.

A replica of the Elizabethan Globe, near the site of the original,
opened on April 23, 1995, celebrating the 431st anniversary of
the birth of Shakespeare. The ghosts of William and his actor
friend Richard might be seen smiling in the wings.

17th Century: Pockets. Sometime during this century pockets
appeared in trousers. A simple idea at the time, it's sure been a
boon to us all. Now we had a place to put things instead of
dangling them from a belt.

1600: We Discover Electricity. Electricity has always been
with us, of course; it's one of the forces of nature. We could
never see it or hear it or feel it, except in the form of lightning.
Ancient Greek women used to amuse themselves by placing pieces
of amber on their spinning wheels and watching it attract and
repel little pieces of wool. They didn't know they were creating
static electricity. The Greek philosopher Thales also noticed that
amber, when rubbed, attracted straw and feathers; he called this
phenomenon *electric*, from *elektron,* the Greek word for "amber."

A little over two thousand years later, in 1600, William Gilbert
of Colchester, physician to Queen Elizabeth I, demonstrated that
other substances could also attract and repel. He coined the term
electricity. During the next one hundred years several scientists devised electrical machines that would create electricity, sometimes
with shocking results. Many of these instruments were looked
upon as merely diversions, nothing more than parlor tricks to
entertain one's guests.

In 1650 Otto van Guericke, the German physicist who invented
the air pump, demonstrated the first electric machine. It was a
large sulfur ball that was cranked by hand, and as it spun, he
rubbed it with his hand, creating static electricity. In 1700 an
Englishman, Francis Hawksbee, created the first electric light. He
pumped the air out of a glass bulb with a vacuum pump and
twirled it at high speed as he rubbed it with his hand. The glass
bulb emitted a dim glow. The Dutch scientist Pieter van
Musschenbroek devised the Leyden jar, about 1745. It was a
water-filled glass bottle lined on the bottom half, inside and out,
with tin foil. A metal rod was inserted into the jar, and when charged

by an electric machine, it stored electricity. We all know the story of Benjamin Franklin, the kite and the key and his invention of the lightning rod. Alessandro Volta of Pavia, Italy, demonstrated that electric current flows when two different metals are separated by moisture. In 1800 he made discs of copper and zinc and piled them on top of one another, each separated by a wet paper disc. When he touched each end of the pile he felt a continuing shock. It was a current of electricity. He had invented the first battery. From this time on, scientists in many countries seriously began research into the properties of electricity. We had at last harnessed this phenomenon. Now the geniuses in the laboratories would invent the machines that would change our lives and modernize the world.

1603: Football. It's difficult to date exactly when football began to be played as a real sport, but in 1603 James I of England lifted the ban against playing it and the game began to gain some respectability as well as rules. Before then, as far back as the first century, an air-filled bladder was kicked and tossed by two opposing groups as they fought, pummeled, shoved, and nearly killed each other in an attempt to get the ball back to one of their towns. This mass chaos eventually became part of special town celebrations, particularly on Shrove Tuesday, which became known as football day. By the twelfth century, the game was being played on a large field marked by boundary lines with fifty men on each side, more or less. It was still a rough and barbaric free-for-all, similar to today's football game without rules and uniforms. Successive kings banned it because so many men were injured, it kept them from such military pursuits as archery. After 1603, however, physical contact was reduced and the ball had to be kicked across the goal between two sticks. English football eventually evolved into three different games: what we Americans call soccer, the game of rugby, and American football.

Young college men in the United States had played a form of soccer since about 1820, and the first intercollegiate game was held at New Brunswick, New Jersey, on November 6, 1869, with Rutgers beating Princeton six goals to four. A week later, in a return match, Princeton won eight goals to zero. Soon Columbia and Yale joined in the play, but Harvard insisted on playing its own game, more akin to rugby, in which a player could run with the ball. Harvard played three games against McGill University in 1874, first using its rules, and then McGill's rules, which Harvard apparently liked better, and soon Yale was also playing by the new rules. By 1876 the Intercollegiate Football Association had been formed and a fall schedule was set up. The rules were still similar to rugby, with fifteen men on each side; only kicked goals could score, and a team kept the ball until it scored or the other team took it away. It was Walter Camp, the Father of American Football, who was a star player for Yale and later returned as its athletic director and football coach, who initiated many of the rules we have now, including the system of downs, which changed the game considerably.

On August 31, 1895, the first professional game was played when a team from Latrobe, Pennsylvania, paid a former college football quarterback ten dollars to play against the nearby town of Jeanette. Latrobe won, twelve to nothing, and all the Latrobe players shared in the profits. As football became more and more popular, many college stars began playing professionally for various teams as well. The American Professional Football Association was organized in Canton, Ohio, in 1920, collapsed, and was reorganized again the next year; franchises were sold for fifty dollars. In 1922 the name was changed to the National Football League, or NFL, as we know it today. In the 1920s college and professional football players and their coaches began to take on heroic proportions for their athletic feats, and names like Red Grange, Notre Dame's famous Four Horsemen (Stuhldreher, Miller, Crowley, and Layden), Knute Rockne, and Jim Thorpe were becoming known to everybody.

After World War II, and with the advent of television, professional football became big business. College and university teams are now the training grounds for those athletes seeking a career in pro ball. "Monday morning quarterbacking" is a national pastime as fans replay Sunday afternoon's game the way they would have called it, while awaiting the next game on Monday night.

1607: Jamestown Settled. The first permanent English settlement in the New World is founded on May 14, 1607, and named after King James I.

The plucky band of 144 colonists experienced great hardships, but were held together by their stalwart leader, Captain John Smith. When he left for England in 1609, the settlers nearly starved and welcomed the arrival of Lord Delaware, whose aid saved them. Although plagued by disease, polluted water, poor shelter, a miserable climate, and hostile Indians, the colony survived. A tribute once again to the courage of the human spirit.

1609: Astronomical Theories. Johannes Kepler, the German mathematician and astronomer, publishes his important finds: planets take elliptical paths as they revolve around the sun, and they travel at different speeds. He figured this out while drawing up astrological charts for emperors and nobles. A job is a job.

1609: Hudson Explores River. The Florentine navigator Verrazano had discovered what is now New York Harbor and the river in 1524, but it was not until 1609 that it was explored. The English navigator Henry Hudson had been looking for a northeast passage around northern Europe to China and had failed. On his third try he sailed under the auspices of the Dutch. This attempt was also in vain, and to placate his mutinous crew, Hudson turned westward, hoping to find a route through Virginia. On September 3, with his ship the *Half Moon,* he entered New York Harbor, then sailed up the river that now bears his name.

Hudson's reports of friendly Indians and fertile lands prompted the Dutch East India Company to establish a trading post at what is now Albany. And, of course, in 1626 Peter Minuit purchased Manhattan Island from the Indians and New Amsterdam was born, later to become one of the world's most important cities, New York.

1610: Galileo's Universe. Galileo taught mathematics at the university in Padua and supplemented his meager stipend by inventing and selling surveying and mathematical instruments in the small shop he owned. He had heard about an instrument called a telescope and, knowing how it had been made decided to build one for himself. He continued to improve the first one he constructed and finally had an instrument that would magnify to the power of thirty. He made a gift of the device to the Venetian senate, which had awarded him his job originally, and they in turn were so delighted, they renewed his professorship for life and doubled his salary. This, naturally, did not sit too well with some of his colleagues, who were more than a mite envious.

In January of 1610, Galileo turned his telescope towards the heavens and was overawed by what he saw. There in the sky were more stars than anyone ever imagined existed. The moon was thirty times larger, with a rough surface full of mountains and valleys, not smooth as had been thought, and there were spots on the sun. Four planets never seen before were orbiting around a star. (They would later be known as the moons of Jupiter.) What Galileo observed finally convinced him of Copernicus's theory of heliocentricity, that the earth and its moon did revolve around the sun. He published his findings in his book *Siderius Nuncius (Starry Messenger)*.

Apparently Galileo felt all was not perfect in Padua and he began looking elsewhere for a place where he could pursue his scientific studies. He wisely sent a telescope to the Grand Duke Cosimo II de Medici in Florence and named the four moons of Jupiter the "Medicean planets." His tactics proved effective and the grand duke appointed Galileo chief mathematician of the University of Pisa and philosopher of the Grand Duke, with a handsome salary. Galileo settled into his estate at Arcetri near Florence, where he would spend the rest of his life writing and experimenting and, unfortunately, battling the church and its doctrines. Protestantism was in its riotous infancy, and the Catholic church was in the throes of self-preservation. The theory of geocentricity, which put the stationary earth at the center of things (maybe we should call it egocentricity), was the only acceptable belief, and those who declared otherwise were heretics. Galileo was caught in the middle of what was part politics and part jealous vendetta. At the age of seventy-seven he was made to face a trial by the Inquisition and was forced to recant. His books on the subject were forbidden and he was confined to his house for life. During this period, Galileo produced a new work written in the vernacular and smuggled to Leyden for publication. The subjects were dynamics and gravitation, and laid the groundwork upon which later scientists would develop theories.

Galileo died just before his seventy-eighth birthday. He had upset the applecart and become the father of modern science. In 1989 we launched a spacecraft named after him to explore those worlds he first observed one starry night 380 years before.

1614: Logarithms. If you are mathematically illiterate, logarithms are probably of no importance to you—maybe you've never heard of them—but back in the seventeenth century they were a boon to every scientist. It was a way of multiplying and dividing large numbers by adding and subtracting exponents, and took the drudgery out of calculating. The tables of logarithms (coined from the Greek words *logos,* "ratio," and *arithmos,* "number") were compiled by the Scotsman John Napier and published in 1614. The tables will appear at the back of every student's math book and be used until the advent of calculators and computers.

1619: Harvey's Discoveries. How the blood circulates in the body seems to have been lost in history and found again. The Chinese apparently had it figured out, at least in theory, about two thousand years ago. Al-Nafis, an Arabian medicine man of the thirteenth century, described the movement of blood between heart and lungs, and in 1553 the Spanish physician Michael Servetus concluded that blood passes from the pulmonary artery to the pulmonary vein. Unfortunately he got mixed up in theological theories and was executed as a heretic. About the same time, the Italian surgeon Realdo Colombo had also figured out pulmonary circulation and explained that blood passed from the right side of the heart to the left by way of the lungs and also described the two beats of the heart. There were still missing pieces and misconceptions, and it took William Harvey, an English physician, to fill in the blanks. Harvey realized the heart was a pump, described its chambers and contractions and the steady flow of blood through the body, and noted that the heartbeat corresponds to the pulse beat. After some mathematical reasoning he concluded that the body had a small supply of blood that circulated over and over again, with the valves in the veins allowing the blood to flow in only one direction. In 1628 Harvey published his findings and a new era in medicine began.

In 1661, four years after Harvey died, the Italian physiologist Marcello Malpighi, using a microscope, unavailable to Harvey, discovered the tiny capillaries that move the blood and connect the veins and the arteries. It was also Malpighi who first saw the circular red cells in the blood through his powerful microscope.

1620: Mayflower Compact.

When the English colonists were blown off course due to storms and rough seas and landed at Cape Cod rather than their destination of Virginia, they realized they were outside the jurisdiction of the English government. Fearing mutiny among those who were not Puritans, the leaders of the venture drew up a document that bound them all to accept whatever government was established when they landed. A "Civil Body Politick" was created to enact "just and equal Laws, Ordinances, Acts, Constitutions, and Offices" for the "general good of the Colony." Forty-one men signed the Mayflower Compact on November 21, 1620.

1621–65: King Philip IV, the Ultimate Angel.

During the reign of Philip IV of Spain, over three hundred comedies were produced under his auspices. A lover of and patron of the arts, Philip spent as much as five hundred thousand reales on a single production. (According to the Spanish novelist Cervantes, at the time a man could live comfortably on a real and a half a day.) He frequently had plays presented in his gardens, with the actors and audience floating on artificial lakes. In his later years he built the palace gardens, which could be used for exterior settings. Philip spared no expense. Broadway producers would have loved him.

1623: Shakespeare's First Folio.

Two actor friends of William Shakespeare, John Heminge and Henry Condell, gather together all of the existing manuscripts of his plays and have them published under the title *The Workes of William Shakespeare*. And it's a good thing they did or we probably wouldn't have them today. Not many plays were printed then, and few manuscripts from the Elizabethan era of drama have survived.

1624: Louvre Palace Completed.

Charles V of France built the original Louvre Palace during his reign (1364–80). Known as Charles the Wise, he commissioned many buildings during his prosperous and peaceful reign and, feeling the need for more cheerful surroundings, had the old arsenal converted into a spacious palace. Under the reign of Louis XIII (1610–43), the palace was completed, and the former medieval castle had been rebuilt in the Renaissance style. Over the next two centuries, the palace was enlarged several times. After the fall of the monarchy the Louvre became a museum and is now one of the greatest repositories of art and archaeology in the world. In 1989 a new entrance to the museum, designed by I. M. Pei, of metal and glass in the shape of a pyramid, was added amidst much controversy. The modern concept does, however, bring the architecture up-to-date.

1626: Manhattan Island Purchased.
In May, Peter Minuit, director-general of the Dutch West Indies Company, buys the island of Manahatin from the Canarsie Indian chiefs for sixty guilders worth of trinkets.

This has something been called the greatest real estate bargain in history. Sixty guilders was about the equivalent of twenty-four dollars, or two cents an acre. The name Manahatin is from the Algonquian *manah*, "island," plus *atin*, "hill," and it is the island on which the Dutch colony of Nieuw Amsterdam will be established. The island will eventually be called Manhattan and the colony's name will change to New York. You couldn't buy a square inch of it now for twenty-four dollars.

1627: The Forbidden City.
The Pao-Ho-Tien, the building used for state banquets, is completed as one of the three great halls of the emperor's "Forbidden City" in Beijing, China. The city is laid out according to the ancient Chou Dynasty (1122–256 B.C.) achitectural principles of enormous courtyards and massive buildings on raised earthen platforms. The "Forbidden City" encloses several immense stone-paved squares connected by huge rectangular buildings with brightly painted tiles and hipped roofs. The major courtyard is two hundred yards wide, ending at a stepped terrace upon which are the *T'ai-ho-tien*, the throne hall, the *Chung-ho-tien*, used as a waiting room, and the *Pao-ho-tien*, the banqueting room. Beyond the first group of buildings are several more huge courtyards with living quarters and structures for supporting services.

The city, once closed to everyone except the emperor, his courtiers, government officials, and servants, has been open to everyone since the country became a people's republic and is now one of China's great tourist attractions.

1628: Petition of Right. Charles I of England needed money. The Parliament was inattentive, so Charles forced a loan from some of his wealthy subjects. Seventy-six gentlemen, including several from Parliament, were imprisoned for refusing. The king's word was law. When he again needed money in 1628, he summoned Parliament once more and found them against him. This time they demanded he agree not to borrow money without the consent of Parliament and not to imprison anyone without due process of law. Charles acknowledged he had violated the rights of his subjects and acceded to Parliament. The Petition of Right was a landmark of English law.

1636: Four Hundred Pounds for a Colledge. The General Court of the Massachusetts Bay Colony votes four hundred pounds to establish a "schoale or colledge" at "Newetowne."

Since they landed just sixteen years before, the colonists lost little time in establishing a school. According to the colonists' own words, after God had safely carried them to New England, they had built houses, provided the necessaries for their livelihood, built churches for God's worship, and settled a civil government. What remained to be done was to advance learning, and desiring to leave a literate ministry, they charted a college for "the advancement of all good literature, arts, and sciences" and "the education of the English and Indian youth."

"Newetowne" was changed to Cambridge in honor of the town in England where many of the leading men of the colony had received their education, and the college was named Harvard in honor of the Puritan minister John Harvard (a Cambridge graduate), who bequeathed 780 pounds, half his estate, and four hundred books to the nascent institution.

By 1701 the politics and theology of the Connecticut colonists had strayed somewhat from the beliefs of the Bay Colony, and although they had been supporting Harvard, there were those who preferred to establish an institute of their own. The general court convened in New Haven and granted a charter to found and endow a collegiate school in their own colony. The students studied at a parsonage in Killingworth until the rector died, after which they dispersed to various towns where their tutors lived.

When the school suddenly became the owner of a collection of one thousand books, a building was needed to house them and the colony voted money for a site, which was granted in New Haven. A Bostonian, Elihu Yale, a member of the East India Company, gifted the school with a cargo of books and goods from the company, and for this beneficence the new college was named for him.

Harvard and Yale are now two of the most prestigious universities in the world, with students from all over the globe attending their graduate and undergraduate schools. Harvard can boast six presidents of the United States among its graduates and the largest university library in the States, perhaps in the world. The first art gallery in America was built on the Yale campus, and the Peabody Museum of Natural History, one of the oldest in the United States, is part of the university system.

Although Yale had the best college football team in the early days of the intercollegiate sport, they don't make the news much these days, except when they play Harvard.

1642–1727: Sir Isaac Newton. The year Galileo died, Isaac Newton was born in Lincolnshire, England, proving that not only does life go on, but it keeps producing great minds. Newton's uncle, a Cambridge graduate, recognized his nephew's mathematical propensities and soon the young Isaac was enrolled at Trinity College, Cambridge, where he pursued studies in chemistry and math. He voraciously read the works of the likes of Kepler, Galileo, Fermat, Huygens, and Viète, and later would write, "If I have seen farther than Descartes, it is because I have stood on the shoulders of giants." It was nice of him to give others credit.

Unfortunately, just after Newton received his degree, Trinity College was closed because of the plague that was devastating the country. Fortunately, Newton left Cambridge and went home to think. During this period he developed the binomial theorem, invented calculus, discovered the law of gravity, and analyzed the composition of white light and the nature of colors. It just shows what you can do if you have a couple of free years to cogitate on things. Of course, being a genius helps. In 1668 Newton became a professor of mathematics at Trinity, experimented with optics, and developed the reflecting telescope, which used a mirror instead of lenses to gather light. For this he was elected a fellow of the Royal Society of London. The first thing he did was present a paper on prisms and the nature of light and colors, demonstrating that white light is a mixture of all colors and that a prism separates it into colors by refraction at different angles. In 1687 Newton published his famous *Philosophiae Naturalis Principia Mathematica,* or *Principia* for short, which became the basis for modern science.

Newton did have a secret weakness: He dabbled in alchemy. Alchemists were those medieval and Renaissance figures who attempted to turn baser metals into gold. Newton didn't succeed, either. Nobody's perfect.

1642: Compulsory Education. The Massachusetts government passes a law mandating that a parent or master teach his children and wards to read and write. The law provides for a board to be formed which could periodically check to see that the law was being heeded. If a parent or master should be remiss in his duties, a fine could be levied by the board.

Until this time, education had been the responsibility of the parents and the masters of apprentices. The new law made it a public function. In 1647 Massachusetts went a step further. It mandated that all towns with fifty or more families must hire a teacher for reading and writing, and all towns with one hundred families or more must have a Latin grammar school to prepare boys for university study. Noncompliance carried a fine. In 1852 Massachusetts again passed another first. It required that all children attend school. Parents loved this law.

1642: Rembrandt Paints *Night Watch.* One of the most illustrious geniuses in the world of art completed his painting known as *The Night Watch,* which now hangs in the Rijksmuseum in Amsterdam.

Although the name sticks, it was found, after a thorough cleaning in 1946, that it is actually a day scene depicting the local civic guard just coming into view in the sunlight from the shadows of an arch.

Rembrandt Harmensz van Rijn was born in Leiden, Holland, on July 15, 1606, into a lower-middle-class family. He enrolled at the university in 1620 but soon knew his talents lay elsewhere. He left to spend three years apprenticed to an artist and then to study further in Amsterdam. In his early days he often painted his family and friends, using them as character studies. Fortunately for posterity, he also sketched himself, which he continued to do throughout his life, enabling us to know what he looked like at different periods. He quickly became well known as a portrait painter, married the wealthy Saskia van Uylenburch, worked hard, and began to develop his genius. His first big commission was for the Surgeons Guild in Amsterdam in 1632, depicting the guild's officers and titled *Anatomy Lesson of Professor Tulp*.

In his lifetime of sixty-three years, Rembrandt painted many different subjects, including biblical stories, family groups, landscapes, and an assortment of people. His ability to translate facial expressions resulted in some of the most affecting portraits ever painted. His etchings are as wonderful as his paintings. He remains one of the world's most brilliant and revered artists.

1642: The Adding Machine.

Blaise Pascal's father determines taxes at Rouen, France. Blaise is a mathematical prodigy. So, of course, Blaise does what he can to help his father with his computations and invents the first machine that adds and subtracts. It consists of wheels and a ratchet mechanism that will carry the one to the next place when a number is greater than nine. Pascal also contributes to the modern theory of probability and advances differential calculus. He conducts experiments with atmospheric pressure and barometers and his work in physics with fluids will lead to the invention of the hydraulic press.

When he is about thirty he experiences a profound religious feeling and turns to writing on theology, of which his most famous work is his *Pensées*. Three hundred years later his genius will be remembered when a computer language, PASCAL, is named for him.

1648: Treaty of Westphalia.

Signed on October 24, the peace treaty between the Holy Roman Emperor, Ferdinand III, Louis XIII, king of France, and their respective allies ends the Thirty Years War.

The war, which had begun in 1618 as a religious conflict between rival coalitions of Catholics and Protestants within the Holy Roman Empire, pitting Hapsburgs against Bourbons, devastated Europe, and many parts of the continent were reduced to ruins. The treaty ended an era of religious wars, with the various rulers within the Holy Roman Empire gaining the power to establish public worship as they pleased.

1654: The Taj Mahal. The mausoleum complex near Agra, India, in memory of Shah Jehan's favorite wife, Mumtaz Mahal, is completed and becomes the jewel of Mogul architecture.

Architects from Persia, India, and central Asia were consulted in its design, and the over twenty thousand builders and craftsmen employed in its construction came from all over India and central Asia. The complex, consisting of the marble mausoleum, with an identically symmetrical mosque and meeting hall, surrounded by a red sandstone wall, is set in a lovely garden of trees and fountains. The Taj Mahal has been acclaimed as one of the most beautiful buildings in the world.

1658: Molière Turns Defeat into Triumph. On October 24 a small company of actors appears in the guardroom of the Louvre in Paris to perform in front of King Louis XIV. The play they have chosen is *Nicomede,* a tragedy by Corneille. Appearing in the drama is Jean Baptiste Molière, playwright as well as actor. He is badly miscast and the result is a total disaster. Immediately after the performance, Molière, with the king's permission, presents what he calls a little entertainment that he has written titled *Le Docteur Amoureux.* As the saying goes, it brought the house down and launched Molière on a career in comedy writing and acting that rarely has been equaled. Among his plays still performed today are *Tartuffe, Le Misanthrope, Le Bourgeois Gentilhomme,* and *Le Malade Imaginaire.* Moliere was one of those rare playwrights who wrote for the actor and invented some of the greatest comedic characters ever to appear on the stage. Although he was disappointed at not doing tragedy, his acting ability in playing comedy roles has led some critics to compare him with Charlie Chaplin. Ironically, the man who is frequently called the greatest of the French writers literally worked himself to death. Frequently suffering from ill health, it was while playing *The Imaginary Invalid* on February 17, 1673, that he became ill on stage and succumbed a few hours later. To this day he can still make us laugh.

1660: It's Comedy Tonight! The monarchy has been restored and Charles II is on the throne of England. After a decade of suppression by the Puritans, the theater is once again alive and Restoration comedy begins to reign supreme. Rollicking comedies of manners, parodies of love and romance, satires on court mores, all reflecting the society of the time, delight audiences. It is the

age of the flowering of some of England's best-known poets and playwrights: William Congreve, Sir John Vanbrugh, Sir George Etherege, William Wycherley, Colley Cibber, and John Dryden.

A century later Richard Brinsley Sheridan will revive the theater again with his wit in such plays as *The Rivals* (in which the character Mrs. Malaprop appears, giving us our term *malapropism* for the misuse of words in ridiculous fashion) and *The School for Scandal,* and Oliver Goldsmith will write *She Stoops to Conquer.*

1660s: Revising Shakespeare. Sir William D'Avenant,
poet, playwright, and producer, tries to give the audience what they want by rewriting some of Shakespeare's plays, along with a little help from Dryden, a fellow poet. *Romeo and Juliet* is given a happy ending; *Macbeth* appears with flying witches, along with a little singing and dancing; *The Taming of the Shrew* moves from Italy to Scotland, as evidenced in the title, *Sawney the Scot, or the Taming of the Shrew;* and *The Tempest* is converted into an opera.

To give him his due, D'Avenant, who was Shakespeare's godson (or his biological son, according to the gossip of the day), was quite innovative, aside from revamping his godfather's plays. To the English stage he introduced opera, painted scenery, and the first female to act and sing. He was also appointed the second poet laureate of England after the death of Ben Jonson.

We can't fault him too much. Over the years Shakespeare's works have been cut as various directors saw fit and turned into ballets, musicals, and movie spectaculars. But a happy ending to *Romeo and Juliet?* Unthinkable!

1675: The New St. Paul's Cathedral Begins. The old
Gothic-style church had been destroyed, as had most of London, in the Great Fire of 1666. Sir Christopher Wren, scientist, mathematician, and architect, who had earlier been commissioned by Charles II to restore the old church, presented plans for the new cathedral as well as schemes for rebuilding the entire city and its damaged churches. There was much controversy over Wren's original plan for St. Paul's since the clergy preferred a medieval style and Wren had conceived the structure following the great domed designs he had seen in France. He finally altered his design and construction began in 1675. As it was built it was altered again and was not completed until 1711. It is today renowned for

its triple dome and is a monument to Wren, who is buried there. In fact, his epitaph reads: *Si monumentum requiris, cirumspice*—"If you seek a monument, look about you."

1678–82: La Salle Claims Louisiana Territory. The French missionary and explorer René La Salle had emigrated to Canada in 1666 to a grant of land on the St. Lawrence River. From there he and his men explored the wilderness to the south, establishing trading posts and cementing good relationships with the Indians. In 1677 La Salle sought financial assistance in France and was awarded a monopoly on the fur trade and permission to build forts. In 1682 he led an expedition down the Mississippi to the mouth of the river and claimed it and all its tributaries for the king of France, Louis XIV, for whom he named the territory.

1685: Bach Is Born. The end of the Baroque period of art and music is approaching when Johann Sebastian is born into the Bach family, whose remarkable musical abilities go back several generations. With such a family background, it is only natural that little Johann should follow in his relatives' footsteps. He will become, however, the most famous Bach of all.

Among his most celebrated works are the Brandenburg Concertos and *The Well-Tempered Clavier*." He is a composer's composer whose analytical mind, belief in God, and melodic genius led him to create some of the greatest religious music we have. He was also the most famous organist of his time and frequently held appointments as church or court organist and director of music. His creative output was enormous, but as so often happened with true geniuses, it wasn't until after his death at sixty-five that his true worth began to be known. Several of his sons followed in his footsteps and made their mark, as well as more money than poor Dad. There were many in the Bach family whose first name was Johann, including Johann Sebastian's father, a brother, and two of his sons. It's a name to reckon with.

1681: Matches Invented. The Englishman Robert Boyle, one of the founders of modern chemistry, dipped a wooden stick into sulfur, drew it through coarse, phosphorus-coated paper, and ignited the stick. The first "match." The word originally meant a fuse to fire a cannon, and comes from the Latin word *myxa*,

meaning "wick." There were other inventive forms of matches produced through the next century; most of them involved glass tubes and phosphorus and were not too practical.

The first friction match was probably made in 1816 by François Derosne, a Frenchman, and in 1827 Englishman John Walker began producing his version of matches. All of these matches were difficult to light, rather dangerous, and gave off a pungent odor. In 1845 red phosphorus was discovered, which is nontoxic and much less flammable and was soon used in matchmaking. By 1856 so-called safety matches were being produced. Some of the ingredients needed to ignite a flame were placed on the outside of the box of matches. One need only to scrape the wooden match alongside the box to ignite it. Our ubiquitous book matches came into being in 1892 when Philadelphia patent attorney Joseph Pusey developed them.

The match, therefore, common as it may be now, is rather a modern device, and a convenient one, too. Think about it the next time you light those birthday candles without a torch from the fireplace.

Ca. 1690: Bustles and Hoops. A hilarious item of fashion, the bustle originated about this time when fashionable women gathered their full skirts around them and anchored them in the back, forming a big pouf. This style lasted until about 1711, when hoop skirts came in, went out, and came back again. As skirts began to narrow, the bustle reappeared once more about 1869, then slowly slipped downward to a mere fullness at the skirt bottom. When skirts became very narrow, the bustle once again arrived on the fashion scene in 1884, and this time stuck straight out like a shelf. Sitting was not comfortable. It didn't last long, and fortunately, we haven't seen it since.

Equally as ludicrous were the flexible steel contraptions the fashionable wore when hoop skirts hit their greatest expansion in 1860. These replaced the stiff horsehair and linen petticoats used to extend the skirts. Either way, getting close to someone, or something, couldn't have been easy. Neither of these styles will return; those hoops just won't fit behind the wheel of a car.

18th Century: Dominoes. Another ancient game very similar to our dominoes was played in Egypt, and the Chinese invented their own game, but modern dominoes probably originated in

Italy and soon spread throughout Europe, where it became very popular.

18th Century: Off-the-Rack. Ready-to-wear men's suits are sold for the first time in London.

No man of fashion or even minor wealth would be caught dead in one of these ill-fitting, baggy garments, but for the lower classes, it was the opportunity to own a "Sunday best" outfit. Until this time clothing for men and women had been custom-made, either at home by the women in the family or by a professional tailor or seamstress. The suits caught on and it wasn't long before production increased as the working class tried to become gentlemen in their newfound sartorial splendor. Naturally, the tailor's guilds were upset at the thought of the loss of business and even went so far as to petition Parliament in an attempt to outlaw ready-made clothing. However, the "if you can't beat 'em, join 'em" philosophy soon eclipsed political maneuvering and many tailors began deserting the guilds to enter the business of ready-to-wear. By the nineteenth century the idea had spread to Paris, the epicenter of western fashion.

It took women a longer time before they could buy clothing off the rack. The invention of the sewing machine was the first big step in mass-producing women's clothes. And once again, fearing for their livelihood, seamstresses and tailors protested. All was in vain, however, and the seamstresses themselves turned to the new invention. Standardized sizes were soon adopted and paper patterns invented in the 1860s, and before long a new clothing industry had sprung up. Women still continued sewing their own dresses, and the wealthier employed seamstresses, but as the fashion business flourished and technological advances made the mass production of clothing cheaper, the custom faded away. By the early twentieth century almost everyone was buying ready-made clothing in retail stores.

We think nothing of shopping in stores for our clothes now; for many, it's a national pastime. It sure beats trying to thread a needle.

1705: A Comet Is Named Halley. A comet was seen in 1066. It was observed in 1531, 1607, and 1682 also. Edmund Halley, an English astronomer, had seen it in 1682, noticed that it seemed to follow the same path as the previous comets, calculated its orbit, and said it would appear again in 1758. He was right, and it's been around about every seventy-six years ever since. It was Halley, by the way, who subsidized the printing of his friend Isaac Newton's *Principia*. A good man.

1713: Treaty of Utrecht.

The city in Holland is the location of the signing of a treaty between Anne, queen of England, and Louis XIV of France in which England receives Nova Scotia, Newfoundland, and the Hudson Bay area from France, and Gibraltar and Minorca from Spain.

On November 1, 1700, Charles II, the feebleminded, sickly Hapsburg king of Spain, finally did what all of Europe was hoping for: He died. Since he was childless, his death precipitated the War of the Spanish Succession, in which the Bourbon Louis XIV and the Hapsburg emperor, Charles VI, had great stakes. The rest of Europe didn't want the Spanish throne going to either dynasty, so they joined in the fracas. After twelve years, Louis came to terms and his grandson (to whom Charles had left his Spanish inheritance in the first place) gained the throne of Spain. The treaty, however, stated that the crowns of France and Spain were never to be united, which was a relief to everyone else. The emperor got the Netherlands, Austria got Sardinia and Naples, and the Stuart pretender to the throne of England was expelled from France. Western Europe would remain constant for the next seventy-five years, until the French Revolution.

1725: The Spanish Steps.

The 137 steps leading from Rome's Piazza di Spagna up to the Trinita dei Monti church are completed. Not that this is a spectacular architectural feat, but the steps will become a meeting place for students and tourists and a great place to sit and watch the world go round while eating a gelato.

1737: Mathematical Pi.

Swiss mathematician and savant Leonhard Euler adopts the symbol π, the Greek letter pi, for use in mathematical notation. Thus we have the equation $C = \pi r^2$, for the circumference of a circle, which may be the only equation some of us remember from high school geometry class. He also uses i for an infinite number and the Greek letter Σ (sigma) to indicate summation. Euler devises other notations we use today in college math and is the most prolific writer and math analyzer we have ever had, writing an average of eight hundred pages a year during his lifetime.

Euler is also proficient in theology, astronomy, medicine, physics, and Oriental as well as European languages. A fine example of a great human mind at work.

1741: Alaska Discovered. The Danish navigator Vitus Bering, under service to the Russians, had earlier explored the strait that now bears his name and sailed into the Arctic Ocean. His pioneering journey proved that North America was not joined to Asia. On his second expedition to explore the coast of Siberia and search for a legendary land near the Aleutians, he became separated from a sister ship, and on August 20 the exhausted crew landed in the Gulf of Alaska. The name comes from the Russian version of the Eskimo word for "great land," Alakshak or Alayeksa. Although Bering died shortly after his discovery, his reports contributed greatly to the geography of the land.

1744: Baseball. The umpire yells, "Play ball," the batter takes his stance at the plate, the pitcher winds up for the throw, and another game of the great American pastime begins. The word *baseball* was first recorded in 1744 in England, and referred to a game of rounders in which a batter hit a soft ball and had to circle round two bases to score runs without being put out by being hit with the ball. It was similar to today's cricket. Batting a ball, or any spherical object, with a stick had undoubtedly been going on since time immemorial, but now we had a game and rules to play by.

The game crossed the ocean and was called *base* by soldiers who played it at Valley Forge in 1778, and in the next century was variously called by such names as *stick ball, goal ball,* and *barn ball.* By 1820 in New England, the players had divided into two teams and were using four bases instead of two base posts, and running around the four bases counted as one run. This was played on village greens and called *town ball* or *the Massachusetts game.* In the late 1830s, the rules changed a bit when someone suggested the runner could be put out by throwing the ball to the base ahead of him or by touching him with the ball instead of throwing it at him. Since the runner was no longer in jeopardy, a harder ball could now be used, which could be thrown faster and hit farther. This meant the game now needed men in the outfield to catch the ball and players in the infield to guard the bases. In 1845 the

New York City Knickerbocker Ball Club devised the first standard rules and the modern game was born, called either the *New York game* or *New York baseball*. The first game was played at Elysian Fields in Hoboken, New Jersey, between the Knickerbockers and the New York Nine in 1846.

After the Civil War, former soldiers who had learned the game from the New York and New Jersey regiments began playing it regularly, and soon people were flocking to ballparks and reading the baseball column in the local newspaper. Big cities had major baseball clubs, and smaller cities had minor clubs, and all the players were amateurs. In 1867 that started to change when the Rockford, Illinois, team began to pay a salary to some expert players to join their gentlemen amateurs. The following year a semiprofessional team was organized in Cincinnati, and in the ensuing year they became the Cincinnati Red Stockings, the first fully professional paid team. The team toured from New York to San Francisco and were so successful that by 1871, baseball had become the great American spectator sport, as well as a blossoming industry. By 1876 we had the National League, and in 1882, the American Association, and in 1884 the World Series began. The American Association later became the minor league, and in 1901 the American League as we know it today was formed from the old Western League.

Throughout the following decades baseball fans were thrilled by such players as Honus Wagner, the first great shortstop; Giants' pitcher Christy Mathewson, who won ninety games in the 1903–05 seasons, and thirty-seven in 1908; Cy Young, for whom the best pitcher of the year award is named; Ty Cobb and Babe Ruth, two of baseball's immortals; the Brooklyn Dodgers' Jackie Robinson, who broke the color barrier; Joe Di Maggio; Lou Gehrig; Ted Williams; Willie Mays; Hank Aaron; Mickey Mantle; Reggie Jackson; Nolan Ryan, and hundreds of others who have made the game of baseball what it is today.

1759: Roller Skates. The first roller skates had only two wheels on each skate and were invented by a Belgian to wear at a masquerade party. Unfortunately he didn't know how to stop when he rolled in and literally crashed the party. Ice-skating was still the safer pastime. Oddly enough, in the mid-nineteenth century an opera and a ballet were performed in which ice-skating scenes were simulated by using roller skates. It wasn't until the late 1880s that roller bearings were introduced, technology improved, and skating began to be popular. And although most of us learned to skate with four wheels on each skate, we have come full circle with in-line roller skates imitating ice skates once again.

1760: School for the Deaf. Educating the deaf seems to have begun as early as 1578 with the efforts of an unidentified Spanish Benedictine monk. However, it was not until 1760 that Abbé Charles de l'Epée began the first school for the deaf in the city of Paris. L'Epée also created a system of sign language, which he used to communicate with his students. In 1790 this school was changed from a private institution to a state-supported school, thereby making it more accessible to deaf children throughout France.

Others besides l'Epée also showed concern for the education of the deaf. In the early to late nineteenth century Thomas Braidwood worked with the deaf in Edinburgh, Scotland. Germany established a school for the deaf in Leipzig in 1778. It began with government money from the elector of Saxony and became the first school for the deaf to receive official state recognition.

Thomas H. Gallaudet established the first American school for the deaf in 1817 in Hartford, Connecticut, using sign language and writing as the fundamentals of instruction. Despite the fact that it was a private institution, certain states paid the costs to send deaf students to Gallaudet. Kentucky inaugurated the first state-funded school for the deaf in 1823.

In 1864 a college offering bachelor's and master's degrees was founded in Washington, D.C., and is now known as Gallaudet College.

1762: The Safety Razor. Men have always shaved, although one wonders why they thought they had to. Maybe a beard just got in the way. Archaeologists have found cave drawings of beardless men, and grave sites containing sharpened flints for shaving. The American Indians methodically plucked their beards out with clamshell tweezers. With the coming of the Iron and Bronze Ages, razors made out of these metals appeared, and over the centuries men nicked and cut themselves while shaving, and no doubt swore when they did. American colonists used a hooked-type razor resembling a small scythe, but the straight razor was also prevalent. The first safety razor was invented by a French barber who used a metal guard along one edge of the blade, which stopped the blade from slicing into the skin. Early in the eighteenth century an improved model was manufactured in Sheffield, England.

The safety razor as we know it today was invented by King Gillette, who was looking for an item to manufacture that would make him rich. Men were already using a T-shaped razor, but the blade was permanent and had to be professionally sharpened. The idea came to Gillette one morning as he stared at his dull blade. Six years later, in 1903, the razor and paper-thin steel disposable blades were on the market. Out went the clamshells, tweezers, and straight razors, as more and more men were introduced to this convenient new invention. When America entered World War I, the government issued these razors and blades to the troops, who continued using the Gillette Safety Razor after the war and made Gillette a millionaire.

In 1931 Jacob Schick marketed his invention, the electric razor, which was slow to catch on until about 1940 when electric shavers began to gain popularity. The safety razor is still with us, though, now in plastic and entirely disposable.

1762: Mozart Mesmerizes Maria. The six-year-old musical prodigy plays the piano magically for the emperor and empress of Austria, then jumps into Maria Theresa's royal lap. He later tells their daughter, Marie Antoinette, that she is very pretty, and when he grows up he is going to marry her. They both may have been better off if he had; Marie would have kept her head, and Wolfgang would have had her money to live on.

Joannes Chrysostomus Wolfgangus Amadeus Mozart was born on January 27, 1756, in Salzburg (then in Bavaria, now in Austria). It was an auspicious day for the world of music; the baby with the lengthy name would grow up to become what many consider to be the greatest musical genius of all time. At the age of five the precocious Wolfgang had already begun composing and displayed an astounding grasp of music, not only on the pianoforte but on the violin and harpsichord as well. His father, Leopold, a musician and composer himself, embarked on a series of European tours beginning in 1762 to show off his son's musical talents as well as those of his daughter, Nannerl. While in Paris for the winter, the seven-year-old Wolfgang published his first compositions, four violin sonatas. They hit the road again, performing in London, Holland, Brussels, Geneva, Bern, and Munich before returning to Salzburg. Soon they were off again, this time to northern Italy. And all the while Wolfgang was composing, composing, composing. In fact, throughout his entire life, music just poured from him, and it seemed to come out in perfect form. He was thirteen when he composed a German operetta and an Italian opera, and fourteen when his second opera was performed at La Scala.

For all his genius, Wolfgang had a hard time keeping a job during his lifetime, although the archbishop of Salzburg appointed him concertmaster for a while, and in 1779 he was appointed court organist in Salzburg. He spent time in Vienna, being called there by the archbishop, who refused to let him play in anyone's house but his and made him eat with the servants. Eventually Mozart sought to resign his post and was kicked out, as he later wrote, "on his behind" by the archbishop's steward. He was now on his own and had to support himself and his new wife, Constanze, by his own compositions and commissions from patrons on a freelance basis. He held his own concerts and played his own concertos as well as improvisations, and eked out a living. All the while he was still composing and composing and composing one masterpiece after another. He wrote at least forty-one symphonies, twenty-seven piano concertos, seventeen piano and forty-two violin sonatas, thirty string quartets, and much chamber music. Of the eighteen or so operas, he composed, *Don Giovanni* is deemed by some musicologists as the most perfect opera ever written, while others contend that *The Magic Flute* is even superior. Operagoers, however, love the melodious *Marriage of Figaro*. As Mozart said, "Music . . . should never offend the ear, but should charm it, and always remain music."

Overworked, finances failing, and in poor health, Mozart died at the age of thirty-five. The composer Franz Haydn had once told Wolfgang's father, "I declare before God as a man of honor that your son is the greatest composer I know, either personally or by reputation." He could still say that today.

1768: Spontaneous Generation Debunked. The theory that living organisms arise from nonliving matter had been held for centuries. Lazzaro Spallanzani, however, finally disproves it when he states that an egg must be fertilized by a spermatozoon to reproduce another animal and that microscopic organisms do not reproduce in broth that has been cooked and kept in closed containers. There are diehards who still believe, however, that lower forms of life are spontaneously generated.

Spallanzani was an interesting fellow. He was an Italian priest and biologist who also studied law at the University of Bologna. He researched the circulation of blood, respiration, eel breeding, regeneration in aquatic creatures, and successfully artificially inseminated a dog.

1768–79: Captain Cook's Voyages.

The greatest of all maritime explorers and one of the most admired, James Cook was born in Yorkshire, England, in 1728. Early in life he was attracted to the sea, and at the age of seventeen was apprenticed to John Walker, a Quaker shipowner and coal shipper who took him under his wing, sent him to sea, and made him study navigation and mathematics. He later joined the British navy, was rapidly promoted, and became master of the flagship *Northumberland*. Cook continued his studies in mathematics and astronomy, gained an excellent reputation as a surveyor, and had his observations and work published in several reputable journals.

In 1768 Cook was commissioned as a lieutenant in command of HMS *Endeavor Bark*, with instructions to sail to Tahiti with observers from the Royal Society on an astronomical mission, and to continue geographical and natural history studies in the Pacific. Cook sailed around Cape Horn at the southern tip of South America, and landed in Tahiti on April 13, 1769, eight months after he had left England. Although the astronomical endeavors were not too successful, the botanical studies were invaluable. To Cook's credit, excellent relations with the native Tahitians were formed, which later proved useful. After leaving Tahiti, Cook explored the Society Islands, which he named, then circumnavigated New Zealand and sailed along the east coast of Australia, scrupulously charting the land wherever he went before returning to England.

His curiosity piqued by stories of a continent below the fortieth parallel south, Cook suggested another voyage to round the globe and was put in command of two ships. He left England on July 13, 1772, sailed around the Cape of Good Hope at the southern tip of Africa and into the Indian Ocean. This expedition explored various sections of the Antarctic on three different cruises but did not find the continent Cook was convinced lay beyond the ice. On this voyage Cook discovered and rediscovered territories from

Easter Island to New Caledonia, including the Marquesas, Tonga, New Hebrides, South Georgia, and the South Sandwich Islands. He was back in England on July 30, 1775. For his explorations and navigations as well as for his methods of combating scurvy to maintain the health of his crew, Cook was made a fellow of the Royal Society.

A year later he was at sea again. This voyage was to explore the northern Pacific coast of America, once more to search for that elusive Northwest Passage. He sailed on the same ship, rounding the Cape once more and on to Tasmania, New Zealand, Tonga, and the Society Islands. From there he ventured north and discovered the Hawaiian Islands. He reached the American coast and sailed around the Aleutians into the Bering Strait as far north as he could before the ice stopped him. Reversing course, he headed to Hawaii for the winter. Unfortunately he never made it back to England; he was killed in a fracas with the natives. The two ships of his third and last expedition returned to England on October 4, 1780.

1769: The Circus. The modern circus began in England when Philip Astley, a trick rider, found he could stand on the back of a horse while it galloped around in a circle. Prior to that the few horsemen who entertained crowds had ridden back and forth in a rectangle. Having accomplished this singular feat, Astley soon opened his riding ring establishment, called the Royal Grove, and we have been watching performers riding around in circles ever since. A few years later, a rival, Charles Hughes, opened a similar institution and called it the Royal Circus. The name stuck.

The time was ripe for a circus. The fairs that had been so popular for centuries were on the wane. The populace was tiring of the rowdy and sometimes lawless crowds that the fairs drew, and the new enterprising theater owners begrudged the competition. So the acrobats, jugglers, trained bears, trick monkeys, rope-dancers, and other performers did the only thing they could do: They joined the circus.

Astley took his circus on the road and eventually established nineteen circuses throughout Europe. His old rival Hughes took his circus to Russia and entertained Catherine the Great.

In the United States, the circus made its debut in August of 1785, when John Poole displayed animals, did trick riding, and hired a clown to entertain the customers in his newly erected establishment in Philadelphia. Eight years later, John Ricketts arrived from England and opened his Ricketts Circus and Riding Academy in Philadelphia, which became famous after George and Martha Washington attended a performance.

The first circuses were mostly equestrian shows with a smattering of vaudeville acts. There were a few wild animal acts, however, the most famous being that of Isaac Van Amburgh in the first half of the nineteenth century. He was reputed to be the first person to put his head in a lion's mouth, at least the first one who lived to repeat the performance. In 1859 a daring new act arrived at the circus when the French gymnast Jules Leotard invented the flying trapeze and the outfit to wear when performing his aerial acrobatics. The same year Charles Blondin crossed Niagara on a tightrope, and soon trapeze artists and tightrope walkers were big features of the circus, surpassing the equestrian acts by the turn of the century.

The circus flourished in the United States, especially after Phineas T. Barnum opened his Greatest Show on Earth in Brooklyn, New York, in 1871. Barnum, the consummate showman, introduced such acts as the Bearded Lady, the Thin Man, the Wild Man of Borneo, Siamese Twins, and General Tom Thumb, who became the most famous midget in the world. Barnum also brought Jumbo, a six-and-a-half-ton elephant, over from London and made him the starring attraction. In 1881 Barnum merged with Bailey's Circus and became the first three-ring circus to perform under the big top, as the circus tent was called. In 1907 the Ringling Brothers Circus combined with Barnum and Bailey and called their show The Big One. The audience thrilled as they watched Alfred Codoma perform his triple somersault from one flying trapeze to the other, and May Worth, the great bareback rider, somersault from one horse to another, and laughed at the antics of famous clowns like Emmett Kelly and Felix Adler.

Nowadays our tastes may be more sophisticated and we may have seen it all on television, but when the circus comes to town, little kids and big kids alike are still drawn to the magic of the big top.

1769: The Steam Engine. Steam is vaporized water, an odorless, invisible gas. Credit for the invention of a practical machine capable of producing steam from water goes to James Watt, a Scottish instrument maker, who patented his reciprocating steam engine machine in 1769, at the age of thirty-three. No longer would we have to rely on animal or human muscle power or the whims of wind and water. Steam power truly transformed our society more than any invention up to its day.

Back in the first century, Hero of Alexandria, the Greek mathematician and writer, conjured up a primitive steam turbine. He called it an aeolipile, or ball of Aeolus (after the god of winds). It consisted of a hollow metal ball with a pair of tubes extending from it, mounted on a vertical axle. The ball was partially filled with water, then heated by a fire under it, creating steam which escaped through the tubes and caused the ball to revolve. In the seventeenth century this action would become Newton's first law of motion: Every action has a reaction. Hero also described other inventive devices such as a siphon, a slot machine, and several instruments using steam.

So much for the idea of steam power. We kept on using manual labor and animals to do our hauling, hoisting, pushing, and powering for the next sixteen hundred years. As the Age of Enlightenment dawned, science came into its own; thinking man was back on track again and ideas proliferated.

In 1690 the Frenchman Denis Papin developed a piston steam engine, but it wasn't too practical. In 1698 Thomas Savery, an English engineer, patented his ungainly steam pump, used mostly to pump water out of mines, but the technology of the times was insufficient to build his engine accurately. Then, in 1712, the English ironmonger Thomas Newcomen built an efficient and practical steam engine by separating the boiler from the cylinder. The new steam pump was used to raise water from the tin and copper mines in Cornwall with which he did business, and later in the mines of northern England.

Along comes James Watt, the working man's inventor. An instrument maker by trade, he had spent a year in London producing quadrants, compasses, and other mathematical devices. Hoping to continue his trade, he returned to his native Scotland and tried to set up shop in Glasgow. The local guild refused to admit him, however, claiming he was neither the son of a burgess, nor had he served the full term of apprenticeship. Fortunately, the university in Glasgow took him in. He had previously cleaned and repaired a group of brass instruments for them, and impressed with his work, they appointed him mathematical instrument maker to the university and gave him a place to work. This also brought him into contact with some of the scientific minds studying there, with whom he had many dialogues, including discussions on how to improve the steam engine. Watt had known about Newcomen's engine and had experimented with steam himself, and in 1764 he was given a model of the engine to repair. A fortuitous event. For the next several years, Watt worked on his own designs to improve the cumbersome and expensive engine. One of his ideas was to separate the condenser from the cylinder. He later devised several other important improvements and patented his refined engine in 1769. The new engine was much more efficient; its pistons made faster strokes and it consumed much less coal, therefore making it much cheaper to operate. The steam engine, once only used for pumping, later became useful for other operations, when Watt added a crank and connecting rod to drive a revolving shaft. With further improvements and inventions over the years, Watt's engine was soon used to drive machinery of all kinds. Watt was fortunate in meeting and becoming friends with Matthew Boulton, a wealthy industrialist who owned a large silver-stamping factory near Birmingham. Together they launched a manufacturing business to produce Watt's engine, which became a rip-roaring success. The Industrial Revolution had already started. Now, with the steam engine to power its machines, it accelerated into high gear.

1769: Dartmouth College; Private Means Private.
Dartmouth College in New Hampshire is chartered by King George III as a private institution.

In 1816 the state of New Hampshire wanted to turn Dartmouth into a public school. The college fought this all the way to the Supreme Court, and its ruling set a precedent for private universities throughout the United States. In 1819 the Supreme Court ruled that the state had no right to tamper with a college or university's charter without due cause and that the desire to force the school to become public was not due cause. In short, the Supreme Court ruled that private educational institutions can remain private.

1770: British Claim Australia.
On August 23, 1770, Captain James Cook formally took possession of the eastern coast of Australia for Great Britain. Nobody else wanted it anyway.

Marco Polo had mentioned a land rich in spices, which geogra-

phers mistakenly thought referred to a southern continent. There
were voyages to locate this mysterious Terra Australis, but none
of the Portuguese, French, or Spanish mariners actually ever saw
it, although some of them came very close. In 1606 Willem Janz,
a Dutchman, was the first to sail close to the northern coast, and
a few months later the Spaniard Luis de Torres sighted the northern tip. The country was reported to be so desolate-looking that
no one bothered to investigate further. The Dutch continued exploring along the west coast while on their voyages to the East
Indies by way of Africa. In 1642 an expedition led by Abel Tasman, seeking a western route to South America, sailed along the
southern coast and discovered the island now named for him,
Tasmania, and then reached New Zealand, which he thought was
part of Terra Australis. Although he had circumnavigated Australia,
he never found the passage to South America. After Tasman's
voyages, the Dutch East India Company lost interest.

In 1688 Dampier, an English privateer searching for lands to
plunder, sailed along the western coast and decided it was not
worth his time and effort. His accounts of his investigations, however, sparked interest in the area. It was not until 1768, however,
that Captain James Cook was commissioned to sail westward and
around South America to Australia, there to establish trading posts
for British goods. On April 20, 1770, he reached the east coast.
This time the country was deemed suitable for settlement. And
also a good place for a penal colony as it turned out.

1774: Priestly Discovers Oxygen.

Joseph Priestly, an En-
glish minister and educator, had a new glass tube. On August 1 he
burned mercuric oxide in it and obtained what he called "dephlo-
gisticated air," which he thought "might be peculiarly salutary for
the lungs in certain cases." He was right. It was later renamed
oxygen by French chemist Lavoisier. (Thank goodness; can you
imagine having to spell the original?) Priestly then went on to
discover more gases: nitrogen, nitrogen dioxide, nitrous oxide,
hydrogen chloride, sulfur dioxide, and ammonia. While doing all
this he also had time to write about education and advocated a
curriculum stressing history, commerce, law, and public administration rather than the classics. A rather novel idea at the time.
He was very sympathetic to American and French revolutionists,
which did not sit too well, naturally, with the English, so he left
for America in 1794 to join his sons. He built a house and labora-

tory in Northumberland, Pennsylvania, where he remained for the
last ten years of his life.

1776: *Common Sense.* The pamphlet written and published
by Thomas Paine on January 10, titled *Common Sense,* urged the
American colonists to rebel against the British and was instrumental in forming public opinion. Paine later wrote *The Crisis,* which
opens with the words "These are the times that try men's souls."
Paine attacked monarchies and advocated a republican form of
government, published his *Rights of Man* and *Age of Reason* pamphlets, championed the rights of women, suggested a progressive
income tax in order to aid the helpless and elderly, proclaimed
equal rights for all individuals, and in general was a great humanist,
appealing to both emotions and reason in his writing.

1776: Declaration of Independence. *We hold these truths to
be self-evident, that all men are created equal, that they are endowed by
their Creator with certain unalienable Rights, that among these are Life,
Liberty and the pursuit of Happiness.* So states the unanimous declaration of the thirteen united states of America, approved by the
Continental Congress on July 4, 1776, and later signed by fifty-
six representatives of the thirteen colonies. The Declaration of
Independence, as we now call it, made history. It was the first
time a whole body of people asserted their right to a government
of their choice.

The purpose of the document was, of course, to declare the
colonies' separation from Great Britain, a declaration King George
III did not take lightly. Nor did he appreciate the delineation of
grievances against him or being told he was unfit to be the ruler
of a free people. You just didn't treat your king that way. What
had been a minor rebellion for over a year turned into a full-
blown revolution. Fortunately, it went our way, and ever since
we have been free to pursue life, liberty, and happiness and to
inspire the rest of the world to do the same.

1781: Uranus Discovered. Using a reflecting telescope that
he constructed himself, William Herschel discovers the planet Uranus, the first planet to be discovered since the ancient Babylonian
era. The German-born Herschel, a well-known musician in Bath,
England, is fascinated by astronomy and spends all his spare time
scanning the skies. His sister, Caroline, is recruited to join him in

England, and she, too, will become a noted astronomer in her
own right. For his discovery, Herschel is elected a member of the
Royal Society and receives the Copley medal. He also accepts an
invitation from King George III to become his private astronomer.
His several books and papers catalog hundreds of new double stars,
star clusters, and nebulae. In August of 1789 he finishes construction of his great telescope with a forty-foot focal length and four-
foot aperture, turns it towards Saturn, and for the first time sees
the planet and its six satellites brightly. In September he discovers
a seventh moon of Saturn.

His son, John, will carry on the work his father began as well
as becoming a well-known chemist and will be the first person to
use the terms *negative* and *positive* for photographic images. Both
father and son are knighted, and Caroline, before she dies at the
age of ninety-seven, will receive two gold medals for her scientific work.

1781: Pestalozzi Publishes. Johann Heinrich Pestalozzi, a
Swiss educator, publishes his novel *Leonard and Gertrude,* detailing
his ideas and opinions on social, political, and moral reforms.

Like many others, Pestalozzi was not satisfied with the prevail-
ing system of education. Born in Zurich in 1746, he began his
contributions to education by starting a school on his own farm
to teach fifty abandoned children. There he taught them not only
the three R's but also the basics of agriculture and trades to help
them lead productive lives. He believed that through education
the poor and displaced could fit back into society and, conversely,
that social reform could be brought about through education. Of
course, Pestalozzi also had plans for reforming education. In the
eighteenth century, most of the schools in Switzerland and Germany were still under some sort of religious control, and the
majority of them taught through memorization of facts. Pestalozzi
felt that this went against the natural grain of a child's learning
ability. Children, he argued, should be allowed to touch and experiment. Each child had his own natural way of learning, and
the job of a teacher was to learn this method and work with it.
Further, he argued, schools should not only educate children, they
should also help to guide them in their development into adulthood. In other words, schools should help children through all of
their stages of natural development.

He not only argued for hands-on learning, but after the financial failure of his first school and several unsuccessful attempts to teach with the established schools, Pestalozzi opened his own boarding school in Yverdon in 1800 and put his ideas to work. Many teachers were brought from several different disciplines, providing both the manpower and the skills for single-subject classes. His ideas became so well-known and sought after that he added a program to educate teachers at his school in Yverdon, and public schools that had once turned him away as a teacher now sent teachers to him.

Pestalozzi's methods revolutionized teaching. He abolished the harsh discipline so prevalent through the ages and which he believed immoral and replaced it with love and caring. He stressed observation, learning by doing, class discussion rather than individual recitations, physical exercise, field trips, and individual differences. His methods were soon adopted by the Swiss, and before long, many schools throughout Europe, particularly in Prussia, were espousing his philosophy. At the Oswego, New York, normal school, in 1861, his principles became the basis for its teacher training program.

Pestalozzi died in 1827, at the age of eighty-one. Always an advocate for the disadvantaged and the helpless, he led the life he hoped to instill in others by his teachings.

1783: Lavoisier's Chemistry. On June 28, 1783, the French chemist Antoine Laurent Lavoisier announces to the Academy of Science that water is a product of hydrogen and oxygen. (That's H_2O, which may be the only thing you remember from chemistry class.) Lavoisier, called the father of modern chemistry, introduces modern terminology for chemical substances, but keeps the old alchemist's symbols. Lavoisier had one of the most brilliant minds of his day, and aside from his work in chemistry, he was associated with committees on public education, coinage, and hygiene, among others. He started a model farm where he experimented with scientific agriculture and crop cultivation. He also framed a plan to improve economic conditions in his community by means of workhouses, canals, savings banks, and insurance societies. During the famine of 1788 he lent money without interest for the purchase of barley.

Unfortunately, he may have been too generous and too brilliant for his own good. During the French Revolution he was charged with stopping the circulation of air in Paris by the wall that had been erected on his advice. Alas, the philistines of the revolution got their way and Lavoisier, along with many others, was executed. He was only fifty.

1783: Treaty of Paris. The American Revolution is over and on September 3 the Treaty of Paris is signed by Benjamin Franklin, John Adams, John Jay, and Henry Laurens. The British recognize the independence of the colonies, with the Mississippi as the western boundary, but retain Canada and cede Florida to Spain. The colonies are also granted fishing rights off Newfoundland and are asked to treat the Loyalists fairly.

It is now time for the colonies to form a new system of government, not a monarchy, not a dictatorship, but a representative republic with legislative, executive, and judicial bodies; a federalist government with states' rights. It is the beginning of a new experiment. Today we call it democracy.

1784: School for the Blind. The first school for the blind, L'Institution Nationale des Jeunes Aveugles, begins in Paris due to the efforts of Valentin Haüy, who developed a system of embossed letters his students could "read." Originally, a student had to provide his own tuition, but eventually the state assumed some of the burden of educating the blind, and aided the school with partial funding. It was also in France that the first printed material for the blind appeared in 1786.

Shortly thereafter, many other countries began schools for blind students. The first schools in America began in 1832 in both Boston and New York, followed closely by a school in Philadelphia. Among other firsts were the first kindergarten for the blind, founded in Germany in 1861, and the first school for the African-American blind, established in North Carolina the same year.

1787: The Constitution. *We the People of the United States, in Order to form a more perfect Union, establish Justice, insure domestic Tranquillity, provide for the common defence, promote the general Welfare, and secure the Blessings of Liberty to ourselves and our Posterity, do ordain and establish this Constitution for the United States of America.* So reads the preamble to our Constitution. In seven articles this amazing document ushered in a new kind of government, of, by, and for the people, and for the first time established a true modern democracy under which we have lived for over two hundred years.

The yoke of a hereditary monarchy was thrown off and the powers of government were divided into three branches: the executive, the judicial, and the legislative, with checks and balances to assure that one branch does not become all-powerful. Over the years, the Constitution of the United States became a model for other nations and peoples to follow when they, too, wished to secure the blessings of liberty.

1787: Fitch's Folly. You thought it was Fulton's Folly. In any event, the steamboat was not invented by Robert Fulton.

In 1707 Denis Papin, the Frenchman who developed the idea of the steam engine, attempted to turn paddle wheels with his invention. Apparently it worked, but not successfully. In 1783 Count Claude de Jouffroy d'Abbans of France built a steamboat, the *Pyroscaphe,* which steamed along the river Saône at four knots, but was not capable of a long run. The French government under Louis XVI was no help to him (the revolution was brewing and Louis had other things to worry about), and d'Abbans didn't launch another boat until 1816, this time with a better outcome.

It was the unknown John Fitch of Connecticut who, in 1787, designed and operated a steamboat commercially. He, too, failed to get government funds for his projects and had trouble with his stockholders. Although not a success as a businessman, Fitch did operate his steamboat on the Delaware River, making scheduled trips between Philadelphia and Trenton, New Jersey.

On August 17, 1807, Robert Fulton's steamboat, the *Clermont,* made its historic 150-mile voyage up the Hudson River from New York to Albany in thirty-two hours, and "steamboatin'," as it would be called, was established as the new method of navigation.

Steamships revolutionized transportation, and from about 1860, increased rapidly in number. It was a faster and cheaper way to ship goods, especially grain from the Midwest, and a means that enabled vast numbers of European immigrants to journey to greater opportunities in the Western Hemisphere.

1789: Dentures. Any dentist will tell you that nothing is better than having your own teeth, but should you lose them, picture gumming your next taco. You can appreciate modern dentistry by taking a look back. The Etruscans who lived in what is now

Tuscany, Italy, made partial dentures as early as 700 B.C. The teeth
were carved from bone or ivory and the bridge was made of gold.
Good teeth were extracted when a person died, and these were
later also used to make realistic dentures. Of course, only the
wealthy upper classes could afford them. They passed on their
methods to the Romans, but after the Roman Empire fell, the
dentistry profession, like everything else, fell with it.

Dentistry in the medieval and Renaissance periods was crude,
to say the least, and once again it was the wealthy who purchased
teeth from out of the mouths of the poor, and set them in ivory
gums or had their own gums pierced with hooks and wires to
hold them. The practice of collecting teeth from dead soldiers on
battlefields was also rampant until about the 1860s. In 1789, however, a French dentist introduced porcelain dentures with the teeth
baked in one piece, and by 1845 single porcelain teeth were being
made. By the 1880s false teeth were in great demand. Nowadays
plastic is used for dentures, making them less brittle, firmer, and
quieter when chomping on that steak.

1789: University of North Carolina Chartered. The first
state university in the United States is chartered at Chapel Hill,
North Carolina, although no classes will be taught until 1795.

Another claimant for the honor of being the first state university
is the University of Georgia, chartered four years earlier in 1785,
but it did not open its doors to students until 1800, five years
after North Carolina had begun classes.

1789: The Rights of Man. As Dickens wrote in his *Tale of
Two Cities,* "It was the best of times; it was the worst of times."
On August 4, 1789, during the French Revolution, the French
assembly adopted their Declaration of the Rights of Man, and on
October 5, King Louis XVI accepted it. The Declaration was
inspired by constitutions of several states of the United States as
well as by the writings of the French philosophers Montesquieu,
Rousseau, and Voltaire and the Englishman John Locke. The Declaration was incorporated into the preamble of the French constitution of 1791 and stated that man had certain unalienable rights
such as "liberty, private property, security, and resistance to oppression." It declared that all men are born free and remain free
and that liberty is the right to do anything that does not harm
others. Every citizen may speak freely and print his views and not

suffer for his opinions, provided they don't endanger public order.

It was a radical document for ordinary Frenchmen, who had been smothered under the monarchy and nobility and denied their basic rights for centuries. The enlightened leaders of the revolution had produced a far, far better declaration than had ever been done before, to paraphrase Dickens.

1790: Washington, D.C., Planned. Pierre Charles L'Enfant, a French engineer who served as a major in the Continental Army, was selected by George Washington to lay out the plan for the new nation's capital city on the Potomac. He sited the congressional building on an eighty-five-foot-high mound at the west of Jenkin's Heights (which is why we frequently refer to Congress as "the hill") and placed the president's house, which he called a palace, along a broad avenue leading in a northwesterly direction from the congressional building. From the Capitol he planned waterfalls and pools which would empty into canals flowing into the Potomac. The executive office buildings were placed near the president's house. The commercial part of the city was laid out in grid fashion intersected by diagonal thoroughfares, all leading to the Capitol. At the intersections were circles and squares in the middle of which L'Enfant planned to erect statues and fountains.

L'Enfant was dismissed for refusing to cooperate by delaying the printing of his map, which was needed to indicate the areas where lots could be purchased by private citizens. The money from these sales was badly needed to begin construction of the Capitol. Andrew Ellicott, who had been the surveyor of the land, replaced him, and Ellicott hired as his assistant Benjamin Banneker, a free black mathematician, astronomer, and surveyor, to help lay out the city.

The cornerstone of the Capitol was laid by George Washington on September 18, 1793, and in 1800 Congress met in their new building for the first time.

Although L'Enfant's original plan was later forgotten, the basic design of the city remains, which is why driving around Washington, D.C., is so confusing today.

1791: The Whiskey Rebellion. Farmers in western Pennsylvania protested against enforcement of the excise tax on distilled liquors that the federal government had imposed to help pay the national debt.

Surplus grain was commonly converted to whiskey, which was then easier to ship and sell. The protest turned into an insurrection and became more violent when about five hundred men burned the home of the regional excise inspector. On August 7 President Washington ordered the rebels to return home and began negotiations with their leaders, but to no avail. Finally the militia from several states were sent into Pennsylvania and the federal troops quelled the rebellion bloodlessly. The strength of the federal government had been demonstrated and the few rebels who had been convicted of treason were pardoned by Washington.

In 1787 Thomas Jefferson wrote about an earlier rebellion in Massachusetts led by Daniel Shay, a farmer who hoped to get taxes reduced and paper money issued. He said: "What country can preserve its liberties if its rulers are not warned from time to time that their people preserve the spirit of resistance? The tree of liberty must be refreshed from time to time, with the blood of patriots and tyrants. It is its natural manure."

1791: The Bill of Rights. On December 15, 1791, the first ten amendments to the Constitution of the United States are ratified and become what is known as the Bill of Rights, one of the most important documents in human history. The amendments guarantee freedoms of speech, religion, and the press, the right of assembly, freedom from fear, the right to privacy and security in one's home, due process of law, the right to trial by jury, states' rights, and other basic human rights.

The forerunners of this document were the Magna Carta, the English Bill of Rights, and Virginia's 1776 Declaration of Rights, drafted by George Mason. Our rights are inalienable, and any acts of Congress in contradiction of them are subject to Supreme Court decisions. We are free people in a true democracy.

1789–91: First Constitutional Amendment. *Congress shall make no law respecting an establishment of religion, or prohibiting the free exercise thereof; or abridging the freedom of speech, or of the press; or the right of the people peaceably to assemble, and to petition the Government for a redress of grievances.*

The English had long had the right, confirmed over the years, to petition their king; thus it is logical that this right would also be demanded by the American colonists. But the colonists' petitions were constantly ignored by the English king, and in retaliation, the colonists revolted.

The right peaceably to assemble, although first considered not as important as the right to petition, has served us well over the years when we have gathered many times to protest the government's actions and make our wishes known. This amendment most recently protected our rights during the many peace marches on Washington during the Vietnam War and the protest marches led by Martin Luther King, Jr., and others.

The Puritan colony in Massachusetts was tightly controlled by the church and would accept no one who was not of their faith. In 1635, when Roger Williams expressed differences in beliefs, he was banished. He fled to what is now Rhode Island and established a new colony with religious tolerance for all and complete separation of church and state. Years later, James Madison of Virginia thought tolerance was not enough and that people should have the liberty to choose and practice whatever religion they like without discrimination. He was also aware of the violence and persecutions in Europe that had occurred when a state religion was foisted upon the people. We owe our religious freedom to wise men like Madison.

Freedom of speech and freedom of the press are rights we have long taken for granted in the United States. This freedom is not granted to people in many other countries. It is one of the keystones of a democratic government. For centuries criticizing the king or the government had been a crime, and those who did so were severely punished. Writers and publishers were punished for printing seditious material, whether it was true or not. In New York in 1733, John Peter Zenger published in his newspaper a series of articles written by others attacking the royal governor. As the publisher, Zenger was charged with seditious libel and arrested. The case was argued by Andrew Hamilton, who brilliantly defended him by stating that Zenger had not committed seditious libel since the material was true. Zenger was acquitted. It was a step in the direction of freedom to print the truth and express an opinion.

Our right to freedom of speech and the press has expanded over the years until we know more about about what's happening in our government and to the people who run it than at any time in history anywhere in the world. It keeps us informed and the government on its toes.

1789-91: Amendments II and III to the Constitution.

A well regulated Militia, being necessary to the security of a free State, the right of the people to keep and bear Arms, shall not be infringed.

Throughout history people have been terrorized by armies of invading and occupying countries, as well as subjugated by the standing armies of their own kings and governments. The fear of a threatening army imposing on their rights led the English in 1689 to declare in their Bill of Rights that "raising of a standard army, unless with the consent of Parliament, is against the law." In colonial America the fear was met by the institution of armed militias to defend, if and when necessary, the people against an aggressor army. In 1669 the constitution of Carolina stated, "All inhabitants and freemen of Carolina above seventeen years of age, and under sixty, shall be bound to bear arms and serve as soldiers, whenever the grand council shall find it necessary." The Virginia Bill of Rights in June 1776 states "that a well regulated militia, composed of the body of the people trained to arms, is the proper, natural, and safe defence of a free state; that standing armies, in time of peace, should be avoided, as dangerous to liberty." These sentiments are echoed throughout the constitutions of the states. It is interesting to note, however, that those who are conscientiously opposed to bearing arms, such as the Quakers, do not have to do so, and may pay sums of money in lieu of their service.

The Second Amendment has been used in recent history to claim that we all have the right to possess a weapon of any kind. It is not quite what the founding fathers had in mind.

The Third Amendment prohibits the government from quartering troops in our homes in peacetime without the consent of the owner, and only in time of war in a prescribed lawful manner. This amendment came about for the same reason as the Second Amendment. Troops were frequently housed in private homes against the will of the occupants. When the British troops in America were quartered in uninhabited buildings, the colonials declared it an affront to their right of private property. It was acts such as these that prompted the writers of the Constitution to add this amendment.

1793: MacKenzie Explores Canada. Sir Alexander Mac-

Kenzie, a Scottish fur trader, is the first to journey across the North American continent above Mexico. He blazed a path through the Rockies to the Pacific, explored western Canada, discovered the Fraser River, and followed the MacKenzie River (named after him) to its mouth on the Arctic Ocean.

1795: Beethoven's Vienna Debut. On March 29 German composer and virtuoso Ludwig van Beethoven plays his Concerto no. 2 in B flat major at the Burgtheater in Vienna. He is twenty-four years old and on his way to being recognized as one of the most prominent musical geniuses of the world, as well as one of the great egos.

As often happens, Ludwig was born into a musical family in Bonn, Germany, and after the family's fortunes waned, found himself the wage earner at the age of sixteen. By that time he had already had his first composition published, been an assistant court organist, and played for the Bonn opera. In 1787 the archbishop-elector of Bonn sent him to Vienna to study with Mozart, who allegedly said of him, "This young man will make a great name for himself in the world." His stay was short-lived when he received news that his mother had died, so back to Bonn went Beethoven to play the viola in the court orchestra, teach music, and acquire influential friends. As luck would have it, Franz Joseph Haydn passed through Bonn en route to London, saw some of Ludwig's scores, and offered to take him on as a pupil. In 1792 Beethoven, who had already attained a reputation as a great piano virtuoso, took him up on the offer and left for Vienna, never to return.

Beethoven acquired several patrons almost immediately in Vienna at a time when aristocrats found music a safer pastime than politics. At the turn of the century Ludwig began to realize that he was losing his hearing, a blow to any musician, especially one who is a piano virtuoso, and by 1819, at the age of forty-nine, he was completely deaf. He took the bull by the horns, however, and continued composing, completing his last great work, the Ninth Symphony, in this period, as well as several quartets. When he died in 1827, twenty thousand people attended his funeral.

Until Beethoven's time, instrumental music took second place to the vocal arts, and third place to literature and painting. It was Beethoven who raised it to heights of glory, grandeur, and passion. His symphonies soar and rage and move us to tears. He created perhaps the most monumental body of work of any composer of any age.

1796–1859: Horace Mann, the Father of American Public Education. Born and raised in Massachusetts, Horace Mann, who was mostly self-educated, attended Brown University, became a lawyer, served in the Massachusetts House of Representatives, and then in the state senate. In 1837 Mann was heavily involved in the creation of a state board of education and served as its secretary from its creation until 1848 when he left to serve a term in the U.S. House of Representatives.

Horace Mann lectured widely in support of public education based on six fundamentals. He believed that in order to remain free, a republic must educate its people and that the education should be paid for and controlled by the public. He advocated schools that include children from diverse religious, ethnic, and social backgrounds and maintained that schools should be free of doctrinal religious influence. Mann realized that teachers must be properly trained as educators and that harsh discipline and teaching methods were undesirable. Through his efforts state-supported normal schools were established to train teachers. His endeavors resulted in the establishment of a landmark public education system in Massachusetts, which had an influence on many other states.

In 1853 Mann became the first president of Antioch College in Ohio, a new coeducational and nonsectarian institute with equal opportunity for African-Americans. He remained there until his death in 1859. In his last address to a graduating class, he said, "Be ashamed to die until you have won some victory for humanity." Wise words.

1796: Smallpox Vaccination. Smallpox, the bane of humankind, had killed or disfigured twenty million people in Europe in the eighteenth century alone; then immigration spread the disease to the Western Hemisphere, where thousands more were affected. We can thank Edward Jenner, a British country doctor, for developing a vaccine against this scourge.

Jenner was well trained and very astute. Perhaps it was because he chose to practice in his native village rather than pursue a lucrative career in London that he saw the solution that was already there. Basically, he improved a practice that had been used for centuries, but was unreliable. In ancient times various methods, centering on artificial infection, had been tried to stop smallpox. In India babies were wrapped in clothing from smallpox victims; the Chinese collected dried scabs from victims and powdered them; in Asia pus from a smallpox pustule was scratched into a healthy person with a pin. These primitive practices were all immunizing people under the concept that giving someone a mild form of a disease will make him immune when he recovers. It apparently worked, but in the eighteenth century, doctors thought it inhuman. Their attitude began to change, however, when the wife of the British ambassador in Greece had her children effectively innoculated by live smallpox, and in 1722 the British royal family did the same. Some people, however, contracted the disease from this method, and doctors realized it was risky.

Having treated many farm people, Dr. Jenner had heard the old wives' tale that said once a person had been infected with cowpox, a similar but less serious disease of cattle, he was protected from smallpox. The doctor himself had noted that those he had treated for cowpox never came down with the more dread disease. Perhaps there was a connection. He decided to perform an experiment that could, if it failed, cost him his career and the life of the unfortunate subject. He infected a young boy with cowpox. After the child recovered, he injected him with smallpox. Not a sign of the disease appeared. A second injection months later confirmed the doctor's suspicions. The boy was immune.

Through Jenner's pioneering work, the concept of immunity was finally accepted by the medical community. Smallpox vaccination was made mandatory in many countries, and now, except for rare outbreaks in remote areas, the deadly, disfiguring disease has virtually disappeared. We must also remember James Phipps, the little boy who received the first vaccination. A trusting soul indeed.

1799: The Metric System Fixed. We can thank the French revolutionaries for establishing the exactness of the metric system and making it compulsory in France. In May of 1790, a year after the beginning of the French Revolution, the National Assembly of France requested the Academy of Sciences to form a committee to standardize their system of weights and measures. Before this time the system wasn't what you would call an exact science, and a meter in Paris wasn't necessarily the same length as a meter in Marseilles. Not only did measurements differ from town to town and country to country, but many guilds had their own set of rules. It was even worse in Britain, where the length of a yard frequently depended on the whim of the king. It was time for reform.

The committee decided upon the decimal system and defined a meter (from the Greek *metron,* "measure") as equal to one ten millionth of the distance between the equator and the pole, measured on a meridian. And they did this without a computer. The committee also fixed the gram as the mass of one cubic centimeter of water at four degrees centigrade. Although the new system was made compulsory, there were many recalcitrant merchants and farmers, and a more stringent law had to be passed penalizing anyone who did not use the established weights and measures after 1840.

Other European countries gradually adopted the system, and it is now used worldwide. The International Bureau of Weights and Measures, to which most countries subscribe, was established by 1875. And, although we in the United States use the metric system scientifically and for international commerce, we are still measuring everyday items by ounces, pounds, feet, yards, miles, quarts, and gallons. We are, however, catching up to the rest of the world. In 1975 President Ford signed the Metric Conversion Act, moving us toward the metric system. It's gradually creeping onto our food labels and road signs.

Just to keep up-to-date with the scientific community, a meter is now defined by the International Bureau of Weights and Measures as $1/299,792,458$ of the distance light travels in a vacuum in one second. We won't quibble.

1800: Library of Congress Established. Thomas Jefferson,

who believed that legislators should have information on a wide variety of subjects, is the principal founder of the library, which opens with nine hundred books and maps purchased with a Congressional appropriation of five thousand dollars.

Originally established for use by our legislators, the Library of Congress is now open to researchers, scholars, and the general public of all nations. It has become the world's largest storehouse of information as well as one of the greatest resources for culture, research, scholarship, and learning. The three buildings on Capitol Hill in Washington, D.C., contain nearly one hundred million items, including books, manuscripts, films, photographs, maps, newspapers, and graphics in over four hundred languages.

And at the other end of the mall at his memorial, Thomas Jefferson sits with a smile on his face.

1803: The Louisiana Purchase. The greatest sale of land in world chronicles and the biggest bargain in American history takes place on May 2 when, with a stroke of the pen, the United States purchases the entire Louisiana Territory from France for a mere $11,250,000.

In one fell swoop the United States has doubled its size and added what will become the states of Louisiana, Missouri, Iowa, Arkansas, the Dakotas, Nebraska, and Oklahoma, plus most of what is now Kansas, Wyoming, Montana, Minnesota, and Colorado. The territory of 828,000 square miles containing valuable mineral deposits, rich soil, vast grazing lands, and forests was bought for less than three cents an acre. And all we really wanted was New Orleans.

1804: The Steam Locomotive. Before there were railroad trains, there were railroad tracks. Carts and carriages were pulled along them, either manually or by animals. It had been going on for centuries.

Now that we had the steam engine, propelling carts by steam seemed logical. To do this, however, required a small high pressure engine. Richard Trevithick, son of a Cornwall tin mine manager, loved steam engines. Cornish miners had long been using James Watt's engine to pump water out of their mines, and since boyhood, Trevithick had been tinkering with the design. He was the first to build a steam carriage for use on a former horsecar route in Wales. His engines were highly successful except for one problem: The five-ton locomotive was so heavy, it broke the cast-iron track. He then built an enclosed circular track in London and ran his steam engine, *Catch Me Who Can,* around it, charging five shillings to watch it or ride it. He also built a three-wheel steam carriage that held eight to ten people and dashed around London at the daring speed of nine miles per hour. Not enough people took him seriously or were interested, however, and Trevithick gave up locomotives to turn to other steam engine endeavors.

The steam locomotive really came into its own when George Stephenson convinced the directors of the Stockton and Darlington Railway to use steam rather than horses to pull carriages along the track they were building. On September 27, 1825, the first public passenger train using steam locomotion, crowded with six hundred excursioners, made its maiden journey on the wrought-iron rail track resting on stone supports and wooden blocks. The locomotive was designed by Stephenson and built by the company he had organized with his son.

Meanwhile, at the same time in the United States, John Stevens built and operated the first rail locomotive in the town of Hoboken, New Jersey. In 1830 Peter Cooper's steam engine, the *Tom Thumb,* pulled the first trainload of passengers on the newly formed Baltimore and Ohio Railroad.

The invention of a practical steam locomotive led to the great age of the railroads. We could now carry more goods and people overland faster and farther than ever before and in less time. On May 10, 1869, in Promontory, Utah, the Union Pacific Railroad Company, building west from Omaha, linked with the Central Pacific, building eastward from Sacramento. The celebration was capped by driving a golden spike through the rails, joining the two together. The transcontinental railroad was born and we were now truly a United States. Or, as one San Francisco newspaper facetiously headlined, "California Annexes the U.S."

1804: Napoleonic Code. The French Civil Code becomes law on March 21, 1804, and with some modifications, is the law of the land in France today as well as the basis of civil codes in many other countries.

The laws of France were a mishmash, with old Roman laws governing the South, laws based on the old Frankish and Germanic feudal systems holding forth in the North, and family life ruled by the church. Among these laws were royal decrees and ordinances as well as case law from the courts that had developed over three centuries. After the French Revolution, a new uniform body of law became a necessity. Codes were drafted, rejected, and drafted again until finally, under Napoleon as first consul, thirty-six statutes, easily understood by all citizens, became the uniform law for the entire country.

The code abolished previous class privileges and guaranteed equality before the law to all citizens, affirmed religious liberty, supremacy of the state over the church, an individual's right to choose his profession, and covered family relationships, property, and contracts, among other legalities.

The Napoleonic Code was an enlightened document in the Age of Reason.

1804–06: Lewis and Clark Expedition. In the late afternoon of May 14, 1804, Meriwether Lewis and William Clark set out from St. Louis, Missouri, with approximately forty men and three heavily laden canoes on a government-sponsored journey that would take them up the Mississippi and Missouri rivers and across the Continental Divide to the Pacific Ocean.

Both Lewis and Clark had experienced military service, and both loved the outdoors and the wilderness. At the time of his appointment to lead the Northwest Expedition, Lewis was a protégé of, and private secretary to, President Jefferson, and not wanting to be the sole leader, he selected Clark to be co-commander. Their mission, according to Jefferson, was to take copious notes about the Indian tribes, plant and animal life, geography, climate, and the possibility of any commercial development.

By November they had reached what is now North Dakota, where they built a fort near the present site of Bismarck and stayed for the winter. Before continuing their journey, they employed the services of a French-Canadian interpreter and his Shoshone wife, Sacajawea, who were invaluable help with the Indians. The expedition headed west by foot and boat and reached the mouth of the Columbia River at the Pacific Ocean on November 15, 1805. On their return journey they divided into two parties and explored both the Marias and Yellowstone rivers and met again at the juncture of the Yellowstone and Missouri. They arrived in St. Louis on September 23, 1806, and received a hearty and noisy welcome from the townspeople.

The Lewis and Clark expedition brought back a tremendous amount of information, carefully notated in diaries by both leaders as well as by other members of the trek. Lewis and Clark had opened up the Northwest, and for their explorations each was given 1,600 acres of land, while their men received 320 acres each and double pay. Lewis was appointed governor of the new Louisiana Territory, where Clark later served as superintendent of Indian affairs as well as becoming governor of the Missouri Territory.

1811: Special Education. It was during the Napoleonic era that the first school to deal with children who need special attention was established in Austria.

Unfortunately, the school closed in 1835. The first major and lasting efforts came from Edouard Seguin in France, two years later. At this stage, Seguin called his students "feebleminded" and

devoted his time to studying their "mental defects." Within the
following decade, further efforts to establish schools for children
with mental illnesses appeared in England and Switzerland. In 1848
a special section of the Blind Asylum in Boston was set aside to
deal with children with learning problems. It was called the "class
for idiots" and led to the establishment of the Massachusetts School
for Idiotic and Feeble-Minded Youth in 1851. Many other schools
and classes became available for mentally retarded children, but as
the names have so far indicated, few had a great deal of respect,
or an excessively positive outlook, for their students.

By 1892 publicly funded classes in special education had become
available in several European countries. As time went by, many
students with learning problems were given some or all of the
attention they needed within the public school systems, and in
general a healthier outlook became associated with special education and the students' needs.

In the United States, Public Law 94–142, the Education for All
Handicapped Children Act of 1975, dictated that the public school
systems must provide either the means or the funding to fulfill
the educational needs of both physically and mentally handicapped students.

1816: The Stethoscope. This brilliantly simple device enables
us to distinguish the doctors from the patients. It also transformed
medical diagnosis, especially for chest diseases. As the story goes,
the French physician René Laennec had been watching children
playing a game with a stick of wood. One child would tap on
one end while another child listened to the sound at the other
end. When he returned home, Laennec rolled up a piece of paper,
put it to his patient's chest, and listened at the other end. He
heard the heartbeat more distinctly than ever before. Laennec was
also a musician, a flute player, which probably had a bearing on
the instrument he devised after his first experiment, a hollow cylinder of wood with a funnel shape at one end. It was eventually
called a stethoscope, from the Greek words *stethos,* "chest," and
skopos, "observer." The new instrument was quickly adopted by
other physicians and contributed immensely to the diagnosis of
heart and lung ailments. In 1855 the binaural stethoscope was
introduced so doctors could listen with both ears. It's also easier
to hang around the neck.

1817: Rush-Bagot Treaty. On April 28 the United States and Great Britain agreed to limit naval forces on the Great Lakes. The treaty was negotiated by United States secretary of state Richard Rush and Sir Charles Bagot, British minister to Washington. The following year, as minister to Great Britain, Rush negotiated the convention of 1818, which settled the boundary between the United States and Canada as far west as the Oregon Territory.

1819: Chocolate Bar Invented. The idea wasn't exactly new, but François-Louis Cailler of Switzerland was the first to produce chocolate bars on a large scale. The French and Italians had been making rolls and sheets of chocolate, which were then sliced into smaller pieces at the time of purchase. Monsieur Cailler's chocolate was already in a small block and need not be cut. His son-in-law later manufactured the first milk chocolate about 1875. Thank you, Caillers, the unsung heroes of every chocoholic in the world.

1819: Plan for Improving Female Education. Emma Hart Willard presents her plan to the New York State Legislature as a plea for state aid to found schools for girls and to give women educational opportunities equal to those of men.

Emma Willard was a pioneer in the field of women's education and educational reform. Born in Connecticut in 1787, she traveled to several different areas in the northeastern region of the United States, teaching and spreading her ideas, which must have seemed radical in her day. She began teaching at the age of sixteen, and in 1807 headed a female academy in Middlebury before opening a successful school of her own. Her largest contribution to education, though, was her push for female higher education. Willard took advantage of a new law passed in 1818 in New York that provided for the funding and improvement of women's education. Her first attempt was a school in Waterford, New York, but funding ran out after the first year. She then accepted an offer to begin a school in Troy, New York, and opened the Troy Female Seminary, which in 1910 became known as the Emma Willard School. Here she pursued new teaching methods and wrote several textbooks on history, geography, and science. In 1838 she retired from her position at the seminary and returned to Connecticut, where she was elected superintendent of the Kensington schools in 1840, in all likelihood the first woman to be elected superintendent of a school system in the United States. She spent the rest of her life lecturing on educational reforms and, with Henry Barnard, represented the United States at the World's Educational Convention in London in 1854. She was honored for her efforts on behalf of education by New York University when she was elected to its Hall of Fame for Great Americans in 1905.

1820: Quinine Isolated.

An annoying buzz, a quick bite, an itchy lump. Luckily, that's the extent of the mosquito problem most of the time, but the bite of the anopheles mosquito causes the infectious and sometimes fatal disease malaria. Widespread in the tropics, malaria can be found in other areas in the summer months. Although it can be controlled somewhat with insecticide spray and drainage of the mosquitos' breeding grounds, some of the little critters manage to survive.

Quinine, from the bark of the cinchona tree, although not a cure, does reduce the fever of malaria and was used by the Indians in South America in the fifteenth century for that purpose. In the mid-seventeenth century Thomas Sydenham used it in England. In 1820 two French chemists, Pelletier and Caventou, isolated it.

In 1944 American chemists Doering and Woodward synthesized quinine. Although other drugs have since been developed, and preventive medicine is available, in some areas, such as Vietnam, new strains of the disease have developed. Because the more recent drugs are not as effective against the new variety of the disease, quinine is once again being used.

1821: Mexican Independence.

On February 24 Mexico, led by Augustín de Iturbide, declared her independence from Spain. The country was to be an independent monarchy with a European prince. On August 24 Spain signed the Treaty of Córdoba, recognizing Mexico's independence. A year later, Iturbide declared himself emperor, but a military rebellion forced him into exile. Mexico was then declared a republic by its congress.

1821: Antarctica at Last.

Although the English sea captain James Cook had come within seventy miles of it in 1774, and others had discovered islands close by, it was an American, John Davis, in search of seals who was the first to land on the frozen wastes of the actual continent.

1821: High School. Boston, Massachusetts, establishes a public high school. The purpose of the school is to prepare students for a university program.

In 1827 Massachusetts passed a law mandating that towns with a population of five hundred or more must have a high school to teach American history, surveying, bookkeeping, algebra, and geometry. A town whose population was four thousand or more must provide a high school to cover these subjects plus Greek, Latin, general history, rhetoric, and logic.

1822: Franz Liszt Debuts in Vienna. The little boy from Hungary was eleven years old when he made his piano debut on December 1. Franz Liszt will later be known as the greatest pianist in history.

During his lifetime he composed, taught, conducted, gave concert performances, and contributed the symphonic (tone) poem to orchestral music. He was the ultimate showman, generating a following of groupies that would put the Beatles to shame. And he loved it. He toured Europe at the age of fourteen and began a series of love affairs at sixteen for which he was as famous as for his piano technique. To say he had a busy life is an understatement. He was always traveling somewhere to give a concert or conduct one, arranging others' works, answering letters, attending banquets, and teaching students. His first long affair, with the Comtesse Marie d'Agoult, whom he met in 1835, produced three children (one of whom later married Richard Wagner), and after they broke up, he toured Europe for eight years. He took every city by storm and was showered with gifts; the ladies loved him, and he returned their favors. In 1847 he took up with Princess Carolyne von Sayn-Wittgenstein, and after a winter together in Poland, they settled in Weimar, where he was director of music to the court and where he composed some of his greatest work. The princess hoped to marry Franz, so off she went to Rome in 1861 to try for a divorce, which, alas, was not granted. Franz followed and they both remained in separate quarters in Rome for the next eight years. Paradoxically, during this time Liszt received minor orders in the church, though he did not become a priest. He toured for the last time in 1886 when he was seventy-four, visiting cities from Budapest to London. A bout of pneumonia caused his demise in Bayreuth on July 31.

His influence on music and musicians of his time and on the

younger composers was enormous. He also raised the status of performers, who had been treated more or less as domestic servants. The world was changing, and great talent no longer would be subjected to every whim and fancy of the aristocracy; it had come into its own and earned respect.

1825: Carousels and Merry-go-rounds. John Sears receives a permit to erect a "Flying Horse Establishment" in Manhattan, New York.

It was called a flying horse because the horses were suspended from the top rather than bolted to a platform as they are now. What we call a merry-go-round has also been known throughout history as a galloper, a roundabout, a whirligig, steam circus, carry-us-alls (a play on carousels, no doubt), a *carousel* in France, a *stoomcaroussel* in Holland, in Germany a *karussel,* in Italy a *torneo.* Early Byzantine citizens had fun riding similar mechanisms fifteen hundred years ago, and there are drawings of comparable contrivances used in Turkey in the seventeenth century, so it seems merry-go-rounds are not really new, they just keep getting reinvented.

Early merry-go-rounds were turned by a horse, but after the steam engine was invented, methods were devised to use steam power to rotate them. The platform on which horses now sat soon became wider, allowing for three or four riders abreast. About 1870 an overhead cranking device was patented that enabled the horses to move up and down while turning. With the steam engine came the steam organ, called a calliope, and soon amusement parks everywhere were filled with the puffing tones of an organ beckoning to one and all to come for a ride on the merry-go-round.

It's not just children who are fond of carousels. A few minutes on a horse and we're reliving our carefree childhood.

1826: Menai Strait Bridge Completed. The most famous suspension bridge of its time took seven years to build and was constructed to carry stagecoach traffic from Bangor, Wales, across the straits to the Island of Anglesey. The 580-foot span was designed by one of England's engineering geniuses, Thomas Telford. Iron was beginning to be used in construction work, and several bridges had been built using this material. Telford used wrought-iron links pinned together into chains which were hauled across the strait and

lifted into place. The deck of the bridge, twenty-four feet wide, was then suspended beneath it. There were no protective girders and the bridge suffered damage in high winds, causing it to be rebuilt twice. It lasted for 114 years before being completely reconstructed.

1829: Braille.

Louis Braille, a twenty-year-old Frenchman, publishes his system of reading that allows a blind person to recognize letters by touch; in other words, to read with his fingers.

Louis attended the school for the blind in Paris on a scholarship. While there, he was introduced to a system of embossed dots and dashes enabling a blind person to read a message. The fifteen-year-old Louis reworked the system into a six-dot code and published it. A few years later he also published a musical notation system. Braille went on to become a teacher at the school as well as a noted church organist. Over time, the Braille system has been reworked. In 1932 it took its current form and has remained true to the touch since.

1830: Chopin's Concert.

On March 17 Frederic Chopin, who just turned twenty, first plays his Concerto no. 2 for Pianoforte and Orchestra for the Warsaw public. It was the beginning of the career of one of history's foremost pianists and composers.

Frederic Chopin was born near Warsaw, Poland, in 1810, the second child of a Polish mother and French father. He grew up in a middle-class family who, although recognizing his musical talent, insisted he finish high school before continuing his piano studies. When he was sixteen he began studying harmony and composition at the Warsaw Conservatory and continued developing his original piano style. The disturbed state of political affairs in Europe interrupted his journey to study in Germany and Italy, so he ended up in Paris, the cultural center of Europe, where he thrived amidst the greats of the day. It was a time of intellectual excitement, with people like Victor Hugo, Balzac, Delacroix, Liszt, and Berlioz holding sway; a period of enlightenment and romanticism, and Frederic was caught up in it. He was also caught up in the arms of Aurore Dudevant, better known as George Sand, whom he met in 1838, and the two, as the gossip columns used to say, became very close friends. All the while Chopin was teaching and composing and making money. And once in a while he gave a concert. He wrote sonatas, scherzos, polonaises, études, waltzes, mazurkas, preludes, and nocturnes. His music was sometimes lively, sometimes sad, always beautiful. His piano technique was flawless and innovative, and thrilled the small audiences he played for. Aurore and Frederic's relationship ended in 1847, and after a brief stay in England and Scotland, he returned to Paris, where he died of tuberculosis at the age of thirty-nine. He is buried in the cemetery of Père Lachaise among many of history's celebrated personages.

Chopin always had Poland in his heart, and Poland has always claimed him as its own. Just before Warsaw surrendered to the Nazis, the last music heard on the radio was Chopin's Polonaise in A.

1833: The Balloon Frame House.

Home construction was a long and expensive process utilizing many laborers. Large pieces of lumber were fitted together by heavy hand-cut joints, and all nails were handmade. Then the balloon frame was developed. The new framing used lightweight precut two-by-four studs placed sixteen inches apart and factory-made nails, which were beginning to be produced at this time. The milling of standardized lumber and factory-produced nails decreased the cost of housing tremendously and enabled the construction work to be done by only a few men in a very short time. The new framing method was a boon to all low- and middle-income families, who could now afford to build their own homes. This simple design helped build America into a land of home ownership.

1835–1919: Andrew Carnegie, a Self-Made Man.

In his essay "The Gospel of Wealth," Andrew Carnegie wrote that the story of a rich man should be divided into two periods—the first to acquire wealth, the second to distribute that wealth for the general welfare. It is the story of his life. Carnegie played a large role in the industrial growth of the United States and was one of the most generous of American philanthropists.

The Carnegie family, political activists with a love of learning and a strong belief in education, immigrated to the United States from Scotland in 1848 and settled near Pittsburgh, Pennsylvania, where Andrew's father found work in a cotton factory and Andrew went to work as a bobbin boy. True to family tradition, Andrew became an avid reader, thanks in part to Colonel James Anderson, who lent his personal library to poor boys so they could improve their minds. At fourteen he became a messenger in the

Pittsburgh telegraph office, was promoted to operator, and soon found himself as private secretary and telegrapher to Thomas Scott of the Pennsylvania Railroad. For this he was paid the astonishing sum of thirty-five dollars a month. It was the beginning of Carnegie's brilliant career.

Within twelve years, he had advanced through hard work to become superintendent of the Pittsburgh division, and during the Civil War his organizational skills were in great demand by the troop transport division of the War Department. After the war, Carnegie realized demand for steel and iron would increase. It was this foresight that helped raise the United States to great industrial heights. He resigned from the railroad and started his first venture, the Keystone Bridge Company, to construct iron bridges. He was thirty years old. Carnegie also made money in oil and from commissions earned selling railroad securities in Europe. In 1873 he organized his first steel company and in 1901 sold his successful enterprises to J. P. Morgan and his new United States Steel Corporation for $250 million.

It was now time for Carnegie to begin his philanthropic pursuits in earnest. In 1900 he founded the Carnegie Institute of Technology in Pittsburgh (now Carnegie Mellon), and a year later, the Carnegie Institute in Washington, D.C. In Scotland he established educational trusts, donating $10 million to the Scottish Universities Trust and $10 million to the United Kingdom Trust. He was a benefactor of the Tuskegee Institute, funded pensions for former employees, and in 1905 established the Carnegie Foundation for the Advancement of Teaching. He is probably best known for his donations to libraries, a repayment for all the books he was able to read through the kindness of Colonel Anderson. He strongly believed that the cure for all the ills of humanity was enlightenment and insisted that the motto "Let there be light" be placed on all library buildings participating in his endowment of $60 million. A man of peace, he contributed the funds to build the Peace Palace at The Hague, Netherlands, as well as leaving $10 million to the Endowment for International Peace. After all this, he then established the Carnegie Foundation to carry on his philanthropic endeavors.

He could have been the first American billionaire and he could have received a title from the king of England, but his most valuable possession was his American citizenship, and as for his money, he gave it all away where he felt it would do good.

1837: Kindergartens. Friederich Froebel opens a school for young children and calls it kindergarten.

Born and raised in Germany, Froebel studied under Pestalozzi in Switzerland to become a teacher. He was very taken with Pestalozzi's ideas and became interested in the possibilities of music and play in education. A few years after finishing his training, Froebel started his own school in Switzerland, and although a financial failure, it was a success for Froebel and his ideas. Not only did it inspire him to write his most famous work, *The Education of Man,* but it also convinced him that early education needed reform. He returned to Germany and opened another kindergarten ("garden of children"). Unfortunately, the political climate of the time later led to the banning of the schools. Froebel had some enthusiastic followers, however, who helped spread his ideas beyond Germany's borders, and soon the schools for tots proliferated.

1841: Westward Ho! The first group of thirty-two pioneers set out with their wagons from Missouri to traverse the two-thousand-mile Oregon Trail to the Pacific Northwest.

The following year over one hundred emigrants traveled the trail together, and by 1843 the westward movement was in full swing. Some followed the route that began near Independence, Missouri, across the Great Plains, and through the Rocky Mountains to the Oregon Territory; others turned south at Fort Hall, Wyoming, and followed the California Trail across the desert and the Sierra Nevadas to the coast of northern California. Some followed the Santa Fe Trail, used since 1821 as a trade route, then branched off to the Spanish Trail and made their way to California.

Whatever route they took, the pioneers suffered hardships: Cholera and other diseases, Indian raids, hunger, thirst, exhaustion, freezing cold and blistering heat, torrential rains and blizzards, took their toll. But they plodded on, walking beside their Conestoga wagons and prairie schooners, determined to reach what they thought would be a pioneer's paradise. All kinds of people were caught up in the westward expansion: farmers, prospectors, schoolteachers, traders, missionaries, abolitionists, and a few who felt the necessity to escape from foul deeds they had perpetrated. Word had reached Europe, and soon English crofters, joined by German farmers, Irish potato growers, and dairy farmers from Scandinavia, were trekking across the West in hopes of a better life. The financial collapse and depression of 1837 in the United States spurred many to migrate, and the discovery of gold in California in 1848 added even greater impetus.

The journey was long and harsh, taking three to five months. But the travelers endured with what we today call the "pioneer spirit," a determination to reach their destination and make a better life, and faith that they would. During the peak year of migration, fifty-five thousand pioneers walked along the Oregon Trail, along with over seven thousand mules, thirty thousand oxen, nearly twenty-three thousand horses, nine thousand wagons, and over five thousand cows, according to records at Fort Laramie in the Wyoming Territory. By 1869, when the transcontinental railroad was completed, 350,000 emigrants had traversed the Oregon Trail and settled in their new paradise in the Oregon Territory. In the 1850s another 500,000 had turned off onto the California Trail. The West was being won by these intrepid voyagers. They bought land or settled as squatters on a homestead that became theirs if they farmed it for five years. The farms grew into towns, and the towns into cities, and the territories became states, and the nation grew.

The rutted wagon trails can still be seen in parts of the West— a reminder of the indomitable pioneer spirit that drove our not too distant ancestors on their heroic journey across unknown territory in search of a new and better way of life.

1843: *A Christmas Carol.* Popular English novelist Charles Dickens publishes *A Christmas Carol,* introducing Bob Cratchit, Tiny Tim, and Ebenezer Scrooge, thereby giving the English language a new word.

Dickens was a prolific writer (he was frequently paid by the word, which may account for his verbiage) who created some of the most immortal and memorable rapscallions, villains, heroes, heroines, and romantics ever conceived in literature. He is considered by many as the greatest of all English novelists, and his works have been adapted to the stage and movies, and developed into musicals.

Much of Dickens's prose was based on observations begun as a child. Born the second of eight children into a peripatetic middle-class family whose fortunes often failed, Dickens was forced to labor in a blacking warehouse at the age of ten. Fortunately, his father inherited a small legacy two years later, freeing Dickens to attend school once more. He learned shorthand and became a reporter in the law courts, Parliament, and for a newspaper. His literary career began when he contributed articles to the *Monthly Magazine* in which he caricatured the society of the time. These were later published anonymously as *Sketches by Boz* in 1836, when he was twenty-four. From these grew *The Pickwick Papers* and, in 1838, his first novel, *Oliver Twist,* in serial form. From then on he produced work after work with titles such as *Nicholas Nickleby, The Old Curiosity Shop, David Copperfield,* and *A Tale of Two Cities.*

Dickens wrote during the Victorian era in England. He brought to light and literature some of the seamier sides of life: the brutality of many schools, the impracticality of debtors' prison, and the miserable living conditions of the poor. In a way he was a social reformer at the time when such reform was just beginning. His writings no doubt spurred on the reformers.

Of all Dickens's creations, the one that pops up every year at Christmastime is probably the most widely known. It is the transformation of the miserly Scrooge into a compassionate human being that leads Tiny Tim to utter his immortal line, "God bless us, every one."

1845: Ancient Nineveh Discovered. Austen Henry Layard, a British archaeologist and diplomat, begins excavations in what is now Iraq that will uncover Assyrian royal palaces in the ancient city of Nineveh.

1845: Narrative of the Life of Frederick Douglass, an American Slave. Frederick Douglass, aged twenty-eight, publishes his autobiography to prove that he had been a slave. The independent, intelligent, and literate Douglass is an agent for the Massachusetts Anti-Slavery Society and speaks so eloquently from the platform that many doubt his background.

Douglass was born in Maryland, the son of Harriet Bailey, an extremely intelligent slave, and a white father. After a difficult childhood on the Maryland plantation, during which time he was mistreated by his masters, Douglass was sent away to Baltimore so he would not be able to cause trouble. There, Douglass became a house servant and was taught basic reading and writing skills by his mistress (which at the time was quite illegal). When his Baltimore master died, Douglass was sent back to the plantation, where he and a few other slaves planned an unsuccessful escape. After serving part of a jail sentence, he was returned to Baltimore, where he learned to be a ship caulker and was allowed to do extra work in order to earn his own money. In time he might have been able to buy his freedom, but Douglass and his employer had a disagreement and Douglass lost the privilege. In 1838 he escaped slavery, fled to New York City, and from there went to New Bedford, Massachusetts. It was in Massachusetts that Douglass began his career as a crusader.

Once his book had been published, however, Douglass had to leave the country for fear of being captured and returned to slavery. He spent two years living in England and was quite pleased with the treatment he received there. Freedom, to him, was now more than escape from one's master, it was social acceptance and economic opportunity. In 1847 he returned to the States, where he allowed his freedom to be bought, which many of his peers saw as an act that legitimized slavery. Next, he started his own newspaper for African-Americans, which angered many of his fellow abolitionists who didn't think there was a need for such a paper. All the while Douglass lectured against slavery and in support of women's suffrage, and aided Harriet Beecher Stowe in founding an industrial school for African-Americans. During the Civil War, Douglass helped to recruit men for all-black regiments, including the acclaimed 54th and 55th Massachusetts. After the war, Douglass served as marshal and recorder of deeds of the District of Columbia and as United States minister to Haiti and continued to be active in politics until the day of his death on February 20, 1895.

1845: Juba's Jig. His real name was William Henry Lane, his stage name was Juba, and by 1845 he was acclaimed as the greatest dancer of his kind.

While he is known as the father of tap dance, Marian Hannah Winters, a dance historian, has also described him as the "most influential single performer of nineteenth-century American dance." Lane began dancing the Irish jig in minstrel shows, then began to add the African rhythms of his ancestors to the steps to create a new type of dance that wowed the critics and enthralled audiences. He headlined in the United States as well as in England, where he died at the age of twenty-seven.

1846: The Smithsonian Founded. "Every man is a valuable member of society who by his observations, researches, and experiments procures knowledge for men." So wrote Oxford graduate James Smithson, illegitimate son of the duke of Northumberland.

When he died in 1829, Smithson left his estate to his nephew, stipulating that, should his nephew die without issue, the whole of his estate should go to the United States of America, "to found at Washington, under the name of the Smithsonian Institute, an establishment for the increase and diffusion of knowledge among men." Maybe he thought there were already enough institutes of learning in Europe or maybe he thought our fledgling country needed a boost in the knowledge field. Fortunately for us, his nephew died childless, and in 1838 the United States received the munificent sum of $508,318 with which to carry out Smithson's wishes.

The trust was accepted in 1846 and a Gothic-Romanesque–style building, now known as the "Castle," opened on the Washington Mall to house the Institute. Under many able directors it grew to become the repository for every bit of Americana that one can think of and has become a true center of knowledge and research.

We were so grateful to Smithson that in 1904 his remains were brought to Washington and interred in the Castle. It was his first trip to America. He would be pleased at how well we have succeeded in the "increase and diffusion of knowledge among men." Among women and children, too.

1846: Anesthesia. On October 16, at Massachusetts General Hospital in Boston, Dr. Thomas Morton demonstrates the use of ether as a general anesthetic during a twenty-five-minute operation to remove a tumor. The procedure heralds a new era in painless surgery.

The earliest record of controlling pain is the Roman Pliny's notation that the early Egyptians used a mixture of powdered marble and vinegar as a topical anesthesia. Greek and Roman healers used opium and alcohol, and ancient tablets from the Far East tell of drugs that were used, including hemlock. The Greeks even made pills which were swallowed whole or dissolved in water. Sometimes sponges soaked with narcotics were held over the patient's nose and mouth. Mandrake, from which belldonna is extracted, is mentioned in the Bible. Mostly, however, patients were held or tied down during surgical procedures and frequently died of shock (no surprise).

Around 1546, Valerius Cordus first mixed what he called "sweet vitriol" and used it as a solvent. Two centuries later, it became known as ether. In 1771 Joseph Priestly discovered nitrous oxide, but wasn't aware of its potential, and in 1797 Sir Humphrey Davy used it experimentally but not medically. Davy, a chemist who worked with Priestly, experimented on himself by inhaling the gas and suggested its use in surgery. In spite of some success, neither ever followed up on its potential, and the medical world ignored it. However, since a side effect of nitrous oxide is hilarity (hence laughing gas), it was a big hit at parties.

It was Crawford Long, an American doctor in Georgia, who hit upon the idea of using ether surgically when he witnessed its effects at a carnival sideshow in 1844, but he didn't publish his results. In 1847 James Simpson, a Scottish obstetrician, used ether and later chloroform on his patients during childbirth, and six years later, Queen Victoria was given chloroform at the birth of her eighth child, making it an acceptable procedure.

By 1940, anesthesiology had become a separate special branch of medicine, with new methods and new drugs available for use. The development of anesthesia was the first important scientific offering of American medical technology.

1846: The Oregon Treaty. Great Britain and the United States signed the treaty on June 15, ceding the territory below the forty-ninth parallel to the United States, fixing our border with Canada. Our "Manifest Destiny" was nearly complete. The phrase had been printed in the *New York Morning News* in December of 1845 by the editor, John L. Sullivan, who wrote that it was the destiny of the United States to spread its "great experiment of liberty and federated self-government" across the entire continent. In 1818 Great Britain and the United States had signed a treaty by which they would both occupy the region west of the Rocky Mountains and north of the forty-second parallel. The only settlement at the time was that of the British Hudson Bay Company at Fort Vancouver. During the next two decades, however, the covered wagons had begun to make their way to the Oregon Territory, and by 1844, about five thousand American settlers had made it their home. When James Knox Polk was elected president, the country was caught up in the Manifest Destiny philosophy, and Polk decided the British should leave the territory and wanted Congress to revoke the treaty. We actually wanted all the territory up to the Alaskan border and rallied around the cry of "Fifty-four forty or fight," referring to the parallels involved. Since the British prime minister, Robert Peel, had enough to worry about in his own country and considered the territory nothing but an untamed wilderness, he suggested a boundary at the forty-ninth parallel. Polk, who really didn't want to fight a war with Britain and would soon be embroiled with Mexico, accepted his recommendation. So Canada now owns Vancouver Island, and we own everything below the forty-ninth. Our border with Canada has been peaceful ever since.

1848: Treaty of Guadalupe Hidalgo. On February 2 the treaty signed between Mexico and the United States ended the war with Mexico and set the boundary between the two countries.

This is the treaty that gave us California, which had declared itself a republic in 1846 but had a hard time convincing Mexico and the United States that it was independent. The Rio Grande and Gila River delineated the border between Texas and Mexico, and the territories of present-day New Mexico, Nevada, Arizona, Utah, and part of Colorado, as well as California, came into the possession of the United States. In return we withdrew our troops from Mexico and restored all the forts, territories, and possessions we had taken by force and paid the Mexican government $15 million.

On December 30, 1853, the Gadsden Treaty, signed by U.S. minister James Gadsden and Mexican president Santa Anna, fixed the boundary from El Paso, Texas, west to the Pacific after serious inaccuracies were found on the map. The area in contention happened to be the best route for a southern transcontinental railroad line to California, and there were many in Washington who wanted the territory kept in the United States. After a few changes, the treaty was accepted on June 30, 1854. We paid Mexico $10 million and received approximately 29,640 square miles of land, most of which is now in the state of Arizona.

With the signing of these two treaties, the territorial borders on the north and south of what will be the forty-eight states were completed and remain to this day.

1848: The Convention at Seneca Falls. On July 14 an ad appeared in the *Seneca County Courier* announcing "a Convention to discuss the social, civil, and religious condition and rights of

woman" to be held on July 19 and 20 at the Wesleyan Chapel in Seneca Falls, New York. All women were invited to attend.

The convention of unconventional women was the beginning of the women's rights movement, spurred by such women as Elizabeth Cady Stanton, Lucretia Mott, Susan B. Anthony, Lucy Stone, and Amelia Bloomer, and was destined to change society.

These ladies and many others dared to question the status of women who had been subjugated by men through the centuries. They wanted to be recognized as individuals, not appendages of husbands, if married; they wanted to be able to receive the same educational opportunities as men; they wanted to be able to use their intelligence, to make their own decisions, to work at substantive jobs and enter professions, to keep their wages, to control their property, and to have the right to vote.

The women who joined the equal rights movements faced harsh opposition from the church, the press, politicians, lawyers, society itself, and frequently other women. But they persevered and fought prejudice, indignities, and unfair laws. Although it was still a man's world by the turn of the century, the women's movement did much to bring the plight of women to the forefront, and doors were slowly opening. It would take another women's rights movement in the 1960s to finish the work these ladies had begun. They did succeed, however, in winning the right to vote for women, although none of the original ladies lived long enough to celebrate the occasion.

We've come a long way since then.

1849: Speed of Light. Armand Fizeau, a French physicist, establishes the speed of light as 186,300 miles per second.

1849: A Modern-Day Moses. Harriet Tubman escapes from the Maryland plantation where she is enslaved and wends her way north, guided by the North Star and helped by the Underground Railroad.

The so-called railroad was a loosely knit network of abolitionists and safe houses through which many slaves made their escape. Soon after her journey, Harriet began acting as a guide, making several trips into the South to lead other escaped slaves to the North, which soon earned her the sobriquet "Moses." During the Civil War, Tubman worked for the Union Army in South Carolina as a cook, laundress, nurse, guide, and spy. After the war, she became involved with a campaign for African-American schools in North Carolina, but this was short-lived. The majority of her energy from then on was focused on her home in Auburn, New York, where she helped abandoned children and those who could not support themselves, especially the elderly. After she died in 1913 at the age of ninety-two, her work was carried on and the Harriet Tubman Home for Indigent Aged Negroes continued to serve the community for several more years.

1849: First Medical Degree to a Woman. Elizabeth Blackwell is awarded a medical degree from Geneva Medical College in New York, the first woman in the United States to become a degreed doctor.

Elizabeth, whose family immigrated to the United States from England when she was ten, had always wanted to be a doctor, something that a woman just didn't do in those days. While she taught school she privately studied medicine, borrowing books from physician acquaintances. She was admitted to medical school because the male students thought her application was a joke. Elizabeth outsmarted them all, however, when she graduated at the head of her class. Dr. Blackwell interned and studied midwifery abroad, then returned to the United States, where she found no hospital would hire her because she was a woman.

Since no hospital wanted her, she opened a small clinic in a slum area of New York and was later joined by her sister, Emily, and Marie Zakrzewska, who had just graduated from Western Reserve College with medical degrees. By 1857, their practice had grown and was profitable enough to enable them to open the New York Infirmary for Women and Children. In 1868 they established the Woman's Medical College of the New York Infirmary, which offered medical courses and clinical experience to women seeking a medical career. The school remained open until women medical students were accepted at Cornell in 1899.

In 1949 the Blackwell Medal was established and is presented to outstanding women physicians.

1850: Jeans, Levi's, Overalls, and Dungarees. Whatever you want to call them, what was once worn by the working class attained the height of fashion in the 1970s and has remained the most popular item of clothing in our closet ever since.

Levi Strauss arrived in San Francisco in 1859 with bolts of

canvas he intended to sell to the gold miners for tents, and then hoped to stake a claim himself. Instead of tents, Levi fashioned some trousers out of the canvas and sold them immediately. The demand for his sturdy, inexpensive canvas pants grew rapidly, and instead of mining, Levi found himself tailoring. In the 1860s he began using denim (from de Nîmes, France) and dyeing it blue. Denim had been used for pants by Italian sailors from Genoa, which in French is spelled Genes, thereby giving us another name for the apparel. In 1873 Levi started riveting the pocket seams to keep them from splitting, which made them even more durable. For generations these utilitarian jeans were the outfit of choice for cowboys, farmers, and workmen, and Levi made his fortune not in gold, but in denim.

In 1935 they began to come into fashion as western gear and more people started wearing them. It wasn't until the rebellious 1960s that jeans came into their own, especially on college campuses, where they were more a symbol of the antiestablishment movement than a fashion statement. Jeans caught on fast, and soon these original work pants were off the ranch and on our legs. We can now buy them in all kinds of shapes and sizes and colors to fit our fancy, and everybody from toddlers to oldsters, whether rich or poor, can be seen in them, on ships, in school, on planes, at work, at cocktail parties, the theater, and occasionally at weddings. You might say jeans are the great equalizer; the most important garment since the tunic.

As an added note, the Japanese seem to have gone bonkers over American jeans, especially Levi's, and the insanity has spread to other countries. Jeans from the thirties command outrageous prices, and Levi's only ten or twenty years old can be sold for much more than their original price. It's one way of spreading democracy.

1851: London's Crystal Palace. The glass palace is built to house the first Great Exhibition of the Industry of All Nations and causes a sensation. The building, designed by Joseph Paxton, an English gardener, is in the shape of a huge 108-foot-high greenhouse and covers eighteen acres at Hyde Park. The structure, utilizing mass-produced interchangeable parts, is comprised of timber, cast and wrought iron, and glass, and is not only the largest glass-walled building in the world but the world's largest structure. The palace, lit by gaslight, is a marvel to behold and inspires future architects and builders who will copy its design, especially for railway stations, and for the New York Exposition of 1853. It also influenced the design of twentieth-century skyscrapers. Unfortunately, it was destroyed by fire in 1936.

1851: Ophthalmoscope. The instrument that allows your doctor to see inside your eyes was invented by Hermann Helmholtz, a German scientist and philosopher. A doctor can check for near- and farsightedness, diabetes, blood pressure, cataracts, and other disorders thanks to this wonderful device. In 1847, however, Charles Babbage, that mathematical wizard in England, had apparently invented the same thing. He asked a doctor friend to try it out, but the good doctor didn't think it was important enough, or forgot, or was overbooked, or maybe it was his day to play golf. Babbage's device went untested and unnoticed.

1852: Mr. Otis's Elevator. Elisha Graves Otis, a builder and master mechanic in Troy, New York, had already invented several labor-saving devices. Sent to Yonkers, New York, to build a factory, Otis installs the first elevator to use an automatic safety mechanism to keep it from falling. Called a "safety hoister," it uses teeth and ratchets which catch when the rope raises and lowers the elevator. In 1853 he sells his first machine, and after he demonstrates the safety of the elevator at the Crystal Palace exhibition in New York, orders begin coming in. In 1857 the first passenger elevator is installed in a store in New York City.

His sons carried on the business and continued to improve on the design. In 1889 the first electric elevator built by the Otis brothers appeared in a commercial building in New York City.

The elevator was an inventive mechanism that eventually enabled us to reach great heights in places like the Empire State Building and the Sears Tower.

1853: Take Two Aspirin . . . and call me in the morning, is the old joke about a doctor's prescription for almost anything that ails us. Joke or not, aspirin has long been the panacea for everything from arthritis and the common cold, to curing the "morning after" headache. In ancient times a powder ground from willow tree bark was prescribed for reducing fevers. As we now know, the bark comprises a salicylic compound similar to aspirin. In 1853 Karl Gerhardt, at Montpellier University in France, first synthesized the substance but didn't think it was an improvement over another extract commonly in use. In 1893, however, German chemist Hermann Dreser wrote of its effectiveness, and Felix Hoffman synthesized it.

Acetylsalicylic acid, under the name Aspirin (from the plant used in its synthesizing, *Spiraea ulmaria,* and the *a* in acetyl plus the suffix *in,* popular in medicines of the day), was then marketed as a powder by the Bayer Company in Germany, and almost immediately became the most prescribed drug in the world. In 1915 the tablet form appeared. After World War I, the trade name was part of the reparations the Germans paid to the Allies, and after a court battle over the use of the trade name, it was finally judged to be generic and no one drug company could collect on its use. We now take aspirin with a lowercase *a* for a variety of ailments even though medical science still hasn't figured out quite how or why it works. But ours is not to reason why, as long as it does.

1853: Private Baths. The Mount Vernon Hotel, accommodating two thousand guests, opens at Cape May, a beach resort on the southern tip of New Jersey. The innovative hotel is the world's first to have private baths.

1853: Potato Chips. Thomas Jefferson had eaten French-fried potatoes while he was our ambassador to France and enjoyed them so much, he served them to his guests at Monticello. To make them, potatoes were cut into thick slices and deep-fried. This was how the American Indian George Crum always prepared them when he was a chef at the posh Moon Lake Lodge in Saratoga Springs, New York. One evening a disgruntled guest sent back his potatoes, complaining that they were too thick. George sliced them thinner and fried up another batch. Again they were sent back. Now furious and hoping to irk the exacting guest, George sliced the next batch as thin as possible, fried them up to a crisp, and served them to the demanding guest. To George's chagrin, they were an instant success. For years they were called Saratoga chips, and meticulously sliced by hand. By the 1920s after the mechanical potato peeler was invented and production increased, sales multiplied and potato chips became the biggest-selling snack food in America. What's a sandwich without them?

1854: The Mortarboard. The term for this academic cap is recorded for the first time in England.

The odd-shaped hat adorned with a tassel is worn by most of us at least once in our lifetime. The close-fitting cap evolved from a short, brimless, cone-shaped hat worn by the ancient Greeks, who copied it from a similar, taller hat devised by the Egyptians. It was called a *pilos,* the Greek word for "felt." The style was around for centuries, and by the time the universities arose during the Middle Ages, it had become a four-sided felt head covering *(pileus quadratus)* for scholars. The top of the pileus was tied together, and the cloth lapped over somewhat. Gradually the excess cloth got lengthier and stuck out in a boardlike manner. Back in the fifth century, eminent people were often depicted with a square nimbus, or halo, known in artistic circles as "glory," which represents spiritual character through symbolic light. The symbolic and the realistic joined together and became the ridiculous in the shape of the square board surmounted on the cap.

I suppose when you march down the aisle heading for your diploma, you might say you are going out in a blaze of glory.

Ca. 1855: Ice Hockey. No one is quite sure of the origins of ice hockey, although it could have developed from field hockey, which was played by the Persians around 200 B.C. It could also have sprung from the Irish game of hurling, or from a game Indians in Canada played a few hundred years ago. By 1855, ice hockey was being played in Canada, and twenty years later, students at McGill University in Montreal had established the rules of the game. It came to the United States by way of two Yale University students who had played it in Canada, and by 1890 had spread throughout the northeastern United States. It was a game that was played outdoors on the local pond or lake and was, therefore, popular only in the more northern climes. With the advent of indoor skating rinks, however, the game moved indoors and gained favor. And, as with our other sports, television gave it a big boost.

In 1917 the National Hockey League was formed with teams from Canada, and in 1924 the first United States team, the Boston Bruins, joined, followed by teams from Detroit and New York. The National Hockey teams vie each year to win the coveted Stanley Cup, awarded to the best team in the play-offs.

1855: The Parker House. Harvey D. Parker opens his hotel in Boston, which serves meals all day long, not just at required times, and is the birthplace of those soft rolls named after it. In 1925 a new Parker House will open on Tremont Street. The rolls will be the same.

1855: Niagara Bridge. Designed and built by John Roebling, the Grand Trunk Bridge, as it was called, was the first suspension bridge strong enough to withstand winds and heavy railway traffic. The double-decker bridge spanned 820 feet and utilized stiffening trusses and, since Roebling owned a wire rope factory, a wire cable system he had patented. Roebling designed several more suspension bridges but is best known for one in particular; we call it the Brooklyn Bridge.

1856: Neanderthal Man Discovered. Feldhofer Cave is a few miles east of Düsseldorf, Germany. It was there that workmen found parts of a human skeleton, including the skull, that would be named Neanderthal, after the Neander Valley in which it was found. In 1886 two similar skeletons were found in a cave in Belgium, verifying that the fossils are, indeed, those of prehistoric humans. The Neanderthals lived during the last half of the last interglacial stage, about 120,000 years ago, and inhabited what is now Europe and western Asia. They had a large cranial capacity, a compact body, and strong muscles which gave them great physical strength. They had tools and a rudimentary sense of art, sometimes buried their dead and decorated the grave, and may have believed in an afterlife. We don't know their fate. They may have died out or they may have interbred and merged with *Homo sapiens sapiens,* modern humans. We may know someday.

1857: Toilet Paper Packaged. One of the refinements of life, toilet paper did not appear commercially in the United States until the middle of the nineteenth century, and then not with success. What was used? Outhouses and bathrooms stocked newspapers, old catalogs, and any other paper of that nature. Twenty years later a British manufacturer produced paper in rolls but couldn't sell the idea either. At the same time the Scott brothers in New York began a paper business and started producing small rolls of tissue. By the late nineteenth century, public sewer systems had been completed in major cities, hotels had installed indoor

plumbing, and apartment buildings as well as private homes had
moved the bathroom indoors. It was an idea whose time had
finally come. Thank goodness!

1858: A New Theory. On July 1 the gentlemen of the Lin-
naean Society in London listen intently, if somewhat skeptically,
as a paper is read to them, presented by Alfred Russel Wallace
and Charles Robert Darwin. The paper details the theory that
both men had come to individually, that the species is perpetuated
by natural means of selection and the survival of the fittest.

Wallace, a naturalist, had come to his conclusion while collecting
plants in the Amazon and studying animals in the Malay Archipelago.
Darwin, also a naturalist, had come to the same way of thinking
after his famous round-the-world voyage on the HMS *Beagle*. Both
had been influenced by the English economist and demographer
Thomas Malthus's "Essay on Population," in which he stated that
population will always increase faster than production.

1858: The Basic Cell. Rudolf Virchow, a German pathologist,
publishes his work on cellular pathology in which he states,
"Omnis cellula e cellula," that every cell comes from another cell
and that cells, the basic unit of life, must be studied to gain knowledge of disease. Among his discoveries are leukemia, embolisms,
myelin, and thrombosis.

Virchow was also interested in archaeology, founded the German Anthropological Society, and went with Schliemann to the
excavations at Troy.

1859–1952: John Dewey. Born October 20, 1859, in Ver-
mont, philosopher-psychologist John Dewey became one of the
outspoken proponents of progressive education.

Dewey stressed the need to teach more in the classroom besides
volumes of information learned by drill and memorization. He did
not disagree with book learning, but he felt that it was not
enough. Children needed to learn by doing, he argued, and the
practical should therefore be worked into the learning process. He
applied this theory to such subjects as science and math as well as
to the larger concern of preparation for adulthood. Dewey wanted
to see the classroom become a social environment in which children could begin to prepare for adult life in addition to the school
curriculum.

Dewey taught philosophy and education at several universities during his career, including the University of Chicago and Columbia, from which he retired in 1930. As a professor, he spread his ideas not only through his classrooms and public discussions but also through books such as *School of Society* and *Creative Intelligence*. He was honored internationally for his efforts in educational reform and for helping to reorganize the school systems in several countries, including Turkey, China, and Chile.

1859: The Origin of Species. On November 24 the English naturalist Charles Darwin publishes his monumental *On the Origin of Species by Means of Natural Selection, or the Preservation of Favoured Races in the Struggle for Life,* explaining his theory of evolution, and creates an uproar.

Darwin did not actually originate the idea, but he did offer proof of the process as he detailed his theory of natural selection in the struggle for survival.

1860: *The Woman in White.* English writer Wilkie Collins publishes his novel *The Woman in White* and pioneers the detective story genre. Collins is known as one of the first and best of mystery writers. His *The Moonstone*, published in 1868, is also a classic in detective work.

1860: Married Women's Property Acts. Under common law, married women had no property rights. Once a woman was married, everything she owned became the property of her husband, and she could neither keep, buy, or sell property, keep her wages, or sign a contract. This gradually began to change, and in 1860 the new Property Acts Law was passed in the state of New York, allowing a married woman the right to buy, sell, and own property, maintain joint guardianship with her husband of their children, and keep her own wages. By the turn of the century, almost all states had passed similar laws. Another twenty years, and women, married or single, would get the right to vote. The wheels of progress sometimes turn very slowly, but they do turn.

1861: Mary Walker Volunteers. Mary Edwards Walker, a twenty-nine-year-old medical school graduate, is commissioned a lieutenant and named acting assistant surgeon in the Union Army during the Civil War, becoming the first woman doctor in the military.

Dr. Walker was captured by the Confederates near Chattanooga, Tennessee, and spent four months in prison, where she insisted the diet be improved to include wheat bread and fresh vegetables. She was eventually traded along with a group of doctors in exchange for Confederate surgeons. She remained in the army and was instrumental in aiding women to find missing relatives and friends. It was Walker who came up with the innovative idea at the time of a return address on envelopes and return-receipt registered mail when she saw mail being thrown away that couldn't be delivered.

In November 1865 Dr. Walker received the Medal of Honor from President Andrew Johnson.

1861: Pasteur's Germ Theory. Louis Pasteur, a French chemist and microbiologist, publishes his paper refuting spontaneous combustion and propounds his germ theory of disease.

As a very young man Pasteur painted portraits and thought he wanted to be a teacher. When he entered college he had no special interests, and after receiving his degree, he became a math teacher. It was while studying for an advanced degree that he attended lectures on chemistry at the Sorbonne and was so inspired by the lecturer Jean Baptiste André Dumas that he embarked on a career in chemistry. Fortunately for us. From chemistry, Pasteur branched out into biology and medical research and became one of the greatest contributors to science we have had.

The process of pasteurization, which obviously bears his name, was discovered by him. He had been working with wine producers who had had batches of wine go bad. In his experiments with fermentation and spoilage, Pasteur discovered that bacteria in the air were the cause. This led to the "pasteurization" or gentle heating method of sterilization of food and beverages. His work saved the wine and beer industry. In 1865 he rescued the silk industry by detecting the bacilli that were causing disease in silkworms and finding a way to prevent it. After that he worked with farm animals and in 1881 developed an anthrax vaccine that immunized cattle from this fatal disease by a process he called vaccination.

By this time, Pasteur was suffering from partial paralysis suffered during a stroke, but it didn't slow him down. He cured cholera in chickens by inoculation and salvaged the chicken industry, which had been suffering losses. He then went on to develop a vaccine against rabies.

In 1888 the Pasteur Institute was dedicated in Paris to further the investigation of rabies. Pasteur headed it until he died in September of 1895, at the age of seventy-two. Thanks to the inspiration of Dumas, the world acquired a great scientist and a great achiever.

1862: The Homestead Act. The act, passed on May 20, granted any United States citizen (or intended citizen) over twenty-one or head of a family 160 acres of public land for a small registration fee and the provision that the family live on the land continuously for a period of five years. After that time, for an additional fee, the grantee could receive title to the land. Settlers willing to purchase land for $1.25 per acre could do so after a six-month residency.

1862: Emancipation Proclamation. On September 22, 1862, President Abraham Lincoln issues his proclamation declaring all slaves in the Confederacy to be free as of January 1, 1863. Slaves held outside rebel territory were freed by other legislation. The abolitionists who had worked for years for their cause now had a president who was committed to end slavery.

1863: The London Underground. In 1853 the British Parliament authorized the building of a 3.75-mile underground railway in London between Farringdon Street and Bishop's Road, Paddington. Construction began in 1860 with the digging of deep trenches along the streets, bricking the sides, then covering the trenches with girders and brick arches and restoring the street above. The tunnel was seventeen feet high and twenty-eight and a half feet wide to accommodate the two tracks.

On January 10, 1863, the Metropolitan District Railway, the world's first underground, opened, with coke-burning steam locomotives carrying the passengers. In its first year of service it carries 9,500,000 passengers.

The now-automated electric transport system has over 257 miles of track stopping at 278 stations, and carries nearly three quarters of a billion passengers each year. Londoners call it "the tube."

1863: Soccer. What we call soccer and the rest of the world calls football is difficult to date, but the rules were drawn up in 1863 by the London Football Association, who called it *association* *football,* later shortened to assoc football, then to soccer. Our present football, soccer, and rugby all evolved from the rough-and-tumble free-for-all kicking ball games that had been going on for centuries. Soccer rules are uncomplicated and easy to understand, team upkeep is relatively inexpensive, and it's an exciting game to watch, all of which no doubt accounts for its worldwide popularity. Unlike our football, where brawn counts, or basketball, where height is mandatory, soccer can be played by almost anyone who doesn't mind butting a ball with his head.

1863: National Academy of Sciences. On March 3, by act of Congress, the National Academy of Sciences is created to advise the United States government on scientific and technological matters and to promote research.

1864: Dunant's Good Deeds. Jean-Henri Dunant is the man largely responsible for the formation of the Red Cross. After helping the casualties of the Battle of Solferino in 1859 (estimated to be around forty thousand men), Dunant proposed an idea for an international organization of trained volunteers to help the wounded in a wartime situation. He wrote a book, *A Memory of Solferino,* outlining his thoughts. It caught the attention of several prominent Europeans, and some of them arranged for a committee to address the subject. Dunant was, of course, appointed a member. The committee held its first conference in 1863 and a second in 1864. The Geneva Convention, which set the guidelines for the Red Cross and the treatment of the wounded during wartime, was the product of the second conference.

By trade, Dunant was a banker. He had been in Solferino on business during the battle, but after witnessing the horrors of that day, his business affairs seemed less important. What was the world's gain was Dunant's loss. He became so involved in his pursuit of what would become the Red Cross that he let his affairs slip and was forced to declare bankruptcy. At the time, this was a very disreputable thing, and Dunant was exiled from Switzerland, his home, for roughly twenty years. However, the world had not quite forgotten him. In 1901 Dunant, along with Frédéric Passy, shared the honor of being awarded the first Nobel Peace Prize. Nine years later in 1910, Dunant died at the age of eighty-two.

1865: Mendel's Laws. Gregor Johann Mendel, an Austrian monk and botanist, reads a paper to the Natural Science Society in which he illustrates his theories of heredity and formulates the dominant/recessive trait laws. Mendel had been experimenting with sweet peas, cross-pollinating them and observing the traits that appeared in successive generations. He called these units that carried the traits factors. We call them genes. Unfortunately not many people paid attention to him, and it wasn't until the turn of the century that others, experimenting on their own, confirmed his studies.

Gregor Mendel's experiments formed the basis for the science of genetics. Not bad for someone who failed miserably on the biology section of his test for a teacher's license.

1865: Antiseptic Surgery. With the development of anesthesia, surgeons could work more carefully, but they were still faced with problems of infection. The Italian researcher Spallanzani and Louis Pasteur had proved that bacteria were carried by air. In 1847 Hungarian obstetrician Ignaz Phillipp Semmelweis found that what had been called puerperal fever (childbed fever) was really blood poisoning and that doctors spread the disease by working with unclean hands. His insistence on hand washing with a mixture of soap and chlorine greatly cut the infection rate. He later included the washing of bed linens and instruments in his crusade, but problems still persisted.

Joseph Lister, an English surgeon, began working with the problem of infection in 1865. After much experimenting with various substances, he settled on carbolic acid. During surgery the wound was sprayed with a diluted mist of the chemical, then sealed with a dressing. His system was highly successful and was soon widely used. In 1877, remembering Semmelweis's work, he expanded the antiseptic concept to everything and everyone in the operating room. New methods of sterilization, such as the autoclave for instruments, have been developed since, and rubber gloves were added to the arsenal in 1890 by William Halsted, the well-known American surgeon.

1865: Thirteenth Amendment Ratified. On December 6 the amendment abolishing slavery in the United States was ratified. The amendment states: *Neither slavery nor involuntary servitude, except as a punishment for crime whereof the party shall have been duly convicted,* *shall exist within the United States, or any place subject to their jurisdiction. Congress shall have the power to enforce this article by appropriate legislation.*

The Northwest Ordinance of 1787 banned slavery in the territory north of the Ohio River and east of the Mississippi, and Congress had passed a law ending the slave trade in 1808, but it was not enough. White indentured servants performed most of the labor in early colonial times; it was one way of escaping the hardships of Europe and migrating to America. About 1680, however, indentured servitude began to decline and African slave labor gradually increased. Between 1774 and 1804 slavery was abolished in the North but expanded in the South until slaves comprised one third of the population by 1860. The abolitionist movement started in the 1830s was the beginning of the end of slavery, but it took a Civil War, a presidential proclamation, and finally a constitutional amendment to end this heinous and degrading institution.

1866: Transatlantic Cable. The first successful transatlantic cable was laid by the iron ship the *Great Eastern,* designed and built by one of the world's greatest engineers, the Englishman Isambard Brunel, and his partner, John Russell. The cable linked the two continents together and expedited communications between them.

1866: Musical Comedy Germinates. New Yorker Henry Jarrett and his financial partner, Harry Palmer, imported a troupe of European ballet dancers to perform at the Academy of Music. Just before opening, the theater burned down. The one other theater, Niblo's Garden, had booked a new melodrama, *The Black Crook,* based on Faust. Jarrett and Palmer, not wanting to lose their money, talked the theater manager into combining the two productions. This unlikely combination was the genesis of that truly American theatrical form, musical comedy.

The audiences loved it. The *New York Tribune* critic wrote, "The scenery is magnificent, the ballet is beautiful, the drama is rubbish." The crowds didn't go to see the drama, anyway, they went to see five and a half hours worth of spectacular production numbers in which trapdoors opened and closed all over the stage, machinery raised and lowered sets, fairies flew through the air, gilded chariots rolled in on clouds, and best of all, scantily clad

women in tights cavorted on the stage. It ran for 474 performances. From 1868 to 1892, it was revived eight times, and several
companies took it on the road. The display of women's bodies
was decried by the church and newspaper editorials, but the louder
they hollered, the greater the attendance.

On the sublime side of early musical comedy was *The Brook,*
an unpretentious little show that played for two weeks in New
York in 1879. It was a simple comedy with a cast of five who
acted, danced, and sang, with only a few costumes and no big
production numbers.

The seeds of musical comedy had been sown. By the 1920s
they had blossomed into the great American art form.

1868: Cro-Magnon Man Discovered.

In the Dordogne region in the southwestern part of France, workmen are building a
railroad when they unearth several skeletons, animal bones, seashell
necklaces, and stone tools. They are the remains of old Stone Age
people we now call Cro-Magnon who lived in Europe about
40,000 to 30,000 B.C. Tall, muscular, and with a large brain, they
were similar in appearance to modern humans. They gathered
food and they hunted; they used animal skins for clothing and
shelter, and they buried their dead. They were also artists. It was
the Cro-Magnon who painted the magnificent and beautiful cave
paintings at Lascaux, Altamira in Spain, and elsewhere.

They apparently survived, perhaps because of their intelligence,
and gradually mixed with new strains of people migrating from
the East until modern humans developed.

1869: DNA Discovered.

Friederich Miescher, a chemistry student at Tübingen, Germany, extracts from the nuclei of a cell a
substance he calls nuclein. We now call it deoxyribonucleic acid,
or, for obvious reasons, DNA. Nobody thought it was particularly important.

1869: Wyoming Women Vote.

In December 1869 the legislature of the newly formed territory of Wyoming granted
women the right to vote in all elections and later confirmed it
in an equal-suffrage clause of their state constitution. Wyoming
thus became the first state to grant women the right to vote.
Of course, there weren't many women in the territory at the
time, and maybe this was a ploy to lure them there.

1870: The Fifteenth Amendment. This article of the Constitution was declared on March 30, 1870, and stated that the right
to vote shall not be denied any citizen on account of race, color,
or previous condition of servitude. This gave the former slaves
the right to vote. They had been declared citizens in the Fourteenth Amendment.

1870: Schliemann's Dig. Heinrich Schliemann had a dream.
When he was a young boy in northern Germany, his pastor father
had regaled him with stories and legends about the heroes of
ancient Greece. When he read about the battle of Troy, of Helen
and Paris and Achilles, he was enchanted, and when his father
told him that Troy had disappeared and no one knew where it
once had been, he was determined. When he grew up, he told
his father, he would go to Greece and find the lost city and the
king's treasure.

Heinrich's formal education ended at the age of fourteen when
he was apprenticed to a grocer. It was during this time that he
used to listen to a customer reciting Homer's *Iliad* and his fascina-
tion with Troy increased. When he was nineteen, after being
shipwrecked while a cabin boy, he became an office worker and
bookkeeper in Amsterdam. Eager to learn, he taught himself
Dutch, Spanish, Italian, Portuguese, and Russian, and eventually
during his lifetime mastered thirteen languages. Schliemann turned
out to be a good businessman, and during the next twenty years
of his life, his many ventures brought him a fortune. (It also
brought him United States citizenship, since he was in California
at the time it was admitted into statehood and automatically became a citizen.) It was now time for his greatest adventure.

He had already mastered ancient and modern Greek, and in
1866 he went to Paris to study archaeology. In 1868 he moved
to Greece, married a young Greek girl, and began to seek his
dream. With a copy of the *Iliad* in his hand, Schliemann surveyed
the countryside and concluded that, contrary to the thinking of
other scholars, his Troy was beneath a large mound at Hissarlik.
His dream came true. He not only discovered ancient Troy, but
nine cities that had been built one atop the other. He also found
a treasure trove of gold jewelry that he thought was Priam's gold,
but turned out to be that of a lesser king. Thrilled with his discoveries, Schliemann turned to other areas to excavate. He began
work at Mycenae in Greece, where he uncovered ancient royal

graves and treasures greater than anything ever before found. At Tiryns, where the god Heracles was supposedly born, he excavated traces of an ancient city and discovered a culture now called Minoan-Mycenaean. He also returned to Troy, where he continued his excavations.

Schliemann died in Naples, Italy, in 1890, having realized his dream and more, and given to the world some of its greatest archaeological finds and sites.

1871: Stanley and Livingstone. The Scotsman David Livingstone is celebrated as the greatest nineteenth-century explorer and missionary in Africa. Henry Morton Stanley is known as the newspaperman who "found" him and greeted him with his now famous words.

Livingstone, of humble origins, hardworking and self-educated, began studying theology and medicine in Glasgow when he was twenty-two. By 1840, he had his medical degree and became a missionary in southern Africa. Disregarding comfort and quickly adapting to the rough travel and tribulations he encountered, he pushed farther into Africa than anyone had gone before, to establish his missions. During the next several years he learned the native languages, was attacked by a lion, which disabled his left arm, married Mary Moffat, and met William Oswell, a wealthy sportsman who would help him in the future.

On his third effort to push north into the unknown, to find Lake Ngami, and to meet the powerful tribal chief of the Makolo tribe, Livingstone and his family, along with Oswell, were finally successful. In order to undercut and fight the slave trade he abhorred, he took it upon himself to explore Africa for new trade routes to bring in industry. He sent his family back to England, returned alone, and set up headquarters on the Zambezi River, guided by the tribal chief he had befriended.

In November 1853 he started his journey westward with twenty-seven tribesmen and reached the coast at Luanda, now in Angola. He refused the offer by British sea captains to take him back to England and, although wracked by bouts of fever, thought it only honorable to return with his men and guide them to their homeland. Their arrival was greeted with great wonder, but Livingstone was disappointed that his route was not suitable for trading. Undaunted, he set out to find a way to the east coast, and in 1855 embarked with one hundred natives down the Zambezi River. En route he discovered Victoria Falls, which barred his navigational plans, but he reached the coast with greater ease than he'd experienced during his journey to the west. This time he left his tribesmen in comfortable means, and took a ship back to England, where he was welcomed with great acclaim. He stayed for a year, giving lectures and writing his classic on exploration, *Missionary Travels*.

In contrast to the public's appreciation of his heroic accomplishments, the London Missionary Society did not approve of Livingstone's explorations and severed their ties with him. In 1858 he was appointed as a consul to the Zambezi region and given command of an official expedition. During this exploration he discovered Lake Nyasa and a route to the interior, took many of his tribesmen back to their homeland, and explored East Africa. Tragedy struck when his wife, who had traveled to join him, died of fever on the lower Zambezi River.

After another year in England, Livingstone returned once more to Africa, sponsored by his friend Sir Roderick Murchison, this time to search for the sources of the Zambezi, Congo, and Nile rivers. After reaching Lake Nyasa, he continued on, again observing, mapping, and recording everything in a scientific manner. He was in very ill health with recurring dysentery and had to rely on the Arab traders for help, although he despised their slave trading. On this journey he discovered Lake Tanganyika and Lakes Mweru and Bangweul. By 1869 he had reached Ujiji in western Tanzania, then the headquarters of the ivory and slave trade, and found that his desperately needed provisions, which should have been waiting for him, had been looted. For the next couple of years he explored the upper Congo River, still looking for the source of the Nile, then returned to Ujiji, disappointed and ill once again.

John Rowlands was an illegitimate child ignored by his mother, and spent his Welsh childhood with indifferent relatives or suffered humiliations in the workhouse. This institution did, however, educate him to a degree, taught him cleanliness, and provided him with a religious faith. At the age of seventeen, he signed on as a ship's cabin boy and sailed from Liverpool to New Orleans, where he landed in 1858. There he met Henry Morton Stanley, a kind merchant who took him under his wing, gave him his own name, and treated him as a son. John, now Henry, had at last found someone who loved him and treated him kindly. Unfortunately, his new father and mentor died shortly, and for the next several years Henry had various careers, as a soldier in the American Civil War, a merchant seaman, a sailor, and a journalist.

In 1867 Henry became a special correspondent for the *New York Herald* and covered the British campaign in Abyssinia as well as the Spanish Civil War. Then, in 1869, James Gordon Bennett, Jr., publisher of the *Herald,* commissioned Stanley to "find Livingstone," who apparently was lost somewhere in Africa and was last heard of near northern Lake Tanganyika.

Thus it was that in November 1871 Henry Stanley, upon finding David Livingstone in Ujiji, uttered his immortal words, "Dr. Livingstone, I presume."

After briefly exploring with Livingstone, Stanley returned to Zanzibar, and from there went on to England, while Livingstone, despite Stanley's exhortations to return with him, continued his search for the source of the Nile. With new supplies and dedicated men sent to him by Stanley, he left on his last journey. In failing health, he tramped the swamps and hacked through trails until he finally succumbed and died in the tiny village of Chitambo. His men, ever faithful to the kind and gentle man who had cared so much about their welfare, embalmed his body and carried it back to Zanzibar, where he was delivered, along with his important papers, to the English.

Backed by his newspaper, and joined by three white explorers, Sir Richard Burton, Sir Samuel Baker, and John Speke, Stanley returned to Africa in 1874, to continue his explorations. Their expeditions opened up the central part of Africa. Stanley discovered and traced the Congo (Zaire) River and explored further under the auspices of King Leopold of Belgium. To him belongs the credit for putting all the geographical pieces together into a map of central Africa, which he detailed in his many journals. And because Henry Morton Stanley was kind to a poor young man named John Rowlands whom he befriended, his name lives on in history.

1871–88: Central Asia Explored.

Nikolai Mikhailovich Przhevalsky, a Russian infantry officer and geography instructor, explores the central part of Asia, including Ulan Bator, the Gobi Desert, China, Mongolia, and other nearby regions. His accurate accounts of the geographical features, plants, and animals serve to enlighten the world about central Asia. Among his discoveries are the wild camel and the wild horse, named for him, *Equus przewalskii.*

1871: *Thespis* Opens in London. Also known as *The Gods Grown Old,* the comic opera is the first collaboration between William Gilbert, librettist, and Arthur Sullivan, composer. The show at the Gaiety Theater isn't too successful. Their second operetta, *Trial By Jury,* runs for a year, however, and succeeding collaborations, including *H.M.S. Pinafore* and *The Pirates of Penzance,* draw crowds. The producer, Richard D'Oyly Carte, then builds the Savoy Theater especially to house Gilbert and Sullivan's comic operas and opens the theater with *Patience* in October 1881.

Gilbert and Sullivan's witty parodies and catchy melodies still delight audiences everywhere, whether performed by professionals or a local amateur group.

1873: Cable Cars. On August 1 the world's first cable streetcar enters service on Sacramento and Clay streets in San Francisco, California. The cars are drawn by an endless cable that runs in a slot between rails and passes over a shaft driven by steam in a powerhouse. The system had been patented in 1871 by Andrew Smith Hallidie, an engineer, as a way to cope with the steep hills of the Bay City and was an instant success. Additional lines were soon added, and the popular cable cars have been synonymous with San Francisco ever since. Rudyard Kipling, the English writer, said of them, "They turn corners almost at right angles; cross other lines, and for all I know, run up the sides of houses."

In 1964 the cable cars were declared a National Historic Landmark and in 1984 returned to service after a complete overhaul of the system. A ride in one of the clanging cars is a thrill, and the views from the hills are spectacular.

1874: The Typewriter. The first practical modern typewriters in America are manufactured by E. Remington & Sons, gunsmiths, in Ilion, New York, from a patent received by Latham Sholes of Milwaukee, Wisconsin. The design was inspired by an article in *Scientific American* detailing a machine invented by John Pratt and patented in England. The one drawback of these first models was that they printed only capital letters, but this was remedied in 1878 with the invention and addition of the shift key.

Mark Twain bought one of the machines and was the first author to submit a typewritten manuscript to his publisher. In 1885 Leo Tolstoy, the Russian author, also began using a typewriter, or rather his daughter did as he dictated to her.

Aside from being a big help to those whose handwriting is illegible, the typewriter veritably turned the business world inside out and wrought a great change in society. Women who once had a subordinate place in the home now entered the world of commerce in droves into paid careers as typists and secretaries. Business schools sprung up to teach office skills, and the once male-dominated profession became the realm of the female. The typewriter had given women a newfound freedom.

1874: We Bridge the Mississippi.

The crowds watch expectantly as seven fifty-ton locomotives start their journey from opposite sides of the river and slowly pull their loads across the new bridge. They meet in the middle, pass each other, and continue across. The bridge holds and the crowds cheer. After a two day celebration, the bridge opens to traffic on July 4, 1874. It is the first bridge over the mighty Mississippi at St. Louis, Missouri. The cantilevered bridge, made of steel, was designed by James Buchanan Eads, an American engineer who was known for his work salvaging sunken Mississippi steamers utilizing a diving bell he had invented and patented. His new imaginative engineering techniques enable piers to be sunk to a greater depth than ever before under compressed air, and the bridge, once thought impossible by others, is constructed. *Impossible* was not in Ead's vocabulary.

Ca. 1874: Lawn Tennis.

The Englishman Walter Wingfield devises what he calls "a new and improved portable court for playing the ancient game of tennis." The game is played outdoors in the court erected on the grass, is called lawn tennis, and soon becomes very popular.

At about the same time, the All England Croquet Club had been ruining the lawn of one of its members, and had decided to look for another place to play. They found just what they needed in the Wimbledon area of London and rented the meadow. The club members soon began playing lawn tennis and badminton as well and changed its name to the All England Croquet and Lawn Tennis Club. Naturally the members wanted to have a tournament, so they formulated the rules for tennis, and on July 19,

1877, the first tournament was held at Wimbledon. The rest, as the saying goes, is history.

Tennis was introduced to the United States about 1874 by Mary Outerbridge, who had spent the winter in Bermuda, where she watched it being played by British officers. The first official championship matches were played in August of 1881, in Newport, Rhode Island, the same year the United States National Lawn Tennis Association was formed.

In 1915 the national championships moved to the West Side Tennis Club in Forest Hills, New York, where they remained until moving to Flushing Meadow. By this time, speed rather than accuracy was making tennis a more dramatic game, and spectators were flocking to watch the matches. A new stadium was built at Wimbledon, and soon the competition became truly international, eventually evolving into the fast, hard-driving, ace-smashing thriller it is today.

1876: Rules of Order. General Henry Robert publishes, with his own funds, one thousand copies of his *Pocket Manual of Rules of Order*. It's been a best-seller ever since, but we usually call it *Robert's Rules of Order*.

Robert was presiding over a chaotic church meeting when he realized there was a need for some sort of parliamentary uniformity in order to accomplish anything. He decided to formulate the rules. From the ladies' garden club to the senate, we've been following them ever since.

1876: The Dewey Decimal System. *A Classification and Subject Index for Cataloguing and Arranging the Books and Pamphlets of a Library* is published by an Amherst College librarian, the twenty-four-year-old Melvil Dewey. The Dewey Decimal System, as it became known for obvious reasons, sure makes finding books in the stacks a lot easier.

1876: The Telephone. The instrument that connects us all, keeps our businesses moving, our governments in contact, and our friends in touch is invented and patented by Alexander Graham Bell. His famous words, uttered on March 10, 1876, *"Mr. Watson, come here, I want you!"* usher in a new era of communication that changes our way of living.

The word *telephone,* from the Greek *tele,* meaning "far," and *phone,* "sound," had been used to describe any instrument that sent sound from one point to another, from a megaphone to a speaking tube. In Germany in 1860, Philipp Reis, a physics teacher, was working on a telephone of his own. He built a replica of the human ear made of wood and fitted with a hammer, anvil, and tympanum, then connected two of these ears by wires and a battery. The words spoken into one ear could softly be heard in the other. He came close to a workable telephone, but gave up, since the scientific community didn't seem interested.

It was one of Reis's telephones that intrigued Bell while he was studying at Edinburgh University in Scotland. Upon his return to Boston, Massachusetts, where he was a teacher of deaf students, Bell continued experimenting with the device he hoped would help in training his students to speak. He also had another motive; his fiancée, Mabel Hubbard, was one of his deaf students. Her father supplied some of the financial support, and Bell and his assistant, Thomas J. Watson, toiled for two years to devise the instrument.

Bell's telephone was a sensation at the Philadelphia Centennial Exhibition that year, although a few scientists in Europe thought the whole thing impossible. Within a few years Bell had improved his invention, and in 1877 in Salem, Massachusetts, in front of an audience, he carried on a telephone conversation with Watson, eighteen miles away.

The first telephones were sold in pairs with a direct wire between them. By 1878, however, telephone cables were carrying many different wires to a central office, where one caller could then be linked with any number of different people, and by 1880 there were sixty thousand phones in the United States. The Bell Telephone Company was formed in 1877 and made Alex, his father-in-law, and Thomas Watson very rich. During his lifetime Bell continued working on various inventions and generously supported other inventors in their endeavors. His interest in teaching the deaf to speak never waned and he was constantly devising new methods for accomplishing this.

We can now call around the world in seconds by a touch of our telephone, know if there is a "call waiting," have incoming calls transferred to another number automatically, or carry on a three-way chat. The technology seems endless. Just like a teenager's telephone conversation.

1877: Low-Rent Housing. As the country moves from an agrarian society to an industrial one, more and more workers move into the cities of the United States, and housing becomes a problem. Private associations and individuals build housing for workingmen's families, and among those is Alfred Tredway North, who constructs the first low-rent housing development in Brooklyn, New York. His cottages are eleven and a half feet wide and contain six rooms, and his four-room apartment buildings rise to six stories around a central court and include community bathing facilities in the basements.

1879: We Light Up the World. On October 21, 1879, Thomas Alva Edison and his assistants watch in his laboratory while the light bulb he has just created glows, and glows, and glows. It burns for forty hours straight. Edison has just invented the first successful incandescent light bulb. The electric bulb would shed light brighter and longer than any other means of illumination in history.

Early humans lived in darkness at night with only moonlight to guide them. Until they discovered the use of fire. Torches then lit their way for tens of thousands of years, and torchlight is still used in many parts of the world. Oil lamps came along in the Stone Age, and again, for centuries, nothing changed. Candles appeared around the beginning of the Christian era, and about 400 A.D. the Phoenicians were making wax candles. It was still pitch-black at night; torches, oil lamps, and candles were the only sources of light, and their illumination was dim and not very far-reaching.

In the late eighteenth century, gas was used in experiments for lighting, and in 1792 the Englishman William Murdock lit up his house in Cornwall with natural gas and later installed it in a factory. (The Chinese had discovered this use for natural gas even before the Christian era and had piped it through bamboo to light up mines.) By 1820 most cities in Europe had gaslights on their streets, and it soon became the method of illuminating homes and public buildings.

Experiments with electricity for lighting had been going on for two hundred years, since the German Otto van Guericke discovered in 1650 that light could be produced by electricity. Many experiments followed by scientists and inventors in England, France, Russia, and the United States. While Edison was working in New Jersey, the Englishman Sir Joseph Swan had developed an incandescent bulb of his own, which he called the electric glow lamp, utilizing cotton thread treated with sulfuric acid as a filament. It was Edison, however, who invented the practical electric light bulb. In 1881 a factory in New York city installed the new electric lights. It was the beginning of the commercial and domestic use of electric lighting. We had come out of the darkness and lit up the sky.

1880: Cologne Cathedral Completed.

Begun in the thirteenth century, the cathedral in Cologne, Germany, is finally completed, making it the largest Gothic cathedral in northern Europe. With spires 515 feet high, it was also the world's tallest structure until the Eiffel Tower was built nine years later.

1881: Booker T. Washington Heads Tuskegee Institute.

The state legislature of Alabama had just chartered a normal school for African-Americans, and Booker T. Washington, former slave, janitor, dormitory manager, and secretary, is chosen to start it.

Born on a Virginia plantation in 1856, Booker, his mother, brother, and sister walked to Malden, West Virginia, after emancipation. Booker studied at night and worked in a salt furnace by day. At the age of seventeen he headed for Hampton, Virginia, Normal and Agricultural Institute, where he worked very hard to get an education and eventually earned a degree. He taught for two years, then attended Wayland Seminary in Washington, D.C., where he became secretary to General Samuel Armstrong, who recommended him for the post at Tuskegee.

When Washington began his work there were forty students, two dilapidated shanties, no equipment, and barely any money. A firm believer that education best served the interests of his people, it was Washington's labors that instilled dignity and knowledge in his students, and Tuskegee graduates became known for their high character and leadership ability. Thirty-four years later, at the time of his death, the Institute had one hundred well-equipped buildings, over fifteen hundred students, a faculty of two hundred teaching almost forty different professions, and a two-million-dollar endowment.

In 1893 Washington gave a now famous speech at the Cotton States and International Exposition in Atlanta, Georgia, in which he stated: "In all things that are purely social we can be as separate as the fingers, yet one as the hand in all things essential to mutual progress." It was this speech that won him international recognition as a leader among African-Americans. During his lifetime he wrote a dozen books, gave a multitude of speeches in the States and abroad, dined with President Theodore Roosevelt, and received an honorary degree from Harvard. All the while, Tuskegee and the welfare of its students was uppermost in his mind.

1882: St. Gothard Tunnel. The first Alpine railroad tunnel opens May 20, runs slightly over nine miles beneath St. Gothard's Pass in the Swiss Alps, and connects Lucerne to Milan, Italy.

1883: The Brooklyn Bridge. The famed bridge celebrated its centennial over a decade ago with crowds, fireworks, music, and dance. The crowds were just as ebullient when the first bridge linking Manhattan and Brooklyn opened to pedestrians on May 24, 1883. The suspension bridge over the East River is a record 1,595 feet long and has four cables, each 15¾ inches in diameter, with steel wires running parallel to them forming a truss to keep the bridge from swaying.

Aside from its beauty, the beloved bridge gained fame in jokes when con artists attempted to "sell" it to unsuspecting immigrants. If the New York City deficit gets too bad, you could always make an offer.

1883: Time Zones Adopted. If you get confused about which way to turn the clock for daylight saving time, you can imagine how baffling train schedules must have been before time zones came into effect. Although Greenwich Time had been adopted by British astronomers in 1850, every city in the United States still operated on its own sun time, which frequently meant mass confusion. In 1872 the railroads devised a system of four time zones that the government agreed upon eleven years later, and on Sunday, November 18, 1883, at twelve noon, all clocks in the country were adjusted accordingly. We now have Eastern Standard, Central Standard, Mountain, and Pacific Time, which certainly has simplified traveling. And remember, it's spring ahead, fall behind, when you change your clocks for daylight saving time.

1885: The First Skyscraper. American architect and engineer William LeBaron Jenney designs and builds the first of what we would forever after call skyscrapers, the ten-story Home Insurance Building in Chicago, Illinois. The marble structure is supported almost completely by an iron and steel skeleton, the first time steel is used as a structural material. Jenney's innovative techniques will revolutionize our skylines.

1885: The Automobile. Of all our means of transportation, the automobile, or car as we call it, will be the vehicle to have the greatest impact on the way we live.

Many inventors had been trying to develop an engine-powered carriage for the road. As early as 1771, a Swiss engineer, Nicolas Cugnot, while working for the French, constructed a large three-wheeled, wood-framed, two-cylinder steam engine vehicle he called a *fardier*. It sped along at 2.3 miles per hour, but he seems to have had trouble controlling it. Successful steam-driven carriages were built in England in the early nineteenth century and were used as buses. However, they were somewhat impractical, very uncomfortable, and opposed by stagecoach owners and the new railways. About 1862 the French engineer J. J. Lenoir built an internal combustion gas engine and ran a car with it. Siegfried Marcus and August Otto also invented internal combustion engines operated by gas.

It was Gottlieb Daimler and Karl Benz, both from Germany, and unknown to each other, who are credited with inventing the first practical motorcars. Daimler improved Otto's engine by using an electrical ignition inside a cylinder, replacing the flame outside the cylinder to explode the gas. Benz worked on the same principle, decided that petroleum would be a useful fuel, invented an electrical ignition, and modified the steering mechanism. At the 1887 Paris Exhibition, Benz displayed an improved model of his "horseless carriage," but not many people were interested. The following year, he drove it through the streets of Munich, engendering much excitement and a few orders for his model. In 1889 Daimler exhibited his four-seater automobile in Paris, and a French firm began building them.

In the United States, the Duryea brothers were credited with being first to build a gasoline-powered motorcar in 1893, although John Lambert of Ohio seems to have driven one in 1890, and George Selden had been granted a patent for inventing the automobile in 1879, although he never built one. By 1898, there were over fifty companies producing motorcars, which was shortened to "car" by 1910. By 1908, Henry Ford was building cars on the assembly line, producing eighteen million Model-T Fords between 1908 and 1927.

After World War II, production of automobiles increased rapidly. A car was no longer considered a luxury; it enabled us to move to the suburbs, and was now a necessity. We could go where trains, trolleys, and buses could never take us. The car had become our own personal travel machine. We were on the road, and we would never get off.

1885: Marie Lloyd Debuts. On May 9, 1885, Matilda Alice Victoria Wood, a fifteen-year-old cockney, appears as an extra act at the Grecian Assembly Rooms of London's famous Eagle Tavern. Her two songs are so well received, she is booked again the same night at another nearby hall, and from June on, appears as a regular at the Grecian under the name Marie Lloyd.

Thus began the career of England's most celebrated and beloved music hall performer. A year later she is a star, and at twenty-one, Drury Lane's principal girl. Audiences clamor to see her, and by the end of 1891 she is playing four to five different London halls each night and earning one hundred pounds a week. Her career takes her to South Africa, Berlin, Paris, Melbourne, and the United States. At one point she makes over four hundred pounds a week, an astonishing figure in those days. The poet T. S. Eliot wrote of her, "No other comedian succeeded so well in giving expression to the life of the music hall audience, in raising it to a kind of art. It was, I think, this capacity for expressing the soul of the people that made Marie Lloyd unique."

The famous and beloved entertainer died in 1922, three days after collapsing onstage, ill and overworked. Most of her money had been given to friends in need over the years and to the homeless and destitute. She is remembered as epitomizing the true spirit of the British music halls with such folksy yet saucy songs as "The Boy I Love Is Up in the Gallery," "She'd Never Had Her Ticket Punched Before," and "You're a Thing of the Past, Old Dear."

1886: Soda Pop. This is a big year for the soft drink market. Coca-Cola goes on sale in Atlanta; Moxie in Lowell, Massachusetts; Dr Pepper in Waco, Texas; and Hires root beer goes into bottles.

These concoctions of carbonated water and various dried roots, barks, leaves, and berries are marketed as good for the body and the brain. The bubbly water that fizzes throughout wasn't made commercially until about 1782 in England, and by 1807 the method had traveled overseas to America, where soda water fountains began to appear. Then someone got the bright idea of flavoring the carbonated water, and soon we were swigging sarsaparilla, ginger ale, and root beer, all stirred up for us by a soda jerk. Now there aren't too many places in the world you can go without seeing a sign for Coke.

1889: The Eiffel Tower. Named after its designer, French engineer Alexandre-Gustave Eiffel, the 984-foot-high tower is the centerpiece of the Universal Exhibition in Paris, France, and a triumph of industrial technology. Eiffel, known for his bridge-building techniques, designed the tower as an open-framework latticed-steel girder with vertical diagonal steel bracing. Work began on the tower in January 1887 and was completed in the spring of 1889. It contains more than seven thousand tons of iron, two and a half million rivets, and over eighteen thousand girders and plates. For over forty years the tower was the tallest man-made structure in the world. A television antenna now adds another fifty-five feet to its height.

The most famous symbol of Paris today draws over three million tourists every year who ride to the top to view the vistas of the historic city below.

1889: The Birth of the Movies. From humble beginnings, the motion picture industry has grown into a billion-dollar business, disseminating entertainment and information to hundreds of millions of people around the world. Movies have had a profound influence on society and culture, and probably a greater impact than the invention of the printing press had.

In 1887 Thomas Edison was tinkering with a device in which a series of pictures seem to move when one looked through its peephole. Edison realized that he would need a roll of material in order to make his invention practical. At the same time, George Eastman, a maker of photographic equipment in Rochester, New York, had patented his new system of roller photography for his Kodak camera which would take one hundred pictures on what he called stripping paper. In 1889 Hannibal Goodwin, a clergyman, invented and was granted a patent for a flexible celluloid-based roll of material covered with a film of photographic chemicals. Eastman then manufactured the film, which Edison obtained for his Kinetograph camera to take moving pictures, and his Kinetoscope device, which showed them. On October 6, 1889, he demonstrated his invention at his laboratory in New Jersey. Motion pictures had been born.

The first movie Kinetoscope parlor opened on April 14, 1894, in New York City and showed parts of vaudeville acts and a few rounds of a boxing match. The Kinetoscope proved very popular in penny arcades in the United States as well as in London and Paris. In Europe two French brothers, Louis and Auguste Lumière, built a camera and projector in their photographic equipment factory. On December 28, 1895, they opened their movie show in a room in the Grand Café in Paris and projected various scenes they had taken with their camera. The twenty-minute show was a sensation, and eight weeks later, it opened in London. Their *Cinématographe,* a combination of camera and projector in one compact portable instrument, became the basis of the early film industry. It was an industry that would grow and grow and provide us with some of the greatest entertainment ever seen by the masses.

1889: The Savoy Hotel. Opening on August 6, the Savoy Hotel in London, England, is the first British hotel to include private baths for its guests. The hotel, built of concrete and steel, is also the first fireproof hotel in Britain.

1890: Java Man. Eugene Dubois, a Dutch paleontologist, discovers fossils on the island of Java that scientists call *Pithecanthropus erectus,* or erect ape-man, an extinct species that lived around seven hundred thousand to one million years ago.

1890: Tetanus Vaccine. In 1889 the Japanese bacteriologist Shibasaburo Kitazato, working in Berlin, isolated the tetanus bacilli, and the following year he and Emil von Behring at the Koch Institute develop the first antitoxin.

Tetanus is a deadly disease caused by a bacterial infection that enters the body through wounds or scratches. It is now preventable by vaccination and booster shots every ten years or so.

1891: Basketball. The one sport that can claim it was "made in America" is invented by James Naismith, a physical education instructor at the YMCA Training School in Springfield, Massachusetts.

The marching and calisthenics the students performed in the gymnasium were rather boring, so Naismith was asked to devise a game that would provide no bodily contact, use a lightweight ball, and give each player an equal chance to make plays. Naismith's new game had nine men on each side, and was played with a soccer ball. The object was to throw the ball into an overhead box tied at each end of the gym balcony in order to score a point. Unfortunately, there were no boxes available at the Y, so peach baskets were used instead, which turned out to be fortuitous. The game quickly spread to other YMCAs across the country, and a few years later, was being played worldwide. It also helped increase membership in the YMCA since the Y usually had the only gym in town.

Originally, after scoring a "basket," a player had to climb up a ladder to retrieve the ball. This situation was improved when an iron hoop with a string net attached replaced the peach basket. Then the player just had to reach up and poke the ball back out of the basket, until one day someone got the bright idea of cutting the net so the ball would drop out. By 1895, a basketball screen behind the basket had been erected, mostly to keep spectators in the balcony from batting the ball away from the basket. These, of course, evolved into the backboards now used.

Women started playing basketball a week or so after the first men's game. Teachers from a Springfield grade school played at the Y gym in their long dresses and leg-o'-mutton sleeves and were taught by Naismith, who also refereed. When one of the young ladies did not like a foul called on her, she swore at him, making Naismith the first referee in history to be cursed by a basketball player.

A year after the game was invented, college basketball began, introduced by Springfield YMCA graduates. By now, five players had become the standard, with a center, two forwards, and two guards the rule by 1922. The first officially recognized intercollegiate game was between the University of Chicago and the University of Iowa on January 18, 1896. Chicago won fifteen to twelve, coached by Amos Alonzo Stagg, who is better known as one of the greats of football.

As far as the YMCAs were concerned, Naismith had created a monster. The game was so popular that the Y gyms were being monopolized by basketball players, leaving little room or time for those who wanted to pay fees for calisthenics and gymnastics. Basketball was being banned. Professional basketball was about to be born. Players began renting halls to play in and charging fees to those who wanted to watch.

Meanwhile, college basketball was on the rise, and soon we had tournament play-offs. Coaches and players became famous, and some of them went on to play professionally as new teams were formed.

With the advent of television, basketball, like baseball and football, has become one of our major sports. If Naismith could see the players now, he'd probably wonder why he hadn't placed those peach baskets two feet higher. It's not quite the game he first invented, especially that "no bodily contact" part.

1893: First Ferris Wheel Rides. The Ferris wheel was the talk of the Chicago World's Fair as millions experienced the thrill of riding on the gigantic wheel and gasping at the fairgrounds below. Invented by the American engineer G. W. G. Ferris, the Ferris wheel has become a staple of amusement parks and fairs everywhere. Fun! Fun! Fun!

1895: X rays Developed. Wilhelm Roentgen, a German professor of physics in Würzburg, unintentionally invents the X-ray machine.

Roentgen was devoted to research. The device that intrigued him during the winter of 1895 was the Crookes tube, an early form of cathode-ray tube. When electric current passes through the vacuum tube, a greenish light is emitted. In his darkened lab, with the tube completely closed in a box, Roentgen saw a specially treated paper glowing. The light from the tube was going through the box. The invisible light was also turning photographic plates black. Roentgen decided to develop a plate that had been in his desk drawer, and on it was the image of a key that had been on the top of the desk. While working further with these rays and trying to find a material that would block them, he accidentally photographed part of his hand and saw the bones outlined on the plate. After working for a while to prove what was happening, he shared his secret with his wife. Poor Frau

Roentgen; when she saw the bones of her hand, she thought she was doomed.

The scientific world, however, welcomed Roentgen's X (for "unknown") rays. He had invented one of the most important machines in the advancement of modern medicine. For this he was awarded the first Nobel Prize for physics, in 1901.

Ca. 1896: Fudge. The students at Vassar, Wellesley, Smith, and a few other women's colleges would stay up after hours and "lights out" time to cook up a batch of candy made with sugar, butter, milk, and chocolate. They called it fudge. At the time, the word *fudge* meant to cheat or to talk nonsense, or a hoax. Whatever nonsense they were surreptitiously cooking up, it tasted great, and soon fudge was a popular treat. It's not recorded how their after-hours activities affected their grades. Personally I'd give them all A's.

1896: The Modern Olympics. The ceremonies open with great fanfare as the athletes of all nations march into the stadium, the Olympic flag is raised, the doves of peace are released, the torch is lit, and the oath is pronounced.

"In the name of all competitors, I promise that we will take part in these Olympic Games, respecting and abiding by the rules which will govern them, in the true spirit of sportsmanship, for the glory of sport and for the honor of our teams."

Baron Pierre de Coubertin, a French scholar and educator, is responsible for reviving the Olympic games. The baron thought that by bringing together amateur athletes from all nations of the world, despite religious, racial, political, or class differences, goodwill could be created among all peoples. It was a beautiful idea.

The first modern Olympics were held, fittingly, at Athens, Greece, in April 1896, with athletes from thirteen countries entered in nine sports with forty-three events. For the first time in modern history, a marathon was held and won by a Greek, who brought great honor to his country as well as himself. James Connolly, a student from Harvard and one of the ten Americans to participate, was the first athlete awarded a gold medal when he won the triple jump (hop, step, and jump) with a distance of 44 feet 11¾ inches. Women, true to tradition, were not allowed to be participants. It wasn't until 1912 that women were able to enter the games in swimming and diving only, and in 1928 they were allowed to participate in separate track-and-field events. In fairness, however, women did participate in the tennis and golf competitions in 1900 in Paris.

The Olympics have been held every four years since 1896, with the exception of the World War I and II years of 1916, 1940, and 1944. The winter Olympics were instituted in 1924, and first held in Chamonix, France. Beginning in 1994, although still on a four-year cycle, the Olympics will be held every two years, alternating the winter and summer games. Originally an event for amateurs only, recent changes in the rules now allow for professionals to participate. Long, grueling years of training are endured by those athletes determined to win the gold and the glory that goes with it. And in addition, those advertising contracts that bring in the cash.

Over the years spectators have witnessed countless thrilling events at the Olympics as each year new records are established and unexpected heroes crop up. The games are a place where the impossible dream is attainable, even for the bobsled team from Jamaica.

1896: We Put Motion in Pictures. On the night of April 23, at Koster and Bial's Music Hall on the corner of Thirty-fourth Street and Broadway in New York, something new is added at the end of the vaudeville show. Thomas Edison's Kinetoscope projects moving pictures onto a screen and delights the audience as they watch a few seconds of a boxing match, a dancer twirling, and waves rolling onto a beach. It's the beginning of the movies and the ending of vaudeville.

1897: Electrons Discovered. Joseph John Thomson, an English physicist, announces during a lecture at the Royal Institution that he has discovered particles smaller than the hydrogen atom. We now call them electrons. He will also show that elements not only have atomic weights, but atomic numbers as well, the atomic number being the number of electrons circling the nuclei of the element's atoms. For this important discovery he was awarded the Nobel Prize in physics in 1906. He also got to be buried in Westminster Abbey.

1898: Radium Discovered. Marie and Pierre Curie work together to isolate the first radioactive element, radium. They also discover polonium (which Marie names after her native country, Poland).

Born in Warsaw, Poland, in 1867, Marie was a child prodigy, the daughter of a mathematics and physics teacher. In 1891 she went to Paris to study and attained degrees in physics and mathematics. Pierre Curie, born in 1859, was a mathematical genius who received a science degree at the age of eighteen and became a lab assistant at the Sorbonne. They met in the spring of 1894 and Pierre realized he had met the woman of his dreams, a true genius. They married the following year and worked together happily ever after.

Pierre's work included studies on crystals, magnetism, and radiation. He proved the existence of positive, negative, and neutral particles, later named alpha, beta, and gamma rays. Marie's studies involved radioactivity, particularly in the field of medicine, and her work paved the way for nuclear physics. After Pierre's untimely death, she was appointed to replace him as a professor at the Sorbonne, the first woman to teach there.

Pierre and Marie received the Nobel Prize for physics in 1903, which they shared with Antoine Becquerel, who discovered radioactivity. In 1911 Marie was awarded a second Nobel, this time in chemistry for isolating pure radium.

1898–1923: Rocket Pioneers. Three men during this period published treatises on the possibility of space exploration that laid the foundation for further experimentation.

The Russian mathematician Konstantin Tsiolkovsky published his work, *The Exploration of Cosmic Space by Means of Reaction Motors,* in which he detailed the theory of mass ratio, and the principle of staging booster rockets. He also suggested that liquid propellants such as hydrogen and oxygen would be a more effective fuel than powder.

Robert Hutchings Goddard, called the father of U.S. rocketry, published his work, *A Method of Reaching Extreme Altitudes,* and is famed for his experiments in rocket propulsion and the concept of stages of rockets to reach the moon. NASA's Goddard Space Flight Center in Maryland is named for him.

Hermann Julius Oberth was born in Transylvania, then a part of the Austro-Hungarian Empire, was in their army during World War I, became a German citizen in 1941, moved to Italy after the war, and in 1955 moved to the United States, where he worked in advanced space research for the army. He experimented in weightlessness and designed a long-range rocket propelled by

liquid fuel. His design was scoffed at and his doctoral dissertation
on the subject rejected at Heidelberg. He published his work
himself, which detailed how rocket speed could be achieved in
order to escape the gravitational pull of the earth.

An example of brilliant minds at work.

Ca. 1900: The Paper Clip. The common ordinary paper clip,
which no office can function without, came into being about the
turn of the century. The Norwegian Johan van Vaaler invented a
clip in 1899 and later patented it in the United States. In 1898
an American, Matthew Schooley, was issued a patent for a similar
device. They were the progenitors of our modern clip, although
there seem to have been variations on the device patented around
the same time. In 1899 William Middlebrook of Waterbury, Connecticut, filed a patent for a paper clip machine that apparently
produced the clip as we know it today. The lowly paper clip was
a blessing. It eliminated the rusty pins and pricked fingers associated with fastening batches of papers together.

1900: Knossos Revealed. The archaeologist Schliemann had
shuffled around the stones and boulders on Crete and was convinced a civilization was buried there. In 1900 the English archaeologist Arthur Evans proves he was right when he excavates the
palace of Knossos and a whole Bronze Age civilization. He calls
it Minoan, after the legendary King Minos of Crete. His discoveries are of great importance to the study of early civilizations in
the eastern Mediterranean. For his work, Evans is heaped with
honors, including a knighthood, after which everyone calls him
Sir Arthur.

1900: The Quantum Theory. German physicist Max Planck
radically impacts the science of physics when he expounds his
quantum theory. Planck states that energy is emitted not as a
continuously variable entity, but as discrete units he calls quanta.
His theory greatly influences Einstein and Niels Bohr. It also influences the Nobel committee, who award him the prize for physics in 1918.

1901: Fingerprint Classification Introduced. Scotland
Yard first instituted the Henry System of fingerprint classification
for identifying criminals. It was immediately adopted by law en-

forcement agencies worldwide and is now the most widely used method.

The system was developed by Sir Edward Henry, later chief commissioner of the London metropolitan police, who based his work on the findings of the English anthropologist Sir Francis Galton. Using thorough, systematic observations, Sir Francis verified the fact that identical fingerprints were not inherited but were different for each individual. He suggested a method of classification based on the patterns of arches, loops, and whorls that comprise all prints.

Very early in the twentieth century, fingerprint files were developed in the United States, and in 1924 the Identification Division of the FBI was initiated. Criminal and civil records are filed separately and include fingerprints of all military personnel, federal government employees, people fingerprinted to comply with local requisites, as well as sets of prints voluntarily filed for use in emergency identification. The law enforcement agencies of nearly one hundred countries share in the international exchange of fingerprints with the FBI.

Fingerprints are used during major disasters to identify victims as well as to identify those who have fallen to foul play. And, of course, to tell the good guys from the bad.

1901: Blood Types Discovered. Karl Landsteiner, an Austrian scientist, discovers that human blood is of more than one type. The four classical types are A, B, AB, and O. Each group has specific substances called antigens on the red blood cells.

Landsteiner's discovery made blood transfusions safe. We now knew that in order for a transfusion to be successful, there had to be a blood-type match between donor and recipient. One of the first reports of a successful blood transfusion on record occurred in 1677, when the English physician Richard Lower performed it between two animals, using quills to inject it at first, and later silver tubes. Around the same time, Jean Baptiste Denis, who was French king Louis XIV's private physician, performed the first recorded successful transfusion on a human, using lamb's blood. This seems quite remarkable since we know the blood from one species cannot be transfused into a different species without a reaction, usually a fatal one. It must have been pure luck. Denis tried this a few more times and finally did produce a fatality. He narrowly escaped being tried for murder. Consequently blood transfusions in France, England, and Rome were banned. It was just as well.

Early in the nineteenth century in England the idea was revived when James Blundell, an obstetrician, saved some of his anemic patients. Late in the century better methods of transferring blood had been devised and scientists realized that animal blood could not be used for humans. Deaths still occurred, however, because of the incompatibility of blood types. Landsteiner's discovery solved the problem.

At first, transfusions were made directly, but in 1914 it was found that by adding certain chemicals, the blood could be stored for up to three weeks. Now it is possible to separate blood into components. When whole blood is not needed, the patient receives the necessary component, such as the clotting factor needed by hemophiliacs. Since these separate components can be frozen and stored for long periods of time, one donation can help several patients.

In 1922 Landsteiner joined the Rockefeller Institute in New York, where he worked on viral diseases and immunology and isolated the poliomyelitis virus. He became a United States citizen and in 1930 was awarded the Nobel Prize in medicine.

1903: The Teddy Bear. The most popular children's toy in the early part of the century was the teddy bear, named after President Theodore Roosevelt. The inspiration for the toy came from a cartoon depicting the president, rifle in hand, with his back turned toward a bear cub. Roosevelt, sportsman that he was, had refused to shoot the cub while on a hunting expedition with his hosts in the South. A toy saleman saw the cartoon, made a stuffed bear, placed it in his window, and called it Teddy's Bear. Customers thronged to his store. In the meanwhile, a toy factory in Germany began producing teddy bears after a visiting American inspired by the cartoon, suggested it.

The teddy bear craze swept the world, and soon cuddly bear-type characters were appearing in books such as the classic *Winnie the Pooh*. Even today, it's a rare home that doesn't have a lovable teddy bear tucked away in some corner.

1903: Electrocardiograph Invented. Although great strides have been made in the medical field, this marvelous diagnostic tool is just as important today as when it was first invented. Heart disease is still the number one cause of death in the United States. It had been known for some two hundred years that the body is a good conductor of electricity, thanks to a few courageous souls who linked hands while one was given a shock, and by the 1790s we knew that electricity caused muscles to move. Since the heart is a muscle, electricity must be involved. Electrodes placed on the body proved it in an 1887 experiment. What was needed was a way to chart this electrical activity. The Dutch physiologist Willem Einthoven's first EKG, which recorded the electrical impulses of the heart, was actually something he called a string galvanometer, made from a wire stretched between the poles of a horseshoe magnet.

Today's modern EKG machine is much more streamlined than Einthoven's first invention, but is basically the same. Once a patient's normal readings, called electrocardiograms, are determined, any changes can indicate a problem. The procedure is quick, pain-free, and saves lives. New units are even capable of sending readings over the phone.

For his work, Einthoven was awarded the Nobel Prize in 1924.

1903: Emmeline Pankhurst and the WSPU. Mrs. Pankhurst founds the Women's Social and Political Union on October 10, at her home in Manchester, England.

Emmeline and her friends were incensed. Before the middle of the nineteenth century, women had rarely been treated as equal to men, and their progress was maddeningly slow. Inequality was still rampant because of religious teachings, laws, and just plain prejudice. Women were routinely denied education, worthwhile employment, the right to vote, and even a legal identity. In 1887 married women in England were given the right to own property, but although most adult males could vote, women were still disenfranchised. Emmeline decided militant action was the only way to call attention to this inequity.

Civil disobedience ensued as the ladies of the WSPU not only gave speeches, held rallies, and printed flyers, but heckled male speakers and taunted politicians and made headlines by being thrown out of meetings and arrested. They went on hunger strikes and were force-fed (which injured several women) and were so disruptive that the government raided their headquarters and arrested the suffragist leaders. When World War I erupted, the ladies joined en masse in the war effort, taking over the jobs of men who could then be mobilized. For their contributions, women over thirty were granted suffrage in February 1918, and ten years later with the Representation of the People Act, voting equality was accorded them.

British politics learned a lot from the ladies and would never be the same again. Stereotypes were broken and females were no longer looked upon as submissive creatures. In 1979 Margaret Thatcher was the first woman to become prime minister of Great Britain.

1903: The Airplane.

The morning of December 17 was cold and windy at Kitty Hawk on the Outer Banks of North Carolina. The two brothers from Ohio, Orville and Wilbur Wright, with the help of a few local spectators, pushed their contraption out of its shed and onto the starting rail in the sand. The craft looked like a glider, a biplane with a forty-foot wingspan, weighing 750 pounds. It had two propellers driven by long bicycle chains powered by a twelve-horsepower engine. They called it *The Flyer* and hoped it would live up to its name.

At 10:35 A.M. the audacious Orville climbed into the machine, settled into a prone position, and grasped the controls. The engine revved, Wilbur released the catch holding the craft on the rail, and *The Flyer* moved down the track. The machine was airborne for twelve seconds and landed safely 120 feet away. The men flew their machine three more times that morning, with Wilbur piloting the last flight at noon. He flew 852 feet in fifty-nine seconds. Unfortunately, after the last flight, the wind rolled the aircraft over and badly damaged it. The Wrights went home for Christmas.

The brothers did not invent the airplane, but they were the first to make sustained flights in a plane of their own design and manufacture. As far back as 1799, the British scientist Sir George Cayley, who founded the science of aerodynamics upon which others would build, had sketched a diagram of a fixed-wing craft and knew the forces that would make it fly: thrust, lift, and drag. He built several gliders, including one in 1853 that transported his terrified coachman on the first man-carrying glider in history. The coachman quit his job after that escapade. Cayley knew it would take a lightweight engine to power his gliders and envisioned a whole world of flight. Of course, most people thought he was crazy.

The first man to take off in a steam-engine-powered craft was the Frenchman Clement Ader, on October 9, 1890. He flew about 160 feet a few inches above the ground. There were many other daring young men in flying machines: Alphonse Pénaud of France designed a control column and glass dome for the pilot; the German Otto Lilienthal contributed much to the design of gliders; Samuel Pierpont Langley, an American astronomer, and his assistant, Charles Manly, built several aerodromes (the name he gave to his airplane). One was launched from a houseboat in Virginia in 1896, and flew thirty-three hundred feet under steam power. In October 1903 Manly himself climbed aboard an aerodrome driven by a gas-powered engine that had taken the men several years to develop. He was catapulted off a houseboat and immediately plunked into the Potomac.

We must give great credit to the men of imagination and genius who devoted their lives to developing and manufacturing a craft that could fly in spite of the ridicule and criticism they frequently suffered, and honor the fearless men who flew these early machines and sometimes lost their lives in the experiment.

We gained our technology about flight so rapidly that within a few decades after that windy day at Kitty Hawk, the airplane had become our fastest means of transportation. It was a leap beyond the wildest dreams of all those early visionaries.

1903: *The Great Train Robbery.* For eleven thrill-packed minutes audiences sit spellbound as they watch the first movie Western projected on the screen. In the sensational final close-up, the villain fires his gun directly into the camera, hence seemingly into the audience. People duck, scream, and faint. It makes their day. *The Great Train Robbery* also made the reputation of its director, Edwin S. Porter, and is considered the beginning of the new art of motion pictures.

Ca. 1904: Hamburger on a Bun. The St. Louis World's Fair launched the hamburger as we know it today, although a hamburger steak sandwich had been around for a while. In the Middle Ages the Tartars of Mongolia and the Baltics had shredded raw meat, seasoned it, and eaten it raw. Today we call this concoction steak tartare. By the fourteenth century the poorer German classes were eating it either raw or cooked, and soon the city of Hamburg became famous for serving it. By 1888, hamburger steak made its way to England, where Dr. J. H. Salisbury, a food faddist who taught that shredded food was good for the digestive system, recommended eating it three times a day. It then became known as Salisbury steak. About the same time, hamburger steak reached our shores with the waves of German immigrants, and after the St. Louis Fair, when people ordered a hamburger, they meant a hamburger meat patty on a bun. It wasn't long before hamburgers began to overtake hot dogs in popularity, and soon we were topping them with ketchup or mustard, onions, tomatoes, pickles, and anything else that struck our fancy. Hamburger stands soon opened up around the country, with the White Castle chain an early favorite. Nowadays a yen for your favorite burger can be assuaged at almost any crossroads in America at a variety of hamburger chains. A little child will be happy to accompany you.

1904: Novocain. No one really enjoys a trip to the dentist, but bless the man who introduced Novocain. It was Alfred Einhorn, a German chemist, who synthesized procaine hydrochloride, to come up with this local painkiller. Cocaine had been used as an anesthetic, but Novocain was a safer alternative. Today, although we now have less painful dental techniques and other methods to reduce pain, Novocain is still being used.

1904: Banana Split Created. Strickler's Drug Store in the small town of Latrobe, Pennsylvania, serves the first banana split. The flavor wasn't recorded.

1904: The Yankee Doodle Boy. After two failed efforts in his own Broadway musicals, George M. Cohan stars in *Little Johnny Jones* and receives lukewarm accolades. Two of the songs are hits, however, and become classics: "Give My Regards to Broadway" and "Yankee Doodle Boy."

It was an upbeat time for America, and nobody epitomized it more than George M. Cohan, who was born on the third of July, 1878, into a family of vaudevillians. His musicals were full of patriotism, the joys of city life as opposed to the country, and good old-fashioned values. From 1906 to World War I, Cohan produced a new musical every year, and his song "Over There" became a big hit during the war. Although the critics couldn't understand the popularity of his shows (they were, after all, using artistic criteria), the people loved them and him.

1905: A Permanent Wave. Charles Nestle (real name Karl Ludwig Nessler) introduces his Nestle Wave in his London beauty parlor. What he calls his "Scientific Everlasting Wave" takes six to twelve hours during which strands of hair are wound around metal rods, covered with a paste, inserted into tubes, and steamed in a Hydra-like contraption.

What women won't do for curls! Nestle left England for the United States and opened a shop in New York in 1915, by which time his "Everlasting Wave" was much quicker and cheaper and also all the rage.

1906: Hot Dog! Wow! That's what the expression means to us. We can thank Hearst newspaper cartoonist Tad Dorgan for the expression and for naming one of our favorite foods. After hearing vendors at baseball games hawking "red-hot dachshund sausages," he drew a cartoon depicting a dachshund on a bun and captioned it "Get your hot dogs." Before they were hot dogs, they were frankfurters, franks, wieners, and dachshund sausages.

As far back as 1500 B.C., sausages were eaten by the Babylonians, who stuffed spiced meat into the intestines of animals. Sausages of various kinds were also eaten by the Greeks and Romans and others throughout history. By the Middle Ages sausage making was practically an art form, with butchers' guilds in various cities developing their own recipes, shapes, and sizes. Sausages from countries in warmer climates were hard and dry, what we call salami; in Scotland, oatmeal was used as a filler, mixed with the meat; from Vienna we get wiener wurst. It was in Frankfurt, in 1852, that the spicy, smoked thinner sausage, packed in a curved transparent casing, was introduced and called, appropriately enough, a frankfurter. Because they remotely resembled the shape of a German dachshund, they were called dachshund sausages.

It was Coney Island in New York that made the hot dog so famous. Charles Feltman was so successful selling frankfurter sandwiches topped with mustard and sauerkraut from a cart along the boardwalk that he was able to open up a restaurant. In 1916 one of his employees, Nathan Handwerker, left to open a stand of his own using a spiced-meat recipe developed by his wife, and sold his frankfurters at half the price of Feltman's. Nathan's Coney Island hot dog stand soon became a landmark.

Even though hot dogs as we know them originated in Germany, they have become associated with the all-American sport of baseball. No game is complete without one.

1906: The Forward Pass. Football was such a savage game of brute force and constant pounding that President Theodore Roosevelt became so incensed after one game that he threatened to ban it altogether. The colleges then "cleaned up their act," so to speak, and abolished some of the more dangerous plays. They also legalized the forward pass, which changed the entire game. Although not readily accepted, the forward pass came into its own during the 1913 game between a powerhouse Army team and a small unknown school in Indiana. Two team members from this underdog college had been practicing passing the football all summer, then taught it to a third team member in the fall. When the two teams met, it was the forward pass that defeated Army thirty-five to thirteen, put a triumphant Notre Dame on the map, and added skill to football. By the way, the team members who accomplished this feat were quarterback Gus Dorias, the back, Pliska, and an end by the name of Knute Rockne.

1906: Equal Suffrage in Finland. The first European country to give women the right to vote is Finland during their parliamentary elections in 1906.

1908: Portable Vaccum Cleaners. James Murray Spangler patents his new invention, the "electric suction sweeper," and sells the rights to William Hoover.

Since necessity is the mother of invention, it was essential that James Spangler invent a suction-type carpet cleaner. He was a down-on-his-luck tinkerer who had taken a job in an Ohio department store to pay his bills. The enormous, clumsy suction carpet sweeper that he used roused more dirt and dust than it picked up and aggravated his chronic lung ailment. So he began to tinker once again and came up with a portable "electric suction sweeper" made from a soapbox, a set of wheels, the roller brush from a carpet sweeper, a pillowcase, and a small motor from an electric fan. It worked so well that he tried to form a company to make and sell his new design. Alas, money problems once more beset him, but help came in the form of William Hoover, whose wife had seen one of these machines. Hoover, a maker of saddles and leather goods for horses, realizing that the horseless carriage would soon make his business obsolete, knew a good thing when he saw one and promptly negotiated with Spangler for the rights to manufacture his invention.

The "Hoovering" of America had been launched. Out went the brooms and sometimes the carpet sweepers as millions of American housewives clamored for the new invention that would remove dust quickly and easily from their homes. Spring cleaning would never be such a chore again.

1909: The Toaster. Since the fourteenth century the English had been attaching pieces of bread to long-handled forks and toasting it over a fire. In 1909 the General Electric Company marketed a simple device of bare wires wrapped around mica strips, but it only toasted one side at a time. It wasn't until 1927 that we had a pop-up toaster, then later a two-slice toaster, followed by a toaster for four slices at once, for the large family. Now we have toasters with wide slots for bagels, pastries, and Pop-Tarts. It sure beats holding a fork over a flame.

1909: Peary Reaches the North Pole. After several years of exploring the vast lands of the Arctic, Robert E. Peary, accompanied by his aide, Matthew Henson, and four Eskimos, reaches the North Pole by dogsled on April 6.

1911: Keystone Company Founded. Mack Sennett, a thirty-one-year-old Canadian-American, leaves D. W. Griffith at Biograph Studios in New York to found his own company in Glendale, California.

Sennett, a former circus and burlesque performer, had been an actor and writer under Griffith, from whom he learned movie technique. He was soon producing hilarious slapstick comedies featuring his Keystone Kops and his daring Bathing Beauties. His movies cranked up the careers of some of Hollywood's best-known early comedians, including Harold Lloyd, "Fatty" Arbuckle, Ben Turpin, Charlie Chaplin, Buster Keaton, and W. C. Fields. It was Mabel Normand who threw the first custard pie in the face of Ben Turpin in a 1915 film. In 1914 Sennett produced the first Hollywood feature-length comedy, *Tillie's Punctured Romance,* starring Chaplin, Normand, Marie Dressler, Chester Conklin, and the Keystone Kops.

His pictures, frequently improvised to take advantage of the events of the day, were often parodies or satires ridiculing the imperfections of society. It was Sennett's comedies that brought audiences to theaters in droves and made "Hollywood" a household word. The advent of sound and the Wall Street crash of 1929 that reduced his personal fortune led to Sennett's retirement in 1933. In 1937 he was given a special award by the Academy of Motion Picture Arts and Sciences for "his lasting contribution to the comedy technique of the screen."

1911: *Vitamines* Introduced. Casimir Funk, a twenty-seven-year-old Polish biochemist at London's Lister Institute, coins the word *vitamines*.

Vitamins are chemical substances needed by our bodies in various amounts for tissue repair, growth, and health. Although the body itself makes some vitamins, the amounts are not usually adequate and other vitamins must come from one's diet or supplements. So far about twenty-five vitamins have been discovered, and it is believed there may be more.

In the early days of exploration, many sailors were lost to a disease we now know as scurvy. Bleeding gums, loose teeth, and other symptoms plagued every voyage. A Scottish naval surgeon, James Lind, considered a quack by his fellow physicians, discovered that citrus fruit could prevent and even cure the disease, and published his findings in 1753. Captain James Cook, the inveterate explorer, prevented scurvy among his men by feeding them citrus fruit (which is why British sailors are called "limeys"), sauerkraut, wild celery, and "scurvy grass." It was this grass that set Lind on his research. A sick sailor, put ashore on a desert island by a captain desperate to save the rest of his crew, began eating the grasses, recovered, and made his way home on a passing ship to tell his story. Lind's experiments not only proved the need for vitamin C, but showed that other diseases were also the results of vitamin deficiencies.

Frederick Hopkins, a British scientist and 1929 Nobelist, is given credit for developing the concept of vitamins. Albert Szent-Györgyi, a Hungarian-American biochemist, succeeded in isolating a goodly amount of the substance we know as ascorbic acid, or vitamin C, from such vegetables as red peppers and cabbage. Szent-Györgyi also discovered riboflavin (B_2) in animal tissues and a substance he named vitamin P. He was a 1937 Nobelist for medicine and physiology.

In 1912 water-soluble B was discovered, and in 1934, B complex. Several scientists came up with Vitamin A in 1913, and in 1922 vitamin D came to light. That same year vitamin E was found in certain foods, and vitamin K was discovered in the 1930s.

Although some in the medical community scoff at the vitamin concept and believe a balanced diet is sufficient to supply the necessary vitamins, others believe supplements are needed for a variety of reasons. In the meantime, drink your juice and eat your veggies.

1911: The Race for the South Pole. In an attempt to be the first to reach the South Pole, five countries, Norway, Germany, Australia, Japan, and Great Britain, embark on expeditions. The honor belongs to the veteran Norwegian polar explorer Roald Amundsen, who reached it on December 14. Amundsen had previously been to the Antarctic and through the Northwest Passage. After learning that Peary had reached the North Pole, Amundsen, who was about to leave for the Arctic, secretly changed his plans and headed south, determined to reach the pole there. He took his ship to the Ross Sea and established a base camp inland. From there he and four companions made the audacious journey by dogsled and planted the Norwegian flag at the South Pole.

About the same time, British explorer Robert F. Scott, with his party of five, also headed for the pole. Delayed by severe weather, they reached their destination a month after Amundsen. Unfortunately, illness and bad weather prevented them from returning to their base and they perished in the Antarctic.

With the discovery of the North and South Poles and the explorations of these polar expanses, the last unknown regions of the earth had been conquered. We must admire these bold adventurers who, for whatever motives, sailed into unknown seas and across great wildernesses to chart the earth as we know it today.

1912: The Piltdown Man. The fossilized remains of the so-called missing link in the evolution of humans are discovered on Piltdown Common near Lewes, England. The find causes a big uproar in paleontology, but a few scientists are skeptical. By 1959, however, enough tests had been done on the remains to conclude that they were a forgery. It remains the biggest joke ever perpetrated on the scientific community.

1912: Tying Up Loose Ends. French-born physician Alexis Carrel, practicing in the United States, is awarded the Nobel Prize in physiology and medicine for developing a technique using sutures to close blood vessels.

Ancient Greek writings tell of using the strings of musical instruments made of catgut to tie off blood vessels. Catgut is from the intestines of animals—usually sheep, not cats—and was used in surgery because it dissolved in the tissues. The Greek physician Galen used it in the second century, but it went in and out of use, being rediscovered every hundred years or so. The French surgeon Ambroise Paré revived the ancient technique in 1552 during battlefield surgery. Cauterization was the usual means of sealing blood vessels, but the shock of the searing pain caused many deaths. When the English physician Joseph Lister began his work in the 1850s, threads or metal wires were used, with the ends left outside the body to be pulled out if infection occurred, which it usually did. With Lister's antiseptic surgical techniques, the incision, though not infected, would have to be reopened to remove the sutures. Lister, to avoid the problem, wanted a suture that would dissolve and remembered catgut. In 1868 he began to experiment with catgut, looking for a way to sterilize it. He used carbolic acid, then saturated the sutures with salts of chromic acid to make them last longer and give more time for healing.

Nowadays, with antiseptic surgery, other methods of suturing are available. Catgut, however, remains in use as the preferred suture in many cases.

1913: The Refrigerator. The Domerle, the first electric household refrigerator, is manufactured in Chicago and is very expensive.

Most families had an icebox, and ice was delivered to households once or twice a week by the ice man. As the ice melted, it would flow into the drip pan under the icebox and would have to be emptied daily. A messy situation, but it kept the milk cool. And if you wanted small pieces of ice, you would have to hack away at the big block with an ice pick.

In 1918 General Motors marketed the Frigidaire, and the name soon became a household word. It wasn't until about 1930, though, that refrigerators became affordable for the average family. Now every home has one and we take it for granted. On hot summer days we just pop a few ice cubes into a cold drink and think nothing of it. Of course, it may not be as much fun as trying to snitch a few pieces from the ice man's truck.

1913: Higher and Larger. The sixty-story Woolworth Building opens in the spring in lower Manhattan, making it the world's tallest. On lower Broadway the Equitable Building is under construction, which, when completed in 1915, will contain 1.2 million square feet of floor space, the largest office building ever.

1913: The Crossword Puzzle. Simple crossword puzzles had appeared in England in the nineteenth century, but on December 21, 1913, the first puzzle is published in the United States in *Fun*, the Sunday supplement of the *New York World*. Within ten years crossword puzzles are being published in almost all newspapers across the country as more and more people became addicted to the mental gymnastics and fun of solving them.

1913: A Hospital in Lambaréné. Alsatian-born Dr. Albert Schweitzer and his wife, Helene Breslau, a scholar and nurse, traveled to Gabon in Africa to build a hospital and provide medical services for the natives.

At the age of thirty-eight, Dr. Schweitzer had already made a mark for himself in the academic world. He had a doctorate in theology and philosophy and had written several acclaimed books, including *The Quest of the Historical Jesus*. While he was teaching and writing, he was also studying music and eventually became an eminent organist, known for his interpretation of the music of Bach, about whom he wrote a definitive biography in French and later in German. All this was not enough, however, for Schweitzer felt he had a mission to accomplish in life. He dropped his university appointments and entered medical school, where, for the next six years, he studied medicine and surgery. The following year he left for French Equatorial Africa, where he and his wife would spend the rest of their lives tending to the needs of the sick.

The hospital site was donated by the Paris Missionary Society, but it was maintained by royalties on Dr. Schweitzer's books as well as fees from his lectures and organ recitals. As his reputation grew and his work became known, people and foundations from many countries began funding the hospital, also. While supplying much-needed medical care to the local peoples, Dr. Schweitzer kept up his writings and his music with seemingly endless energy.

For his devotion to a cause, his philosopy of "reverence for life," and his appeals for peace in the world, Dr. Schweitzer was awarded the 1952 Nobel Peace Prize. He died in 1965, at the age of ninety, and was buried in Lambaréné, where his hospital had grown to the size of a village, with a large staff that included white and black doctors, nurses, and aides. He will be remembered as a true humanitarian as well as a genius.

1913: The Sixteenth Constitutional Amendment. This was declared ratified on February 25, 1913, and reads in part, "The Congress shall have power to lay and collect taxes on incomes, from whatever source derived . . ." If you don't think this belongs in a book for optimists, look around you and see what you get for your money. Not a bad deal.

1913: The Little Tramp. Mack Sennett, producer of the Keystone Comedies, signs Charles Spencer Chaplin to a $150-a-week contract. It marks the beginning of the film career that will make Charlie Chaplin an international star and one of the great geniuses of comedy.

The filmmaker discovered the twenty-four-year-old Chaplin while the English music hall entertainer was touring with the Karno Company in New York. Chaplin put together the outfit for which he became famous from the Keystone wardrobe and prop departments and wore it in his second comedy, *Kid Auto Races at Venice*. In 1915 he first portrayed the humorous and pathetic "little tramp" in the movie *The Tramp*. He quickly soared to stardom, and so did his salary. In 1917 he signed the first million-dollar movie contract for eight pictures with First National, making him the highest-paid star in Hollywood. After that, nobody could afford him, so two years later, along with Mary Pickford, Douglas Fairbanks, and D. W. Griffith, he formed United Artists to produce and distribute independent films. Chaplin wrote, directed, and starred in his pictures, which have become classic. The little tramp appeared in such films as *The Gold Rush, City Lights, Modern Times,* and *The Great Dictator,* his first talkie.

Comedians come and go, but the cocky little fellow with a mustache in tight coat, baggy trousers, and bowler, twirling his cane as he waddles down the street, has endured. Perhaps it's because we see a little of ourselves in him.

1914: Traffic Signals. The first red and green traffic lights begin operation in Cleveland, Ohio. In the early 1920s, the first automatic signals with red, yellow, and green lights will be erected in Detroit, Michigan, home of the industry that required the need for them in the first place.

1914: Air-Conditioning Arrives. We all complain about the heat, but Willis Carrier did something about it. Using his engineering talent, Carrier transformed a steam heater to use cold water, then circulated the cooled air by fans, which also removed the humidity. Although the first air conditioners were used for industrial purposes, air-conditioning soon spread to the new movie houses that were opening up, and from there to office buildings. After World War II, air-conditioning in the United States took hold, and all new office buildings and most new residences were equipped with a central air-conditioning system. And now so are our autos. One of the comforts of life.

1915: Einstein's Theory of Relativity. In 1905 Albert Einstein, a German-born Swiss, was working in the Swiss patent office in Berne. He had been unable to find a teaching job after receiving his degree in physics and mathematics and a Ph.D. from the University of Zurich. His job was not particularly inspiring and left him plenty of time to meditate on theoretical problems in physics, which had always intrigued him. His cogitations paid off and in one year he published four papers, including his famous special theory of relativity. In this theory he states that the speed of light is the same for all observers whether they are on the earth or on a distant galaxy and that the speed of light in the universe is fixed; nothing can go faster and nothing will be seen moving faster. He also stated that any form of energy has mass (mass is a quantity of matter; matter is the substance objects are composed of; an object is anything that occupies space and can be a gas, liquid, or solid) and that matter is a form of energy. From this came the celebrated equation $E=mc^2$. E represents energy (measured in ergs), m represents mass (measured in grams), and c is the speed of light in centimeters per second. The formula illustrates that even a small amount of mass can supply a tremendous amount of energy.

In 1916 Einstein, by now a professor at the University of Berlin, publishes his general theory of relativity, which deals with accelerated motion and gravity and the curvature of space.

Einstein became a member of the Institute for Advanced Study in Princeton, New Jersey, in 1933, and seven years later was granted United States citizenship. For his inestimable contributions to physics he received the Nobel Prize in 1925. He also had a newly discovered element named in his honor in 1953, einsteinium.

1915: The Babe. On May 16, 1915, twenty-year-old George Herman "Babe" Ruth hit his first home run for the Boston Red Sox. In 1920 the Babe became a Yankee and batted himself into history.

1916: The Supermarket. The Piggly Wiggly markets were the first self-serve grocery stores in the United States. The first one was established in Memphis, Tennessee, by Clarence Saunders, and by 1929 there were three thousand of these markets in eight hundred cities across the country. At the same time, grocery chains such as the Great Atlantic and Pacific Tea Company (A&P) were springing up, and many of them bought the Piggly Wiggly stores for their own grocery business. The new stores were referred to as supermarkets by Californians, and soon we were all calling them by that name.

Supermarkets, with everything under one roof, changed the way we shopped. No more did we have to tote our shopping bags daily to the butcher, the baker, the greengrocer, or the dairy. With the advent of refrigerators and freezers, we could now shop once or twice a week for all our groceries and find everything conveniently in one place.

1916: Griffith's Masterpiece. The creative genius of director D. W. Griffith triumphs in his movie *Intolerance,* regarded as his greatest film and one of the greatest films ever. The movie weaves together tales from four periods in history to demonstrate the evils of intolerance and contemplates the day when "perfect love shall bring peace forever."

1916: The Imperial Hotel. Designed by American architect Frank Lloyd Wright, the Imperial Hotel in Tokyo, Japan, opens. The sprawling hotel, with its floating cantilever construction, is so well engineered, it is the only large building to remain intact and survive the great Tokyo earthquake of 1923.

1916: Margaret Sanger Opens Clinic. The first birth control clinic opens in Brooklyn, New York, on October 16.

The Comstock Law of 1873, named for the antivice crusader and professional reformer Anthony Comstock, had classified contraceptives as obscene and prohibited contraceptive information from being sent through the mails. As a nurse on the Lower East Side of New York City, Margaret had seen poor and uneducated women living in squalid conditions, exhausted from giving birth to too many children who were frequently neglected or died, and many women who were the victims of venereal disease. She became determined to fight for the right of every woman to control the size of her family and to legalize contraception. She traveled around the United States to gather support for her endeavors and made trips to Holland, England, and France to bring back contraceptive techniques, which she disseminated in pamphlets.

Margaret was arrested for opening her clinic and "maintaining a public nuisance," and arrested several more times for her activities along with Ethel Byrne, her associate, whose hunger strike created a great deal of publicity until the governor released her. Thanks to Margaret Sanger, the Comstock Law was modified and the United States Circuit Court of Appeals permitted physicians to prescribe contraceptives ". . . for the purpose of saving life or promoting the well-being of patients." In the 1920s clinics opened throughout the country after Margaret Sanger won her fight to improve basic human rights for women. She devoted the rest of her life to her cause and aided in forming what would become, in 1942, the Planned Parenthood Federation of America and was the first president of the International Planned Parenthood Federation, organized in 1953.

Ca. 1918: The Jazz Age Begins. The American novelist F. Scott Fitzgerald coined the term in his 1922 book *Tales of the Jazz Age,* but the era began before the twenties.

The term *jazz* was known in the 1870s in New Orleans, where jazz music, a style of syncopated ragtime improvisational music, had its beginnings. There is no doubt it had strong African ties, its first breath coming to life in the music of the African slaves brought to America by traders. There were also strong Spanish, French, and Caribbean influences incorporated into the style. First thought of as strictly black music and played in New Orleans's Storyville district, jazz became popular with whites in the early twentieth century, and reached its peak in the "roaring twenties." Some jazz aficionados, however, claim this wasn't great jazz but a lukewarm, watered-down, socially acceptable version fit for the big-city ballrooms.

When Harlem got hold of it, jazz soared to new and wondrous heights. Songs like "Minnie the Moocher" and artists like Cab Calloway gained fame and popularity. Jazz produced many great performers and composers, such as W. C. Handy, Billie Holiday, Bessie Smith, Louis Armstrong, Paul Whiteman, Dizzy Gillespie, and Duke Ellington, just to name a few.

In the 1940s and 1950s cool jazz, or progressive jazz, came to the fore with orchestrated music for small groups whose improvisations were not only thematic but modal. New names appeared, such as Miles Davis, Thelonius Monk, and John Coltrane.

Today jazz, ragtime, bop, and blues, America's great contributions to the world of music, continue to draw new fans to their captivating rhythms, and new musicians to improvise on them.

1918: Wilson's Fourteen Points. In a speech to a joint session of Congress on January 8, 1918, United States president Woodrow Wilson outlines his fourteen points for a post–World War I peace settlement. His last point suggested a "general association of Nations" with power for maintaining peace and security throughout the world. It was the basis for the formation of the League of Nations and for its successor, the United Nations.

1919: Two National Parks. In 1908 President Theodore Roosevelt created the Grand Canyon National Monument in order to protect it against land speculators, and in 1919 an act of Congress established Grand Canyon National Park. The park encompasses 673,575 acres of land, providing the public with some of the most awesome and spectacular scenery in the world. The same year Congress also established the 147,035-acre Zion National Park in Utah, another place of beauty and wonder.

1920: Prohibition. January 16, 1920, is the beginning of Prohibition, a date that will live in infamy (with apologies to Franklin D. Roosevelt). The Eighteenth Amendment states, ". . . The manufacture, sale, or transportation of intoxicating liquors within, the importation thereof into, or the exportation thereof from the United States . . . for beverage purposes is hereby prohibited."

The Woman's Christian Temperance Union had won its battle to rid society of demon rum. The Volstead Act, passed on October 28, 1919, provided for enforcing the amendment that had been ratified in January of that year and specified fines and punishments for breaking the law.

Prohibition was somewhat effective and the consumption of alcohol fell. Sales of coffee, tea, soda, and ice cream increased, much to the delight of the purveyors of those items. On the dark side, bootleggers prevailed and organized crime increased.

Legislating morality proved difficult for the federal government, and some Americans wanted revisions to allow wine and beer to be legalized, if not hard liquor. Society and its values were changing; there were those who feared the federal government had overstepped its powers. When the depression hit, it was argued that repeal would provide jobs for many, and taxes on liquor would fill empty coffers. Finally, in 1933, the Twenty-first Amendment repealed the Eighteenth, and Prohibition ended. The states, however, still have the right to control liquor and pass laws regarding its manufacture, sale, and consumption.

1920: Nineteenth Amendment Ratified. Twenty-eight words end years of struggle for women's suffrage. *The right of citizens of the United States to vote shall not be denied or abridged by the United States or by any state on account of sex.*

We thank all of those who exercised their right of free assembly and marched for the vote, especially Carrie Chapman Catt, president of the National American Woman Suffrage Association. You did a fantastic job, ladies!

1921: Band-Aids. Johnson & Johnson begins producing small adhesive bandages invented by one of their employees.

Is there a household that doesn't have a box of Band-Aids? This simple but useful—in fact, downright necessary—item was devised by Earle Dickson, a buyer at Johnson & Johnson, manufacturers of antiseptic surgical dressings. It seems Dickson's wife was accident-prone, constantly nicking and burning herself in the kitchen, and her husband was endlessly bandaging her mistakes. He cut a small piece of gauze from a sterile surgical dressing, put it in the middle of an adhesive strip, and taped it over his wife's wound. When the company president learned of Dickson's method of covering these minor cuts and burns, he was so impressed that he immediately began producing them.

It took a push by the company's marketing department before they gained popularity, but once the public read how Band-Aids would promote healing and prevent infection, they began to sell. More than one hundred billion Band-Aids have been sold since they were introduced. They now come in several different sizes and colors and even with cute designs on them. How fortunate for us that Mr. Dickson's wife was such a klutz in the kitchen.

1921: Chanel No. 5 Introduced. On May 5 the innovative French designer Coco Chanel presents her new perfume, which will eventually become the world's top-selling fragrance.

Perfumes have been with us since at least 4000 B.C. The Chinese burned pleasant-smelling incense with their religious offerings long before this time, and it's from this smoky act that we get our word *perfume,* from the Latin *per,* "through," and *fumus,* "smoke." Archaeologists have discovered dried remnants of aromatic oils in jars at sites everywhere from Egypt and the Middle East to Greece and Rome. Even the Bible, in Exodus 30, gives formulas for making incense and for perfume using myrrh, cinnamon, sweet calamus, cassia, and olive oil, although these were to be used for holy purposes only. The Greeks and Romans studied perfume making and spread their fragrances wherever they went, but as the Roman Empire declined, such indulgences as baths and perfume dropped out of favor, leaving it up to the Persians and Arabs to carry on the trade.

It wasn't until the Middle Ages and the return of the Crusaders from the East that perfumes returned to Europe with them. In 1533, when the Florentine Catherine de Médicis married the future Henry II of France, she brought her perfumes and perfume makers with her (along with other things like broccoli, the double boiler, and macaroons), and the French perfume industry was off to a great start. This was very fortunate since bathing was not an accepted practice; all those perfumed handkerchiefs weren't just for show. By the eighteenth century the flower industry was blooming in France, all for the sake of extracting the oils used in producing fragrances.

Nowadays as many as three hundred ingredients may be found in one formula, which may take years to perfect. Catherine probably wouldn't have wanted to wait that long.

1921: Baseball Is On the Air. On August 25 station KDKA in Pittsburgh broadcasts the first baseball game on radio. The Pittsburgh Pirates beat the Philadelphia Phillies, eight to one. In 1924, WMAQ in Chicago began broadcasting season games regularly.

1921: World Series Broadcast. The first World Series to be broadcast is announced on radio station WJZ, in Newark, New Jersey. The New York Giants beat the New York Yankees, five to three.

1921: Sweden Abolishes Capital Punishment. Sweden takes a stand on human rights and abolishes capital punishment for peacetime offenses.

In a further affirmation of human life, the government will ban the death penalty for wartime crimes in 1972. Sweden's philosophy of punishment is based on reforming offenders by providing them with vocational training and helping them to make a new start after they have served their sentences. An enlightened form of justice.

1922: Ur Uncovered. English archaeologist Leonard Woolley discovers the ancient city of Ur, originally founded nearly six thousand years ago. The site of the capital of the early Sumerian kings is located in the southern part of what is now Iraq. The first settlement predates the flood described in the Bible, and continued excavations of the area uncover several dynasties and civilizations which lasted throughout history until about 300 B.C. Woolley's excavations brought to life a people and sophisticated culture about which little was known except in legends.

1922: Tut's Tomb. The British archaeologist Howard Carter, with wealthy art collector Lord Carnarvon, had been digging in the Valley of the Kings near Luxor, Egypt, for several years. From the few artifacts that had been discovered, Carter was almost certain the tomb of a king known as Tutankhamen was somewhere in the area. The last big job had been to clear away rubble around Ramses VI's tomb, which had previously been excavated (and found to have been looted). At the foot of the tomb was a group of workmen's huts along with more rubble. Carter and Carnarvon had decided that they would spend one more winter excavating and then call it quits.

And so it was that on the morning of November 3, Carter started tearing down the huts. As the soil was removed, a stone step was discovered. Two days later, after clearing away more rubble, Carter realized he was standing before the entrance to a royal tomb. He wired Carnarvon, who was in England, and on November 23 the Englishman and his daughter arrived in Luxor. The next day, after the stone steps had been entirely cleared of debris, Carter read the name of the royal seal. It was, indeed, that of Tutankhamen. But from the appearance of the doorway, he realized that robbers had been there before him.

The following days were spent in clearing the passageway inside the tomb, which led to a second door. It was through a hole in this door that Howard Carter by candlelight peered into the tomb and glimpsed one of the greatest finds in all archaeology. When the door was opened several days later, a treasure trove of antiquities surrounded them: golden couches and a gilded throne, alabaster vases and shrines, replicas of animals, royal statues covered in gold. But no sarcophagus. The task of identifying and removing all the items in the tomb was daunting and would take several seasons of work by archaeologists and specialists. Finally the antechamber was cleared and another door, which had been discovered previously, could now be opened. Again, Carter carefully opened up a hole in the door and shone a flashlight through it. All he saw was another wall, this one of solid gold. When the door was opened, the wall proved to be a shrine, and beyond that, the untouched tomb of the king. Within the yellow quartzite sarcophagus was a coffin on which a golden mask of the boy-king was placed, with a wreath of flowers still on the forehead. Within a third coffin was the mummy itself, wrapped in linen cloth interspersed with jewels. He had lain there undisturbed for over three thousand years.

King Tutankhamen still lies in his stone sarcophagus in his tomb in the hot Egyptian desert. The young king, who died when he was about eighteen, was a minor ruler of no significance in Egyptian history. Ironically, the discovery of his intact tomb catapulted him to a fame no other pharaoh has ever achieved. And the contents of his tomb provided archaeologists and historians with a wealth of knowledge about Egypt that has never been surpassed. Most of the treasure can be seen in the National Museum in Cairo, where a whole room is devoted to Tut.

1922: Nansen Awarded Nobel Peace Prize. Fridtjof Nansen, Norwegian explorer, zoologist, university professor, oceanographer, artist, writer, and statesman, is awarded the Nobel Prize for his great humanitarian efforts. He donates the money to international relief work.

Nansen was involved in the dissolution of the union between Sweden and Norway, about which he stated, "Any union in which the one people is restrained in exercising its freedom is and will remain a danger." Norway gained its independence, became a monarchy, and Nansen was appointed minister to London.

After World War I, he headed the delegation to the League of Nations and was chosen to negotiate with Russia for the return of half a million sick and starving prisoners from the former German and Austro-Hungarian armies. The Soviet government refused to recognize the League of Nations, but did negotiate personally with Nansen, who succeeded in his task. Appointed a high commissioner for the Red Cross, he next took on the job of bringing relief to millions starving in Russia as well as aiding refugees in Europe, many of whom were victims of the Russian Revolution. In 1922 in Geneva, displaced persons were issued identification cards called "Nansen passports," which were recognized by over fifty governments. Through his efforts, thousands were resettled as well as given jobs and food.

His philosophy of "Always look forward, never back" served him and millions of others very well.

1922: Insulin. The story of insulin begins in 1869 when a young German medical student, Paul Langerhans, discovers tiny cells in the human pancreas that are different from any others. These cells would later be named "islets of Langerhans" after their discoverer, and the secretions (termed *hormones* in 1904) they produce would be called *insuline*.

In 1922 Canadian researchers James Banting and Charles Best, in the laboratories of J. J. MacLeod, isolate the hormone and save the life of a patient, after injecting themselves with the insulin to prove its safety. They had developed a new treatment for diabetes that would save millions. For their efforts McLeod and Banting will receive the Nobel Prize for medicine in 1923, which Banting then shared equally with Best.

1923: Work Hours Reduced. On August 2 United States Steel, the largest corporation in America, reduces its twelve-hour workday to eight hours. It will soon be the norm.

1924: Disposable Tissues Marketed. This now indispensable absorbent cottonlike material was first used as bandages and as air filters in gas masks when cotton was in short supply during World War I. After the war, the manufacturer found itself with a large supply still on hand, and advertised it as a disposable facial towel good for removing makeup. Americans soon found out it had another use, for blowing one's nose. It was more sanitary than a handkerchief and better than one's sleeve. Of course, tissues made the old "drop your handkerchief" flirting ploy passé.

1924: Native Americans Declared Citizens. By act of Congress on June 15, 1924, all Indians born in the United States are declared citizens, with the right of participation in the government.

1925: Frozen Foods. Clarence Birdseye and Charles Seabrook patent a process for freezing cooked foods that will eventually revolutionize the way we store foods and eat.

The idea of frozen food had occurred to Sir Francis Bacon, the Elizabethan philosopher and man of letters, who, about three hundred years before, had tried stuffing a goose with snow to see if it would keep. Unfortunately more than the goose got chilled, and Sir Francis and his experiment came to a dead end. Birdseye had more luck. He was a young American fur trader in Labrador, which is a lot colder than England, and observed that a fish caught through the ice froze immediately and would be just as fresh when it was thawed out and cooked weeks later. So back to New York went Clarence to figure out how this could be done outside of Labrador. Birdseye opened a small freezing plant to process and sell his frozen foods, but the public wasn't too eager to buy. Retailers didn't always have the facilities to keep the food packages frozen, and many homes had no place to store them. It wasn't until 1929, when the Postum Company merged with Birdseye to create General Foods, that Birdseye Frozen Foods found a commercial market.

In the 1950s the ubiquitous Swanson's TV dinners appeared, all-in-one meals packed in an aluminum tray that need only be heated in the oven, cutting out all that food-preparation time.

Now we can zap our frozen dinners in the microwave during the commercial and not miss a thing.

1925: Locarno Pact. Agreed upon on October 16, 1925, in Locarno, Switzerland, the pact among several European nations guaranteed the post–World War I boundaries between Belgium, France, and Germany, and attempted to assure disputes would be solved by arbitration and peaceful means. By agreeing to the stipulations, Germany was accepted into the United Nations.

If at first you don't succeed, try, try, again.

1925: The Motel. On December 12, in San Luis Obispo, California, the Motel Inn opens, accommodating 160 guests. It is the first of a new type of lodging catering to motorists, who no longer need to hurry to the city to find a hotel room for the night. The motel, a combination of the words *motor* and *hotel,* will slowly appear on busy highways across the country and be called a motor lodge, motor court, motor inn, and tourist court, but *motel* becomes the generic term we use the most. By the mid-1960s, there were approximately forty thousand motels dotting the highways and byways of the United States, lodging our peripatetic citizenry on business and vacation travel.

1926: Morgan's Gene Theory. United States biologist Thomas Hunt Morgan publishes his *The Theory of the Gene,* proving the chromosome theory of heredity. His works earn him the Nobel Prize in 1933.

1927: Showboat Opens. The first collaboration between lyricist Oscar Hammerstein II and composer Jerome Kern is a smash hit when it opens at the Ziegfeld Theater on December 27, and sets a new standard for musicals. Kern had written some of the great songs for the stage, but his idea that "musical numbers should carry the action of the play and should be representative of the personalities of the characters who sing them," rather than standing alone, had always been sloughed off by producers. With *Showboat,* however, based on Edna Ferber's novel, his ideas are brought to the stage and a distinctly American art form comes to fruition.

After Kern dies in 1945, Hammerstein teams up with Richard Rodgers and the two collaborate on some of the greatest musicals in theatrical history, including the Pulitzer Prize–winning *Okla-*

homa and *South Pacific* as well as *The King and I* and *The Sound of Music.*

1928: Bojangles on Broadway.
On May 9, 1928, *Blackbirds of 1928,* a Negro musical, opens at the Liberty Theater in New York with Bill "Bojangles" Robinson, one of the great dancers in show business.

1928: Mickey Mouse Is Born.
The mouse makes his appearance in *Steamboat Willie,* the first animated cartoon featuring a sound track. Walt Disney's Mickey Mouse becomes an international star, along with Minnie, Donald Duck, and Pluto, and is the basis of Disney's vast fortune.

Along with his animated cartoons, titled *Silly Symphonies,* Disney also produced full-length animated feature movies. The first, *Snow White and the Seven Dwarfs,* was a hit in 1938 and was soon followed by *Pinocchio, Bambi, and Dumbo.* After World War II, Disney studios expanded into full-length live features as well, beginning with the 1954 film *20,000 Leagues Under the Sea,* and continues today to be one of the major studios in Hollywood.

1928: Iron Lung Invented.
Before the discovery of the polio vaccine, the disease not only paralyzed limbs, but sometimes the chest muscles that control breathing. The patient then could not get enough air, and suffocated. The iron lung, invented by Philip Drinker, a Harvard professor, mechanically performs the movement of the chest muscles. The Drinker respirator, a large metal cylinder, draws air out of the tank, the chest rises, and air then enters through the nose and mouth. Air is then pumped back into the tank, compressing the chest so that the patient exhales. This simple device kept many patients alive during severe attacks of polio.

1928: Penicillin Discovered.
Not that anyone was actively looking for it. Sir Alexander Fleming, a British bacteriologist, was, however, searching for something that would destroy the bacterial infections that caused so many unnecessary deaths. One day he discovered that one of the colonies of staphylococcus bacteria he had been growing in a petri dish had been contaminated by airborne spores. Where the mold was growing, there were no staphylococci. By isolating the mold in a pure culture, Fleming

discovered that what he called "mold juice" could kill various forms of bacteria that infect humans such as streptococcus, staphylococcus, and gonococcus. He identified the mold as *Penicillium notatum,* and called his new substance penicillin.

Even greater was the discovery that penicillin had no toxic effect on human cells, unlike the antiseptics in common use at the time, which were more toxic to humans than to bacteria. In a Jekyll-like gesture, Fleming drank some penicillin in a solution and had no ill effects. Penicillin inhibits the synthesis of cell walls in bacteria, and since human cells have no walls, the effect on humans is nontoxic.

When Fleming read a paper on his wonder drug to fellow medical researchers, they seemed unimpressed, and it was not until a decade later than two other researchers, Dr. Howard Florey and Dr. Ernst Chain, found the article in the stacks of a library at Oxford University, and began conducting their own experiments. Unfortunately by this time it was 1940 and Great Britain was at war. Florey traveled to the United States, where he was able to secure the support of drug companies. A short while later, commercially produced penicillin was on the market. After World War II penicillin came into wide use. It has been especially successful in treating that scourge of mankind, syphilis, as well as gonorrhea.

For their contributions to medicine, Fleming, Florey, and Chain shared the Nobel Prize in 1945.

1928: Volunteer Rescue Squads. Julian Stanley Wise organizes the first American volunteer rescue squad trained to help in emergency medical situations. We call these people emergency medical technicians (EMTs).

Today there are over half a million EMTs throughout the world. These rescue crews undergo lengthy rigorous medical training and testing before they are certified. The crews are on the scene administering immediate aid before the ambulance takes victims to the hospital. They specialize in shock trauma and cardiac treatment; start IVs and administer drugs. They treat people for bee stings, poisonings, and heart attacks; are on the scene at fires, floods, car crashes, and train wrecks. They nurture and support and perform heroic deeds and save lives every day. We are truly fortunate to have these volunteers in our communities. Support them, or better still, become one.

1929: The Seeing Eye, Inc. The foundation to train and supply guide dogs for the blind was established in Morristown, New Jersey.

The idea wasn't new. Dogs had been used to lead the blind several centuries ago, and in the seventeenth century a blind man in Germany wrote of training dogs to lead him. In the twentieth century the idea of training dogs to guide blind people was first tested in Switzerland, and just after World War I, a school to train such dogs was established in Germany.

Inspired by an article about their training by Dorothy Eustis, Morris Frank went to Switzerland to acquire and train with a dog. The two exhibited their skills around the States, and with the aid of Mrs. Eustis, the school in Morristown to train dogs was established. There are now several other schools that train dogs, including Guide Dogs for the Blind, Inc., and Leader Dogs for the Blind.

Labrador and golden retrievers, German shepherds, and boxers are good candidates for Seeing Eye dogs. Training in proper behavior begins at about fourteen months, after which the student and dog assigned to him are taught how to work and live with each other. The dog must learn to wear a special harness and to obey certain commands. The owner must learn how to bathe and take care of the dog and keep it healthy.

The guide dog and its master form a symbiotic relationship and prove again the old adage that a dog is (wo)man's best friend.

1929: Kellogg-Briand Pact Proclaimed. In 1927 the French statesman Aristede Briand, who had been awarded the Nobel Prize for Peace the year before, proposed a bilateral treaty between France and the United States renouncing war and agreeing that all disputes be settled by peaceful means. The United States secretary of state, Frank B. Kellogg, suggested the pact be open to all nations. Eventually the pact outlawing war was signed by sixty-three countries and formally proclaimed on July 24, 1929. Provisions of the pact allowed defensive wars and wars in defense of allies, however.

Nice try!

Ca. 1930: Chocolate Chip Cookies. As the legend goes, the proprietor of the Toll House Inn, near Whitman, Massachusetts, added chopped-up pieces of a Nestle's chocolate bar to her sugar cookie recipe and baked the first Toll House Inn cookie. Everyone in America should be grateful to her. The Nestle's people were so enamored of the cookie, they printed the recipe on their label. In 1939 they even invented the chocolate chip, which eliminated having to dice the chocolate. It's the little things that mean so much.

1930: Pluto Discovered. The astronomer Percival Lowell thought there might be a planet beyond Neptune, and on February 18, at the Lowell Observatory in Arizona, Clyde Tombaugh discovered it. The ninth planet farthest from the sun is named Pluto. It takes 248 years to revolve around the sun. You could live your whole lifetime during just one season.

1931: New Delhi. The opening of the new planned city is celebrated on February 8, in New Delhi, the capital of India.

According to historians, there has been a city in the vicinity of Delhi since the first century B.C. when Raja Dillu built the first one and called it Dilli. Throughout the centuries new rulers created new cities in the area, and during the reign of Shah Jahan, 1628–1658, the city we today know as Delhi was built. The shah, of course, had originally named it after himself and called it Shahjahanabad.

When King George V of England announced the transfer of the capital of India from Calcutta to Delhi, a planning committee was formed to build a brand-new city on a hill site about three miles south of Delhi. The planners included the British architects Sir Edwin Lutyens and Sir Herbert Baker, who designed a city with a central mall, wide diagonal avenues, trees, gardens, and fountains, with buildings that combined classical Roman architecture and Indian details.

1931: Statute of Westminster. The British Commonwealth of Nations is created by the statute granting autonomous government to Great Britain's colonial possessions. All the dominions are equal and in no way subordinate to one another in their domestic or external affairs, according to the statute, and all are united in owing allegiance to the crown. The days of the great empires are waning as nationalism is rising.

1931: The Empire State Building. On April 30, at Fifth Avenue and Thirty-fourth Street in Manhattan, the world's tallest building opens for business and quickly becomes a symbol of the great city of New York. The 102-story steel-frame skyscraper rises 1,250 feet from street level, and with the addition of a 222-foot television mast added in 1950, will increase in height to 1,472 feet.

The Empire State Building will soon become famous as the setting for that fabled ape, King Kong, who clings to the side of the building while fighting off an airplane.

1931: Scrabble Invented. One of the two best-selling board games in America, Scrabble was invented during the depression years by Alfred Butts, who wiled away his hours of unemployment devising crossword-puzzle-type games. For years it was played only by family and friends, until one friend, in 1948, suggested he copyright it. Selchow and Righter produced it, and children have been trying to beat their parents at it ever since.

1932: *The Jack Benny Show.* Violin-playing vaudeville comedian Jack Benny makes his debut on radio on May 2. The show will continue for the next twenty-three years, then appear on television for ten years beginning in 1955.

In the cast appear Benny's wife, Mary Livingston, announcer Don Wilson, singer Dennis Day, and sidekick Eddie "Rochester" Anderson. By the time the show ends, Benny, the comedian's comedian, is still "thirty-nine" according to his writers, and has been the butt of jokes about his old car and his stinginess hundreds of times over.

1932: Cardiac Pacemaker. Electricity is a wonderful thing. It lights our offices, runs our appliances, and keeps our hearts pumping smoothly. A glitch in the body's electrical system can speed up or slow down our heart too much, and in some cases cause it to be hopelessly irregular. The problem can be solved with a cardiac pacemaker. A. S. Hyman, an American heart specialist working for the U.S. Navy, developed the first such apparatus and named it as well. The unit was outside the body and connected to the heart by wires. A smaller version that could be inserted into the chest was developed in 1957 by the American physician Clarence Lillehei. When the natural beat of the heart goes out of whack, the pacemaker brings back the normal rhythm. There are several types of irregular heartbeat, and with new developments in the field, we now have different kinds of pacemakers available for a variety of problems.

1932: Sulfa Drugs Discovered. A little package carried by almost every GI in World War II and labeled "wound powder" probably saved many lives. The only instructions with the powder were "Apply to open wound and bandage." The white powder is sulfanilamide, the first of the miracle sulfa drugs that kill bacteria.

The development of sulfa drugs involved many scientists and is international in scope. The medical revolution was started in 1932 by a German biochemist, Gerhard Domagk. While experimenting with organic dyes, Domagk found that one of them, a compound called prontosil, cured miced and rabbits of streptococcal infections. Circumstances, namely a patent and the beginnings of World War II, prevented the drug from being shipped out of Germany. A French team, however, after reading Domagk's report and earlier work done by others with the dye, realized that only one component of the compound was the miracle cure. Since the original patent was for the compound, not sections of it, it could now be manufactured by others.

Although there was initial resistance to injection of such a chemical into the bloodstream, the drug saved the life of one of President Franklin Delano Roosevelt's sons who was suffering from a life-threatening infection. The proof was in the saving and public acceptance was won. Other sulfa drugs followed, such as sulfathiazole and sulfadiazine, all of which revolutionized the way infectious diseases were treated and are still treated today.

In 1939 Domagk joined the ranks of those who received a Nobel Prize for their good work.

1933: The Game of Monopoly. It was during the Great Depression that Pennsylvanian Charles Darrow, an unemployed engineer, devised the game of Monopoly, which would make him a millionaire and be played in over thirty countries around the world in nineteen different languages.

1933: The Incubator. A small enclosed crib used to maintain the life of premature babies or others with life-threatening ailments, the incubator provides oxygen in the right amount, and constant warmth. In 1884 a kerosene-lamp incubator was introduced in France, and in 1933 an electrical model was designed and patented by an American physician, Julius Hess. Incubators have saved the lives of a lot of babies.

1933: Movies Outdoors.

A new phenomenon, a drive-in movie theater, opens in Riverton, New Jersey, on June 6, 1933, and by 1960, there are forty-seven hundred drive-ins in the United States.

The entire family could now sit in the privacy of their car to watch a movie, eliminating the need for a baby-sitter. Teenagers loved drive-ins, too, for other reasons. With the advent of television and videocassettes, however, drive-ins gradually declined.

1934: Indian Reorganization Act.

For years the Native American population of the United States had been in ill health, uneducated and poor. The Reorganization Act is adopted to help reverse this condition. Tribes are now able to adopt written constitutions and to incorporate themselves in order to manage their internal affairs. Funds are authorized to establish a credit program for land purchases, health, and educational programs. The fund will aid tribes to increase their herds, improve economic conditions, and add to their land holdings.

1935: Social Security Act.

During the presidency of Franklin D. Roosevelt, Congress passes the Social Security Act on August 14, 1935, providing old-age retirement benefits and a system of unemployment insurance. In 1939 amendments will provide benefits for the dependents and survivors of workmen. In 1950 the program, which originally applied only to employees in industry and commerce, will be expanded to include farm and household workers and self-employed people.

1937: Fallingwater.

The private house designed by architect Frank Lloyd Wright for department store owner Edgar Kaufmann is completed at Bear Run in Fayette County, Pennsylvania. One of the most famous and dramatic homes ever designed, the flat-roofed wood and stone house sits suspended on cantilevered concrete terraces over a fast-running stream in a natural wooded site. Wright, iconoclastic, unorthodox, and individualistic, is known for his "prairie"-style houses utilizing horizontal design, bands of windows, and wide, flat roofs.

Aside from private homes, Wright's genius can be seen in such buildings as the Guggenheim Museum in New York, the S. C. Johnson & Son Administration Building in Racine, Wisconsin, and at his studio, Taliesen West, near Phoenix, Arizona. He has been called the greatest architect of the twentieth century.

1937: Antihistamine Discovered. Those who suffer with allergies, seasonal or otherwise, can thank Swiss pharmacologist Daniel Bovet for his work in the field. Bovet found several compounds that helped combat the symptoms brought on by allergies. The first of these was introduced as pyrilamine. Since the stuffy head, watery eyes, and sneezing are caused by the body producing histamines, the drugs were called antihistamines. In addition to these symptoms, antihistamines can also reduce the itch of bites, skin allergies, and hives. Antihistamines are not a cure, but they bring blessed relief from the annoying symptoms.

Bovet was also a pioneer in the field of anesthetics. For his achievements in medicine and physiology, he was awarded the 1957 Nobel Prize.

1938: Fair Labor Standards Act. During the late nineteenth century, many states had passed child labor laws, and in 1916 Congress banned interstate commerce of goods on which children under fourteen participated in manufacturing or on which fourteen- to sixteen-year-olds worked more than eight hours per day. Unfortunately, in 1918 the Supreme Court declared the law unconstitutional and an infringement on states' rights. It was another twenty years before the Fair Labor Standards Act was passed, also known as the wage and hour law. It stated that the work week would be reduced to forty hours per week within three years, and overtime must be paid after that. It also set the minimum wage and placed restrictions on child labor, prohibiting children under sixteen from working in mining or manufacturing jobs. In 1949 an amendment to the child labor provisions banned children under sixteen from working in other businesses, such as transportation, commercial agriculture, public utilities, and communications.

1938: Bob Hope on the Air. On September 27 the London-born song-and-dance man Leslie Townes Hope broadcasts his first comedy show from Hollywood.

As did most entertainers of the time, Bob Hope began his career in vaudeville and stepped from there onto the Broadway stage, where he appeared in the Ziegfeld Follies and starred in several major musicals. He also made movies and is remembered most for his comedy roles in the "Road" pictures with Bing Crosby and Dorothy Lamour. The 1938 movie *The Big Broadcast* featured the song "Thanks for the Memory," which was to become his theme song and will be forever associated with him. Beginning in 1939, Bob Hope emceed the Academy Awards show, which he continued to do on and off for the next thirty years. On April 9, 1950, Hope's show moved to NBC television, where we could now watch his antics and laugh at his topical one-liners.

It is for entertaining the troops that Bob Hope is perhaps best known. It began on March 6, 1941, at the March Field Airbase in Riverside, California. From then on Bob and his company traveled all over the United States and to wherever troops were stationed overseas during World War II, Korea and Vietnam, and in between. For bringing a little bit of home and a great deal of laughter to them, GIs everywhere thank Bob Hope for the memories.

1939: Automatic Washers and Dryers. There had been a few so-called automatic washers invented, but they were really hand-cranked and more trouble than they were worth. The first electric machines were introduced around 1915, but proved rather dangerous because of their design. It wasn't until 1939 that the fully automatic washer and dryer came into existence. A lifetime of washday drudgery was beginning to end for the housewife.

1940: The Electron Microscope. We can now see what we've never seen before. On April 1, at the RCA lab in New Jersey, the first electron microscope, ten feet high and seven hundred pounds, is demonstrated. It can magnify to one hundred thousand diameters.

1940: Nylon Stockings. In 1938 the DuPont chemical company invented a new synthetic miracle yarn they called nylon which they displayed at the 1939 New York World's Fair, and on May 15, the following year, nylon stockings went on sale in select stores all over the United States. The new nylons, as women began calling the stockings, lasted longer and didn't run as easily as the silk stockings they had been accustomed to. Nylon went off to war the following year to be used in the manufacture of parachutes, and ever since its victorious return, we have been wearing nylons.

1941: Atlantic Charter.

On August 14, President Franklin D. Roosevelt and British Prime Minister Winston Churchill adopt the Atlantic Charter at a conference aboard the USS *Augusta* off the coast of Newfoundland. The charter states that neither country seeks additional territory, that all peoples have the right to self-government and to choose the form of government under which they will live, that all nations have equal access to trade anywhere in the world, and that all nations should collaborate to secure economic stability, improved labor standards, and social security.

The charter was meant to be a rallying cry in support of World War II against the aggressor countries. The points it made, however, were later adopted into the charter of the United Nations.

1942: Ethiopia Abolishes Slavery.

Ethiopia wanted to join the League of Nations, but slavery still existed in the country, which was against the laws of the League. The Ethiopian government pledged to abolish the practice, but with the loss of its independence to Italy in the mid-1930s, this did not come about until the country was free again.

1942: Super Secret Code.

A select group of Navajo Indians devise a secret unbreakable code in their native language to transmit military messages during World War II.

The idea came from the son of a missionary who had grown up on the Navajo reservation in Arizona and spoke the language. With the assistance of several Navajo friends, he demonstrated the language to marine officers, who, although at first skeptical, realized its potential. The first group of Navajos who joined the marines became the 382nd Platoon and were responsible for inventing the code. Since Navajo, spoken by few outsiders, is basically an oral language and everything is memorized, nothing was ever written down. The completed code used ordinary Navajo words as well as several hundred new ones made up for the purpose. Even the untrained Navajos couldn't crack it. Those who knew the system were referred to as Code Talkers and proved invaluable in the fight against the Japanese in the South Pacific.

It was with the help of the Navajo Code Talkers that the marines were able to take Iwo Jima and fly the now famous flag over Mount Suribachi.

About 3,600 Navajos served in World War II, 420 as Code Talkers. The Pentagon has a permanent exhibit dedicated to their courage and to the supersecret code they invented that no one could decipher.

1943: The Pentagon. Completed on January 15 in Arlington, Virginia, the Pentagon, so called because of its five sides, is the world's largest office building. At a cost of $83 million, the five-story building on thirty-four acres encloses 6.5 million square feet of floor space with seventeen miles of corridors. Originally built to house all the United States War Department offices during World War II, it will later become headquarters for the Defense Department as well as the army, navy, and air force. You could get lost in it for days.

1944: Kidney Dialysis Machine. The basic function of the kidneys is to carry waste products out of the body. Almost three quarters of our body is water. The kidneys maintain this volume of fluid and its composition by a unique filtration system that preserves what we need and excretes what we can't use. The kidneys also control production of red blood cells and maintain the body's blood pressure. Kidneys can be damaged by injury, poisoning, diabetes, and high blood pressure, among other things. One kidney can perform the work should the other be damaged, but lose both and poisons rapidly build up in the body (uremia), causing death. A good many people facing this crisis can be helped by dialysis, wherein a machine takes over the job of the kidneys outside the body. Instead of the blood passing through the kidneys, it is removed from the body, pumped through a machine, and returned. The machine, although referred to as an "artificial kidney," cannot replace the kidney completely; it does, however, remove the waste products to prevent uremia.

A Dutch physician, Willem Koff, developed a machine to perform this function outside the body and used it in secret to save the lives of his compatriots in Nazi-occupied Holland during World War II. Kolff immigrated to the United States after the war and continued to improve his dialysis machine. In 1960 the American physician Belding Scribner and an engineer, Wayne

Quinton, introduced a new cannula (tube), which greatly improved the process, and although there are new variations, dialysis is basically done the same way it was when first originated. Today kidney dialysis keeps thousands of people alive.

1944: Wallenberg's Mission. On July 9 Raoul Gustaf Wallenberg, a Swedish businessman with diplomatic immunity, arrives in Budapest, Hungary, to rescue Jews from the Nazis.

In 1912 Wallenberg was born into a prominent Lutheran banking and industrial family near Stockholm. He studied architecture at the University of Michigan, traveled, and worked for a while in Palestine, where he heard Jewish refugees tell tales of persecution in Germany. He returned to Sweden in 1936 and, just after World War II began, became a foreign trade representative for a Jewish Hungarian exporter. Since Sweden was a neutral country, Wallenberg was able to travel through Europe and became skilled at negotiating with the Nazis.

In March 1944 Hitler sent troops and SS officer Adolf Eichmann to Hungary and began deporting the Jews in the rural areas. At the same time, several neutral countries began issuing Jews protective passports, and the War Refugee Board in the United States asked Sweden to recommend someone to aid the Jews trapped in Budapest. Wallenberg was suggested, and when he was asked if he would take on a humanitarian mission in Hungary that might be dangerous, he agreed, feeling that the job offered him a greater purpose in life than the export business.

Wallenberg did his job well, sheltering Jews in buildings under the Swedish flag, handing out protective passports, administering a volunteer staff to run schools, hospitals, and orphanages, and feeding the hungry, which was practically everyone. Other neutral countries followed his humanitarian example and joined in the rescue. As the Germans began retreating from Hungary towards the end of the war, forcing hundreds of Jews to walk to their death, Wallenberg organized rescue parties in trucks and compelled the Nazis to turn over their victims, claiming they were under the protection of Sweden, all the while handing out Swedish passes to those still without them. As the Russians approached the outskirts of Budapest near the end of the war, the Nazis were ordered to massacre the remaining Jews in the ghetto. Wallenberg sent a messenger to the SS general in charge and threatened to hold him personally responsible and have him hanged as a war criminal if the massacre occurred. The general capitulated.

It is estimated that over one hundred thousand lives were saved due to Wallenberg's heroic efforts. He is one of the great humanitarians of this century. When the Russians arrived in Budapest, they couldn't comprehend why anyone would voluntarily perform such deeds as he did, and thought he was a spy. He was turned over to the NKVD (the then Russian equivalent of our CIA) and imprisoned. His actual fate is still unknown. Adolf Eichmann, for performing his deeds, was tried and executed for war crimes.

1944: The GI Bill of Rights. On June 22 the Serviceman's Readjustment Act, passed by Congress, is signed into law by United States president Franklin D. Roosevelt.

Thousands of returning veterans attended college or vocational school under the GI Bill, as it was commonly called, with the government paying five hundred dollars a year for tuition and fifty dollars a month in living expenses. Among the other benefits provided were no-money-down low-interest mortgages, veterans' hospitals, vocational rehabilitation, and for those who weren't sure what they were going to do, twenty dollars a week for fifty-two weeks. The benefits later covered Korean War veterans, and in 1966 the Readjustment Benefits Act extended them to those who served in the peacetime forces.

In historic terms, the bill was an unprecedented piece of social legislation. It was also a grateful nation's way of saying thank you to those who served.

1944: Blue-Baby Surgery. Helen Taussig, a pediatric cardiologist, devoted herself to the study of heart disease in children, specifically those with valve problems. These children were so short of breath that sometimes their entire bodies were blue due to the lack of oxygen. After much observation, she realized it was basically a "plumbing" problem and what was needed was a new "pipe" to go around the part that was malfunctioning. Uncertain as to how to accomplish such surgery, Dr. Taussig called upon Alfred Blalock, a researcher and surgeon whose field was the heart and circulation. Dr. Blalock welcomed the challenge, and together with his technical assistant, Vivian Thomas, a gifted and talented man who could work magic with his hands, worked out the details.

Dr. Blalock had yet to practice the technique when a desper-

ately ill little girl was presented to them. She would die if nothing
was done, so they decided to operate. Along with their own
technical skills, they had two assistants that day who would later
make their own outstanding contributions to medicine, Dr. Denton Cooley and Dr. William Longmire. On November 9, at Johns
Hopkins Children's Hospital in Baltimore, Maryland, with Dr.
Taussig looking on, this wonderful team of specialists successfully
constructed the first human ductus (valve) and saved the child.
Years later, the girl's mother was still talking about the miracle.
The new surgical procedure would save the lives of thousands of
blue babies in the future.

1944: Streptomycin Developed.

Selman Waksman, a
Russian-born American biochemist, and his assistants isolate streptomycin, supposedly from a clump of moldy dirt from the throat
of a chicken. Since Dr. Waksman is an authority on soil microbi-
ology, he had a reason to be looking down a chicken's throat for
dirt.

The "White Plague," better known as tuberculosis, killed thousands of people in the nineteenth century. Many patients were
sent to sanatoriums, partly with the hope they would recover, and
partly to try to isolate the disease. The bacterium that caused TB
had been isolated by Dr. Robert Koch in 1882, but he could not
find a cure. The mold Waksman found killed the TB bacillus,
and after testing and purification, the new drug was used to save
a patient. Streptomycin and its kin are effective not only against
tuberculosis but several other infectious diseases such as whooping
cough, certain influenzas, and bladder infections for which penicillin proves ineffective.

Dr. Waksman received the Nobel Prize in physiology in 1952
for his work on antibiotics, which helped to cure tuberculosis, the
scourge of humans since time immemorial.

1945: Germany Surrenders.

World War II in Europe ends
on May 7 when the Germans surrender unconditionally. The next
day is proclaimed V-E (Victory in Europe) day by American president Harry S Truman.

In the greatest invasion in history, the Allied forces had landed
in France on June 6 (D-day), 1944, and in less than a year, defeated the German army on the western front while the Russians
closed in on the east. The defeat of Hitler and his Nazis is a

turning point in history and will eventually lead to prosperity and a peaceful union of the nations of Europe never before attained.

1945: The United Nations. On June 26, 1945, in San Francisco, fifty-one nations join together to sign the charter establishing the United Nations organization, with the primary purpose of maintaining international peace and security.

Among its principles, the charter states that disputes are to be settled by peaceful means; members must refrain from the threat or use of force against the independence of any state; each member must assist the organization in its actions; except for enforcement measures, the United Nations shall not intervene in domestic matters within a state. The United Nations also strives to solve economic, social, cultural, and humanitarian problems and to promote and encourage respect for human rights.

1946: The Bikini. The atomic explosion at Bikini Atoll in the Pacific was minor compared to the explosion in the fashion world when the French designer Jacques Heim dropped his own bombshell, the daring bathing suit he called the bikini. The skimpy new swimsuit design, so common now, appeared scandalous on American beaches and wasn't really acceptable until the 1960s, when it gradually crept in from the Caribbean resorts and Europe. Victorian ladies would have been mortified.

1947: Microwave Oven Invented. Microwave cooking was discovered serendipitously when Percy Spencer, who was working with shortwave electromagnetic energy, felt a melted candy bar in his pocket. The waves produce a molecular vibration, which in turn produces heat inside the food. Sort of an inside-out method of cooking, you might say. Commercial microwave ovens became available almost immediately, and in 1967 the compact size now found in our home kitchens was introduced. It has become a staple in college dorms, a convenience for those in the "singles" scene, as well as a boon to working mothers. And a great way to pop corn.

1947: The Truman Doctrine. On March 12 President Harry S Truman, fearing that Greece and Turkey might fall under the control of Russian communism, issues what is known as the Truman Doctrine. It states: "It must be the policy of the United States to support free peoples who are resisting attempted subjugation by armed minorities or by outside pressures."

The Doctrine became the basis of our Cold War policy in our fight against the spread of communism throughout the world.

1947: Levittowns. World War II is over, GIs are coming home, new families are beginning, and they need housing. The GI Bill of Rights provides low-cost mortgages with no money down, and builder Abraham Levitt supplies the houses. The houses he builds on Long Island, New York, are almost identical, sit on concrete slabs with no basements, are assembled with precut material, include major appliances, and are sold for a modest cost. The planned community includes village shops, playgrounds, a swimming pool, and sites for schools and churches and well as a community center. By 1951, there were seventeen thousand Levittown houses, at which time a second community was begun in Bucks County, Pennsylvania, followed by a third community in New Jersey in 1965.

As a result of this new building, and the many other communities that sprang up around the country, thousands of families left the cities and settled in the suburbs.

1947: Carbon Dating. In 1940 the Canadian-American biochemist Martin Kamen discovered the carbon 14 isotope (radiocarbon). In 1947 Willard Libby, a United States chemist, makes the discovery that all organisms contain carbon 14 atoms. C-14 decays at a constant rate and has a half-life of 5,730 years, more or less. This means that in 5,730 years or so, only one half of the original amount of C-14 in an organism remains. Then, in another 5,730 years, one quarter of the original is left. This continues until there's nothing left to measure. This discovery is invaluable to archaeologists and anthropologists, who now have an accurate way of dating their finds.

Libby received the Nobel Prize in chemistry in 1960 for his work on atoms and nuclear studies.

1947: Jackie Robinson Signed by Dodgers. Jackie Robinson had been a football player at the University of California, then went on to play baseball with the Negro major leagues. Dodger president Branch Rickey, impressed with Robinson, signed him up to play for their Triple-A farm team, and the following year brought him up to play for the Brooklyn Dodgers, thereby breaking the color barrier. Robinson hit twelve home runs, stole twenty-nine bases, had a batting average of .297, and won the Rookie of the Year Award.

1947: The Transistor.

In December, at the Bell Telephone Laboratories in New Jersey, William Shockley, in collaboration with John Bardeen and Walter Brattain, demonstrates the transistor.

It is one of the greatest inventions in the field of electronics, and revolutionizes the industry. The transistor is a semiconductor (half conductor and half insulator), a tiny piece of silicon crystal into which electrons flow in a closed circuit. It needs no high-voltage power, no wiring and soldering, and lasts for a long time. The transistor will replace the vacuum tube and enable the miniaturization of radios, television sets, computers, and all kinds of electronic devices.

Transistors are now used in everything from hearing aids to telephones and guided missiles. For their work, the three men received the Nobel Prize for physics in 1956.

1948–52: The Marshall Plan.

Europe was devastated by World War II. United States secretary of state George C. Marshall promised that the United States would support European recovery if the European governments would develop a plan for economic reconstruction. The result was the European Recovery Program, known as the Marshall Plan, which provided more than twelve billion dollars in aid over four years to assist war-torn Europe, and in the process kept the spread of communism in check.

1948–49: Berlin Airlift.

After World War II Germany was divided into four occupation zones, with the USSR, Great Britain, France, and the United States each controlling one zone. Berlin, the capital of Germany, isolated in the USSR zone, was also under shared control. On June 24, 1948, the USSR cut off all communications and effectively blockaded the western sectors of Berlin. The USSR was probably hoping to force the Allies out of Berlin and perhaps undermine the European Recovery Program by starving the population of Berlin. In retaliation, the United States and Britain began a giant airlift of food and supplies to West Berlin, which lasted from June 26, 1948, until September 30, 1949. The

Berlin airfield handled up to one thousand landings each day, while over two million tons of food, medicine, and fuel were delivered by strategic bombers. The blockade was broken.

1948: The Dawn of a New Entertainment Age.

The "Texaco Star Theater" with comedian Milton Berle debuts on television on June 8, and America becomes glued to its TV sets every Tuesday from eight to nine.

At the time of his debut, there were only five hundred thousand television sets in the whole country. By the 1950s, TV sales had zoomed upward while movie attendance plummeted. America had fallen in love with "Uncle Milty" and television. The show remained popular for eight years, finally ending in June of 1956.

Berle was the first comedian to have a show on national television in prime time. His career began at an early age, and by the time he was eight, in 1916, he had appeared in over fifty films at movie studios in New York and Hollywood. He broke into vaudeville and at twenty-one became the youngest person to headline at the Palace Theater in New York. One of the busiest comedians in the business, he sometimes performed a late night club act after appearing in a Broadway show while also doing a radio program in the daytime. A pioneer of television comedy, Berle still appears on cable TV and in an occasional movie, both as a comedian and a serious actor.

1948: Armed Forces Desegregated.

On July 26 the Armed Forces of the United States are officially desegregated by executive order of President Harry S Truman.

African-Americans had served during the Revolutionary War, but later were excluded from the army and marines, but not the navy. They also fought in the Civil War and both World Wars, but always in segregated units.

On October 1, 1989, General Colin Powell, an African-American, was appointed Chairman of the Joint Chiefs of Staff of the United States Armed Forces.

1948: Universal Declaration of Human Rights.

On December 10 the United Nations' general assembly adopts the Universal Declaration of Human Rights, recognizing "the inherent diginity and the equal and inalienable rights of all members of the human family." Article 3 of the declaration states that "everyone has the right to life, liberty, and the security of person."

This is an extraordinary document covering all aspects of civil liberties never completely stated before in history. It declares that slavery should be prohibited as well as cruel and inhuman punishment; everyone is equal before the law and should be protected against discrimination; there should be no arbitrary arrest or detention; a fair trial should be guaranteed and a person should be presumed innocent until proven guilty; people should be able to move freely within their country and have the freedom to leave and be able to own property and marry without limitations because of religion, nationality, or race. There are articles that provide for freedom of conscience and religion and freedom of assembly and speech.

Progress has been a little slow in implementing the entire declaration, but it is happening. The important thing is that the nations of the world finally got together to acknowledge the rights and liberties of individual human beings.

1949: The Computer Age. Our technology is expanding so rapidly, we can hardly keep up with ourselves, especially in the computer field. Back in 1834, the English mathematician Charles Babbage invented the principle for building what was really a modern computer. He called it his "analytical machine." (He had already constructed a "difference engine" which could do mathematical functions.) Babbage was aided in his work by the daughter of the poet Byron, Augusta Ada Byron, who was a mathematical genius. She wrote a set of instructions for Babbage's "computer" to be written on punch cards, which had been invented by the Frenchman Jacquard for his weaving looms. In essence Augusta was the first computer programmer. Babbage's machine would have been of enormous size and impractical to build at the time.

Over one hundred years later, in 1946, the ENIAC, which stands for Electronic Numerical Integrator and Calculator, was demonstrated at the University of Pennsylvania. It was the size of a large garage, contained more than one hundred thousand vacuum tubes, resistors, and switches, and could do five thousand additions and subtractions per second. The program for this demonstration was also written by a woman.

The first electronic computer with a stored program, the EDSAC (Electronic Delay Storage Automatic Calculator), began operating at Cambridge University in England in May 1949, and at the same time IBM unveiled its own computer in the United States. In 1951 the UNIVAC (Universal Automatic Computer) was installed at the Census Bureau and became the first computer in commercial use. It used magnetic tape for storing data and had a memory of 1.5K. In 1953 a high-speed printer was connected which could print six hundred lines per minute, and after 1959, the UNIVAC was run entirely by transistors. By 1955, MIT had built a binary computer to control flight simulators. New technology allowed data from variously located terminals to be processed through a central computer and vice versa. It was a mainframe with work stations.

The new generation of computers produced by IBM from 1959 used transistors rather than vacuum tubes. Transistors enabled computers to be faster, smaller, and cheaper. In 1962 IBM introduced a disk storage system for computer data. By 1963, we had a minicomputer from the Digital Equipment Company, and in 1976 a supercomputer from Cray capable of performing 150 million operations per second. Further generations of computers used integrated circuits, and after the microprocessor was invented, we could get more information than ever before into and out of our computers. By 1975, we had desktop computers, and in 1987 a supercomputer performing 1.72 billion computations per second.

Every day brings new advances, new chips, and new techniques to make our computers run faster, store greater quantities of data, and regurgitate it more rapidly. Computers operate our factories, teach our children, animate our movies, design our automobiles, generate our airline tickets, compute our bank statements, print our newspapers, fly our planes, and amuse us with games. There is hardly an aspect of our lives that remains untouched by computer technology. It's a world of wonder and amazement and genius. Computers are almost as intelligent as we are.

1950: Automatic Elevator Doors. The Atlantic Refining Building in Dallas, Texas, shows off the first automatic doors on its passenger elevators. Of course, this new technology will put all those elevator operators out of work eventually, but that's progress.

1950: "Your Show of Shows" Debuts. Comedians Sid Caesar, Imogene Coca, Carl Reiner, and Howard Morris star in NBC's new hour-long comedy show. For the next five years

America is entertained by some of the most imaginative and wittiest comedy sketches ever seen on television.

1951: "I Love Lucy." The television show starring Lucille Ball and Desi Arnaz debuts on October 15, and keeps America in stitches for six years laughing over Lucy's antics in her wacky comedy skits. All America ends up loving Lucy, and Lucy ends up owning her own studio.

1952: Transistorized Hearing Aids. The first hearing aids using transistors are introduced on December 29, by the Sonotone Corporation in New York.

Back in the eighteenth century there were gadgets available to help people hear. Ear trumpets and speaking tubes were used, along with a device called a dentiphone. This fan-shaped instrument, made of celluloid or cardboard, was held between the teeth and bent in the direction of the sound. The sound vibrations traveled around the skull to the auditory nerves.

In 1901 Miller Hutchison applied for a patent for the first practical hearing aid, after which several other devices were invented. They were made up of bulky, wire-connected parts, all carried on the body. In 1935 the British inventor A. E. Stevens manufactured an electronic hearing aid weighing two pounds.

With the invention of the transistor in 1947, hearing aids could now be developed that were much smaller and almost invisible in the ear. These tiny devices are an asset to anyone who has a hearing loss, enabling one to join in the conversation, answer the telephone, and enjoy the music again.

1953: Heart-Lung Machine. Dr. John Gibbon, a Boston surgeon, successfully uses a machine to keep the blood circulating while bypassing the heart and lungs during open-heart surgery.

Gibbon and his wife, Mary, had worked for twenty years to perfect the device after Gibbon had watched a young girl die during surgery to remove a blood clot from her lungs. Subsequently, Dr. C. Walton Lillehei developed a more reliable machine. It was, however, the bold dream of Gibbon that created the lifesaving technique.

1953: The Double Helix. Scientists had suspected that DNA might be responsible for heredity, and in 1944 three Americans,

Avery, MacLeod, and McCarty, proved that DNA was, in fact, genetic material. In May of 1953 U.S. geneticist James Watson and his English counterpart Francis Crick publish their findings in *Nature* in which they illustrate their model of DNA. They show that chromosomes are composed of two helical strands of DNA coiled around each other in a ladderlike form. The rungs of the ladder are composed of nucleotides. It is the sequence of these nucleotides that spells out the genetic code by which cells copy themselves.

Crick and Watson's work was later confirmed, and they, with Maurice Wilkins of Great Britain, who had also worked on the project, received the Nobel Prize in 1962.

The unraveling of the genetic code is one of the greatest feats in scientific history, and the work continues. We now use DNA in forensic pathology, to identify genes for hereditary diseases, to track outbreaks of disease such as the Hanta virus, for fingerprinting new strains of bacteria, and in the treatment of some diseases. The work goes on; the possibilities are endless.

1953: Mount Everest Conquered.

On May 29 at eleven-thirty in the morning New Zealand mountaineer Edmund Hillary and his Sherpa guide, Tenzing Norgay, stand on the summit of 29,028-foot Mount Everest in the Himalayas. They are the first to reach the top of the highest mountain in the world.

Why do we climb mountains? Perhaps to try the impossible, or to satisfy a sense of adventure or to explore the unknown. Or maybe just because they are there.

1954: The Birthday Present.

Most people celebrate their birthdays with candles and cake, but not Elvis Presley. On the day of his nineteenth birthday, January 4, the unknown Tennessee truck driver enters a Memphis recording studio, plunks down four dollars, plucks on his guitar, and records "I'll Never Stand in Your Way" and "Casual Love."

Two years later in 1956, under the guidance of his manager, Colonel Tom Parker, the dynamic singer was the hottest thing in rock 'n' roll, with his song "Heartbreak Hotel" heading the charts. His meteoric rise to fame was phenomenal. His star continued skyrocketing, and on September 9, 1956, he appeared on the Ed Sullivan TV show "Toast of the Town," gyrating to "Hound Dog" and the ballad "Love Me Tender" from his first movie of the same name. It was a ratings coup for Sullivan; an estimated fifty-four million watched, garnishing an 82 percent share of the TV audience. Because of his pelvic movements to music while he sang, he was nicknamed "Elvis the Pelvis." Teenaged girls loved it, but the parental generation was not so adoring. As one fan so aptly put it in a newspaper account, "He's just one big hunk of forbidden fruit." On his next appearance on the Sullivan show, however, the camera shot him only from the waist up.

Elvis was a true teenage idol. By the time he was drafted into the army in 1958, he had sold over forty million records. After the army, he continued making movies, recording albums, and performing in concert tours. In his twenty years in show business, as the king of rock 'n' roll, he made a tremendous and unique impact on music. His untimely death in August of 1977 created a growing legend which thrives today. Legends die hard, however; the tabloids frequently report sightings of him alive and well at various spots throughout the world.

1954: A Successful Kidney Transplant. Surgeons at Peter Bent Brigham Hospital in Massachusetts successfully transplant a kidney between identical twins. The patient lives for seven more years.

Since identical twins are compatible in tissue and blood there was no rejection of the kidney. Medical science had long dreamed about organ transplants, but our bodies reject things that are foreign, including somebody else's parts, and in the beginning the problem seemed unsurmountable. In 1936 a human kidney transplant was performed by a Soviet surgeon, U. Voronoy, but the patient lived only two days.

By 1963, rejection was overcome with the introduction of drugs such as cyclosporine which suppresses the body's immune response, permitting the acceptance of a donor organ. Organ transplant surgery now includes the lungs, heart-lung combination, the liver, and the pancreas. The pancreas is a piggy-back operation; the donor organ is implanted but the patient's own organ is left in place continuing part of its function. Transplants are one of the major achievements in medicine in the twentieth century.

1954: Brown v. Board of Education. On May 17, 1954, the United States Supreme Court unanimously declares racial segregation in public schools to be unconstitutional. The father of

Linda Brown had brought suit against the Topeka, Kansas, Board of Education in 1951, which operated under the "separate but equal" Supreme Court ruling of 1896, as did all schools in the South. Chief Justice Earl Warren rejected this principle, stating that "separate educational facilities are inherently unequal" and denied black children equal protection under the laws of the Fourteenth Amendment. He ordered states to proceed "with all deliberate speed" to integrate their schools. Although most states in the upper South complied with the law, schools in the Deep South remained segregated. In 1957 President Dwight Eisenhower sent federal troops to Little Rock, Arkansas, to maintain order when several black children attempted to attend the high school there and were refused admittance. Over the years, however, thanks to the Supreme Court ruling, all schools became desegregated.

The 1954 ruling spurred the civil rights movement in the United States and led to antidiscrimination legislation which affected not only blacks, but all minorities, women, and the handicapped.

1955: Disneyland Opens.

July 17 marks the opening day for the amusement park in Anaheim, California, built by Walt Disney. The park will become a major tourist attraction with young and old flocking to enjoy a ride on the Mark Twain paddle wheeler, zoom through Space Mountain, circle in a Mad Hatter's teacup, submerge in a submarine, or drift along a jungle river. Included with all the attractions in Adventureland, Frontierland, Fantasyland, and Tomorrowland are shows and parades and a chance to shake the hands of Mickey, Minnie, Donald, and Pluto, the characters who made it all possible.

Disney has mortgaged himself to the hilt in order to build the park on 244 acres of a former orange grove twenty-five miles from Los Angeles. It is so successful that he gradually amasses 27,500 acres of land near Orlando, Florida, to build a Disneyland East vacation resort. Unfortunately he dies in 1965 before he can realize his second dream. Walt Disney World, like Disneyland, with its fairy-tale castle, amusements, old-fashioned Main Street, and storybook characters, is a world of fantasy and fun enjoyed by hundreds of thousands of visitors every year from all over the world. Thanks, Mickey.

1955: Chlorothiazide Discovered. The drug used by many
to control high blood pressure was discovered by researchers at
Merck, Sharp and Dohme.

Before 1900, hypertension (high blood pressure) as a condition
was not really recognized and was barely treatable. Mild elevation
of blood pressure can be controlled by lifestyle and dietary changes
such as salt restriction, weight loss, and exercise, but serious elevation can cause a great deal of damage to the body. In the 1930s
rest, warm baths, and occasionally bloodletting were suggested. In
1944 a rice diet was tried. It worked as far as lowering blood
pressure, but failed as a remedy because no one could stay on it
too long.

Chlorothiazide lowers blood pressure and has few side effects.
It was made commercially available in 1958 under the trade name
Diuril. Today there are many types of diuretics available, and
doctors use the one that works best for each patient.

1955: Polio Vaccine. Poliomyelitis, or infantile paralysis, has
been with us since the dawn of time. It's caused by a minute
virus in the digestive tract that moves into the bloodstream, spinal
cord, and brain. It enters the body through inhalation or by
mouth, usually from unclean food or dirty hands. Prior to the
twentieth century, when better hygiene and cleanliness began to
hit their stride, many infants had been infected with the virus, had
become mildly ill, then developed a natural immunity. It is a
paradox that better sanitary conditions allowed the disease to develop by not enabling this immunity to occur. By the twentieth
century polio epidemics were ravishing the country, killing and
crippling people of all ages.

In 1938, under the auspices of President Franklin D. Roosevelt,
himself a polio victim, the National Foundation for Infantile Paralysis was instituted as a research organization and the March of
Dimes began raising funds for it. In 1949 Drs. Enders, Robbins,
and Weller, researchers at Children's Hospital in Boston, made a
big breakthrough when they were able to grow the polio virus in
several different types of human tissue, not just in nerve tissue.
For this discovery they shared in the 1954 Nobel Prize for medicine. Another team of researchers discovered there were actually
three types of polio and that vaccines would be needed for each.
In 1952 Drs. Bodian and Horstman discovered the progression of
the virus through the body, which proved to be very important.

At this point, based on previous information, microbiologist Jonas Salk and his team of scientists began the painstaking task of developing a safe vaccine. In 1952 he had accomplished his mission, and by 1954 a national immunization program was started. In 1957 Dr. Albert Sabin produced an oral form of the vaccine that is used today.

All these men and women working together rid us of the dread of polio, and children once more can go out to playgrounds and beaches without the fear that it will strike them down.

1955: Rosa Parks Sits and Stays. On December 1 Rosa Parks, an African-American seamstress in Montgomery, Alabama, refuses to give up her seat on a bus to a white man.

Her daring action results in her arrest and precipitates the 382-day boycott of buses led by Martin Luther King, Jr.

A ban on segregation on interstate buses and trains and in waiting rooms had been ordered by the Interstate Commerce Commission on November 25, but did not affect intrastate transportation. In April of 1956 the Supreme Court takes care of this oversight and outlaws segregation on public transportation within the states.

1956: Perfect Pitch. On October 8, 1956, Don Larsen, playing for the Yankees in the World Series, pitches a perfect game against the Brooklyn Dodgers. The Yankees win, two to nothing. Larsen had pitched the first perfect game in a World Series, as well as the first perfect game in the major leagues in thirty-four years. The crowd roared.

1957: Frisbees, More or Less. The Frisbee craze began in earnest when the plastic toy disk from California called a Flyin' Saucer met up with the pie tin from Frisbie's bakery in Bridgeport that Yale and Harvard students tossed around in a lawn game. The enterprising president of the Wham-O Company, which manufactured the Flyin' Saucers, knew a good thing when he saw it, and suddenly the Saucers were renamed Frisbees and everybody and his dog was playing the game.

1957: European Common Market. Signed on March 25, the Treaty of Rome, signed by Belgium, Luxembourg, the Netherlands, France, West Germany, and Italy, establishes the European

Economic Community, better known as the Common Market. The aim is to end tariff barriers, enable labor and capital to move freely within the signatory countries, and do away with obstacles to free competition. The hope is that eventually a political union of Europe will arise.

1957: The Space Age Begins. On October 4 the Soviet Union launches *Sputnik 1*, the world's first artificial satellite, heralding the beginning of the Space Age and taking the fiction out of science fiction.

1958: The North Pole via Submarine. On August 5 the United States nuclear submarine *Nautilus* crosses the North Pole underwater. The following year, the nuclear submarine *Skate* breaks the ice and surfaces at the Pole.

1958: Baseball on the Move. The beloved Brooklyn Dodgers leave home to become the Los Angeles Dodgers, and the New York Giants migrate to San Francisco. Baseball moves westward while New Yorkers mourn.

1958: The Barbie Doll. Barbie appears on the market as a full-grown adult doll, unlike the baby dolls little girls were used to, and takes the market by storm. Barbie, and her boyfriend, Ken, who arrived in 1961, have their own stylish wardrobes, houses, swimming pools, and all the other accoutrements of the good life. No wonder they are so much fun to play with.

1959: We Become Fifty. On January 3, 1959, President Eisenhower announces that Alaska has been admitted to the United States, and in June, Hawaii becomes the fiftieth state.

Alaska adds 586,400 square miles, and Hawaii, 6,424. Alaska has glaciers, bears, and minerals. Hawaii has sunshine, pineapples, and tourists. We are now a union of fifty states, a nice round number. Of course, we have to reconfigure the stars on the flag again.

1959: The Guggenheim Museum. Designed by Frank Lloyd Wright, the Solomon R. Guggenheim Museum of Non-Objective Art opens on Fifth Avenue in New York City. In a departure from traditional museum architecture, the concrete snail-shaped building features a cantilevered circular inner ramp which spirals upward to the glass-domed top. Everyone has an opinion about this startling building. I love it.

1959: Panty hose Introduced.

The combining of nylon stockings and panties into one garment known as panty hose eliminates garters, garter belts, and corsets. They appear on the market just in time; the miniskirt is just around the corner.

1960: The Sky Above, the Sea Below.

In 1960, three years after the world's first satellite was launched into space, we explore the ocean to a record-breaking depth. On January 23 Jacques Piccard, the French oceanographer, and U.S. Navy Lieutenant Don Walsh, in the bathyscaphe the *Trieste,* dive to 35,800 feet in the Mariana Trench east of the Philippines, the deepest part of the ocean.

1960: Brasilia.

The new city becomes the federal capital of Brazil by order of President Kubitschek. In 1957 ground was broken in the remote undeveloped state of Goiás for a federal district 580 miles northwest of Rio de Janeiro. Many studies had been undertaken as to topography, climate, water systems, geology, engineering, transportation, recreation, scenery, and other factors before the site was selected. A design competition awarded the project to Brazilian Lucio Costas, who developed the city on a plan resembling a bow and arrow, or airplane, and determined the city would be, in his words, "convenient, efficient, welcoming, and intimate." Brazilian architect Oscar Niemeyer was in charge of designing the buildings, all of which are constructed in the modern style inspired by Le Corbusier.

Another planned city with panache.

1960: John, Paul, Ringo, and George Debut.

Four young British musicians perform in public for the first time in a striptease bar in Hamburg, West Germany. A year later, under their manager, Brian Epstein, who thought they had great possibilities, the Beatles were on their way to fame and fortune as one of the most famous, successful, and innovative pop groups in music history.

The young Liverpudlians with their long hair and fitted black suits soon became household names. In 1962 they recorded "A

Hard Day's Night," which became a huge hit and led to a British invasion of America, Beatles style. When their plane touched down at Kennedy Airport, a sea of shrieking teenagers greeted them, and upon their arrival at the prestigious Plaza Hotel, they found fans waving signs and banners announcing, "Beatles, We Love You." The adulation never stopped during their entire stay in the States.

Their appearance on the "Ed Sullivan Show" catapulted their celebrity further, as it did for another musical phenomenon, Elvis Presley, and their two performances at Carnegie Hall were sold out.

In July 1964 their first movie, *A Hard Day's Night,* hit the British theaters, to critical approval. Shortly thereafter, they arrived in San Francisco, greeted again by the customary teenage shriekers, to begin a twenty-three-city tour. By this time their success was astounding. Their songs, written by Paul McCartney and John Lennon, held the top five spots on the music charts at one time, and "Beatlemania" reigned supreme.

The times they were a-changin', however, and so was the Beatles music. Their 1967 recording of "Sgt. Pepper's Lonely Hearts Club Band" reflected the "tell it like it is" disillusioned culture that was pervading society. The Beatles, once the idols of teenagers, had grown up and evolved into serious musicians. The *Sgt. Pepper* album sold 2.5 million copies in three months.

Fame, however, had taken its toll on the group. In 1968 they went to India, and under the guidance of a guru, sought "absolute bliss consciousness." Apparently they didn't find it together since upon their return, they began to branch out into individual musical pursuits. In 1970 Paul McCartney left the group, citing "personal differences, business differences, musical differences, but most of all because I have a better time with my family."

Thus ended the ten-year reign of one of the most creative and influential groups in the annals of musical history. Their songs live on.

1960s: Laser Surgery. *Star Wars* comes to the operating room. Powerful beams of light have long been a tool of destruction in science fiction, but now the tables have turned and lasers (an acronym for Light Amplification by Stimulated Emission of Radiation) are being used in surgery for beneficial purposes.

In 1958 two physics professors, C. H. Townes and A. L. Schawlow, worked on the idea of a laser based on principles Einstein had developed in 1916, and in 1960 another physicist, Theodore Maimen, built the first working laser. Laser beams are now used in many ways, from shooting down missiles to checking out at the supermarket, but almost from the beginning one of the most promising and exciting possibilities was in the field of medicine. In 1961 Dr. Leon Goldman at Children's Hospital in Cincinnati used a laser to treat melanoma, a form of skin cancer. In 1962 lasers were used in eye surgery, sealing off leaking blood vessels, and by 1985, arteries were being unclogged by lasers. Almost painless, and with little bleeding, laser surgery does minimal damage to healthy surrounding tissue and greatly decreases the chance of infection. Lasers can be used to remove some birthmarks, tattoos, and warts. Surgeons have found one of the greatest values of the laser to be its use in treating some otherwise inoperable tumors of the brain.

Drs. Townes and Schawlow are both Nobelists in the field of physics.

1960: The Sit-In. At 4:00 P.M. on February 1 in Greensboro, North Carolina, four black college students sit down at the all-white lunch counter in Woolworth's. The students, from A&T State University, have decided to challenge the laws that bar blacks from public facilities.

The idea spread and soon there were sit-ins at Woolworth's lunch counters in fifty cities in the South. On July 25 all Woolworth's lunch counters were declared open to everyone.

The audacious act was one of many precipitating the Civil Rights Act of 1964.

1960: The Pill. The world's first oral contraceptive pill, Enovid, is introduced.

Birth control, a term coined in 1914 by its greatest American proponent, nurse Margaret Sanger, has been practiced since time immemorial in a variety of ways. The early Greeks knew the plant *silphion* had contraceptive properties, and the city of Cyrene (in what is now Libya), where it grew, became very prosperous from its famous cash crop. By the first century A.D., however, it had become scarce, and other plants, including asafoetida, began to replace it. The seeds of Queen Anne's lace, according to Hippocrates, also have contraceptive properties, along with such plants as pennyroyal, artemisia, and rue. Evidence from archaeological digs as well as ancient manuscripts indicates that women of ancient times knew how to limit the size of their families. This folk knowledge seemed to be available through the Middle Ages but then gradually faded.

While in Mexico in 1941, Russell Marker, an American chemist, developed an oral contraceptive when he discovered that the hormone progesterone could be extracted from the root of the barbasco plant (yam) that grows wild there. Back in the States, chemist Gregory Pincus, with a healthy nudge from Margaret Sanger, tested norethynodrel derived from yams and found it safe, simple, and effective. Since Enovid was introduced, even safer pills have been developed, none of which contains the original norethynodrel. "The Pill," as it has become known, however, was a medical breakthrough and is now used by millions of women the world over to prevent conception.

In 1990 the FDA approved Norplant, which, when implanted under the skin, slowly releases the hormone progestin and can last up to five years.

So far nobody's been awarded the Nobel Prize for these noble deeds.

1961: First Man in Space. On April 12 Soviet cosmonaut Yuri Gagarin becomes the first man in outer space. His spacecraft, *Vostok I,* weighing over ten thousand pounds, takes him on a complete orbit around the earth in one hour and forty-eight minutes.

1961: First American in Space. On May 5 astronaut Alan Shepard, Jr., aboard the *Freedom* 7 space capsule, reaches an altitude of 116.5 miles in a fifteen-minute suborbital flight.

1961: A Record Season. Roger Maris of the New York Yankees breaks Babe Ruth's 1927 record of sixty home runs in one season when he hits his sixty-first home run in his last game of the season.

1962: Outward Bound. On February 20 U.S. astronaut John Glenn orbits the earth three times in the space capsule *Mercury 9* during a five-hour flight.

1963: Spacewoman. Soviet cosmonaut Valentina Tereshkova becomes the first woman in space as she orbits the earth forty-eight times aboard *Vostok 6* on June 16.

1963: Nuclear Test-Ban Treaty. Diplomats from the United States, the USSR, and Great Britain sign a treaty in Moscow on August 5, banning the testing of nuclear weapons in the atmosphere, underwater, and in outer space, but permitting underground testing.

The treaty was later signed by more than one hundred other nations.

1963: Martin Luther King, Jr., Has a Dream. On August 28, civil rights leader Martin Luther King, Jr., stands on a platform in front of the Lincoln Memorial in Washington, D.C., and addresses over 200,000 people who have joined together to protest discrimination. In what will become known as his "I Have a Dream" speech, King fervently proclaims his hope that the descendants of slaves and of slave owners will one day be joined in brotherhood and that we will become a nation where people are judged by their character and not by their skin color. His "dream" will be echoed time and time again.

It is a triumphant ending to the March on Washington led by King and other civil rights activists to peacefully demonstrate and demand passage of civil rights legislation, including the banning of discrimination in public accommodations.

The following year President Johnson will sign the Civil Rights Act, and Martin Luther King, Jr., will be awarded the Nobel Peace Prize for his nonviolent struggle in the quest for racial equality.

1964: The Civil Rights Act. On July 2, 1964, President Lyndon Johnson signs into law the Civil Rights Act, barring discrimination in public places for reasons of color, race, national origin, or religion. The bill has been filibustered for seventy-five days by southern senators before the Senate finally invokes cloture for the first time in history—ending debate by calling for a vote—and passes the bill seventy-three to twenty-seven. The bill prohibits discrimination by employers and establishes the Equal Employment Opportunity Commission to implement it. The new legislation strengthens enforcement of voting rights for African-Americans and aids in furthering school desegregation.

1964: Verrazano Narrows Bridge. On November 21 the largest single-span suspension bridge in the world opens, linking the two boroughs of Brooklyn and Staten Island at the entrance to New York City's harbor. The 4,260-foot span contains 150,000 tons of steel in its structure and has two decks each, carrying six lanes of traffic.

1965: Miniskirt Madness. The young British designer Mary Quant creates the miniskirt, with a hemline six inches above the knee. It causes a sensation in more than just the fashion circles and becomes the rage, especially among the young.

1967: Pulsars Discovered. Jocelyn Bell, a twenty-four-year-old graduate student at Cambridge University in England, discovers pulsars, a spectacular scientific find.

Pulsars are dense, burned-out stars that rapidly rotate and send out radio pulses just like a lighthouse sends out rays of light as it rotates. A pulsar is what remains of a small star after it has used up its nuclear fuel, exploded into a supernova, and collapsed in upon itself. What remains is mostly neutrons (atoms contain protons and neutrons, and each of these contains quarks), so pulsars are also called neutron stars.

Jocelyn Bell had been helping her mentor, Anthony Hewish, build a radio telescope to scan the sky weekly and plot the positions of radio sources from stars. She was in charge of analyzing the data received on charts when she noticed what she called "scruffs" that appeared periodically. These turned out to be pulsars.

1967: Habitat Apartments. A radical new concept in apartment dwelling is unveiled at Canada's Montreal Expo 67. Designed by the young Israeli-born architect Moshe Safde, 158 precast concrete units are hoisted and posttensioned into place. The arrangement creates private outdoor space for each unit in a building of cantilevers and terraces. Another great mind at work daring to be different.

1967: Heart Transplants Pioneered. On December 3 South African surgeon Christiaan Barnard performs the world's first heart transplant at Groote Schuur Hospital in Cape Town.

The operation was a success, but the patient, Louis Washansky, died eighteen days later as a result of the drugs he received to suppress his immune system. He caught double pneumonia and his body couldn't fight the disease.

Fourteen days later, New York surgeon Adrian Kantrowitz successfully completed a heart transplant, but the patient did not recover. In 1968 Dr. Denton Cooley in Houston, Texas, performed the first successful heart transplant in the United States. It was the beginning of a new era in surgery.

1968: The Impossible Dream. Between December 21 and 27, three American astronauts, Frank Borman, James Lovell, and William Anders, become the first men to orbit the moon in their *Apollo 8* spacecraft, circling it ten times.

1969: The *Eagle* Has Landed. July 20, 1969, became one of the most memorable days in world chronicles when two American astronauts land on the moon at 4:17 P.M. eastern daylight time. It was the culmination of President John F. Kennedy's 1961 commitment to land a man on the moon within the decade, and the most expensive scientific enterprise in history.

The historic voyage for Neil Armstrong, Colonel Edwin Aldrin, Jr., and Lieutenant Colonel Michael Collins began at Cape Kennedy in Florida on July 16, when the three astronauts were launched with a lunar module on their *Apollo 11* mission. The flight was near perfect and in three days they were orbiting the moon. The crew woke early on July 20, as the sun was rising over their landing site on the Sea of Tranquility. They were sixty-four miles above the moon's surface, speeding along at 3,660 miles per hour. After breakfast, Armstrong and Aldrin donned their space suits and crawled through the tunnel that connected the command ship, *Columbia,* piloted by Collins, with their lunar vehicle, the *Eagle.* The ungainly-looking craft, with four legs and yard-wide footpads, was thirty-one feet wide and almost twenty-three feet high. If anything should go wrong, the craft, with walls of finely milled aluminum foil, would never withstand reentry into the earth's atmosphere even if it had the rocket power. The two stood at the controls, turned on the power, checked the cockpit panel, and tested communications with the *Columbia* and ground control in Houston. Everything was go.

Colonel Collins fired his command ship's rockets and moved two miles away from the *Eagle* into a slightly different orbit. The two were on their own, riding backwards and facing downwards as the lunar module circled around to the dark side of the moon. The descent rocket was programmed to fire at 3:08 P.M. while the *Eagle* was behind the moon. A hush fell over the control center in Houston while they waited. At 3:46 P.M. Colonel Collins reported from the *Columbia* that things were going beautifully. Two more minutes passed, then Armstrong's voice crackled over the airwaves and announced that "the burn was on time." The module had descended to twenty-one miles and was coasting downward. At fifty thousand feet green lights in the cockpit indicated to Armstrong that he had five seconds to decide whether to proceed with the descent or continue on an orbit back to the command ship. He pressed the proceed button. They had passed the point of no return. The engines fired continuously, thrusting the craft downward. In six minutes they were at twenty-seven thousand feet. At three and a half minutes to touchdown the pair finally viewed the landing site, a barren land full of craters and hills and ridges. They closed in. At three hundred feet Armstrong took over semimanual control to adjust the hovering position. They were headed for an area of large boulders and rocks. Armstrong tilted the craft forward, looking for a smoother landing place. He found the spot and set the craft down perfectly. The *Eagle* had landed. Sighs of relief were heard in Houston while Armstrong's and Aldrin's hearts beat double time at touchdown.

At 10:56 P.M. Neil Armstrong stepped off the ladder leading from the lunar module, put the first human footprint on the moon, and declared, "That's one small step for man, one giant leap for mankind." After testing the moon's crust, he took a few steps and then, like the explorers of the past, planted his country's flag. Aldrin joined him on the powdery, rocky, desolate moonscape, and the two spent the next two hours taking photographs, collecting rock and soil samples, and deploying a solar wind experiment, a laser beam reflecting device, and a seismic experiment. They found working on the moon very comfortable in their space suits as they bounced over the surface under the influence of gravity only one sixth that of the earth. Adding to the wonder of this awe-inspiring event was that fact that we could watch it on our television sets at home 238,855 miles away.

The heroic astronauts returned to earth on Thursday, July 24. They had gone where no human had ever gone before. Neither the world nor the universe would ever be the same again.

1970: Hale House Founded.

Clara McBride Hale founds a home in the Harlem section of New York City to care for drug-addicted black babies. With funds from private and public sources, Mother Hale, as she is affectionately called, and her small staff will care for over eight hundred babies born with drug addiction, and children with AIDS. Hale House provides a warm, loving environment for these children, tended by a caring staff devoted to their well-being.

After Mrs. Hale's husband died when she was in her forties, she began taking care of foster children as a means of supporting herself and her three children. In 1969 a young woman appeared at her home with a drug-addicted baby and later returned with two more children for Mrs. Hale to take care of. Word of her kindness spread and soon Mother Hale found herself ministering to many such afflicted babies just when she had reached the age of sixty-five and was about to retire.

Ronald Reagan, in his 1985 State of the Union speech, will acclaim Mother Hale a true American hero, and the Salvation Army will award her two of their highest honors for her selfless humanitarianism. Her daughter, Lorraine, a Ph.D. in child development, is now the director of Hale House and carries on the work her mother began.

1971: Aswan High Dam Completed.

The first dam spanning the Nile at Aswan in southern Egypt was completed in 1902. It was considered one of the world's great engineering projects. The High Dam was begun in 1960 to increase the amount of farmland and relieve the country of Nile flooding. In order to construct it, about ninety thousand Egyptians and Sudanese farmers had to be relocated. The High Dam also submerged several archaeological sites, some of which were rescued by UNESCO and relocated. The removal and relocation of the temple at Abu Simbel to higher ground was an engineering feat in itself.

1971: CAT Scan.

This has nothing to do with furry felines. CAT stands for computerized axial tomography. While X rays gave us the ability to see through the skin, the hardest area to examine remained—the brain. Until this time, any look inside the brain was very difficult and dangerous, not to mention painful. Unlike the X ray and other wonderful scientific inventions, the person responsible for the CAT scan was Godfrey Hounsfield, a British workshop wizard without a long list of formal academic credits. Although he had some training in electrical and mechanical engineering and had worked with high-tech radar and computer systems, he had no degree. He was, however, fearless in trying new ideas, and he wondered if X rays and computers could be combined to recognize and piece together images. In 1968 the first laboratory model of a CAT scanner was completed, and in 1971 the Atkinson Morley Hospital in London installed the first machine. CAT scans are simple and harmless, and besides the miracle of being able to see inside the skull clearly, they can be used to monitor osteoporosis and take three-dimensional pictures of all the internal structures of the body.

In 1979 Hounsfield shared the Nobel Prize for medicine with the American Allan Cormack, who had worked out the mathematical computations of how such a machine could function.

1971: Doctors Without Borders. Médecins sans Frontières was founded in Paris, France, as a voluntary organization of doctors and nurses who rush to disaster areas without being asked in order to alleviate the pain and suffering of victims.

Based on cofounder Dr. Bernard Kouchner's philosophy that people's needs come before politics and bureaucracy and that it is the agency's "duty to interfere," Doctors Without Borders, along with two other groups it inspired, Médecins du Monde (Doctors of the World) and Assistance Médicale Internationale (International Medical Assistance), have coordinated relief efforts in such countries as Jordan, Ethiopia, Afghanistan, Bangladesh, Romania, Chad, El Salvador, and Cambodia. Wherever there are wars, natural disasters, famines, and epidemics, the medical teams leap in with zeal and compassion to nurse the wounded, heal the sick, and protest against human rights violations. Vive les médecins!

1971: First Space Station. On April 18 the Soviets launch the world's first space station, the *Salyut 1,* sixty-six feet long and weighing forty thousand pounds. On June 7 three cosmonauts arrive to man the station and stay aboard for twenty-three days.

1972: Artificial Hip Designed. British orthopedic surgeon John Charnley designs the first artificial hip made from high-density polyethylene.

Now when our hip joint wears out or is severely damaged, we

can replace it. This type of operation has had a high rate of success, as many who are now walking around free of pain can attest to.

1973: UPC. This is short for the Universal Product Code, those little black lines that now appear on practically everything that's sold. The UPC enables electronic scanners to "read" the price of the item and record it automatically. This makes inventory keeping easier, eliminates errors, and theoretically improves productivity. Naturally people complained about this innovation and retailers thought it would cost them too much money to install, but it caught on quickly. Now we watch the monitor at the supermarket checkout counter as the scanner magically beeps its price to it, totals up everything, and tells us how much change we get. Who needs arithmetic?

1973: The Sears Tower. Architecture and engineering merge to reach great heights. Now the world's tallest building, the Sears Tower in Chicago, Illinois, reaches 1,455 feet into the clouds and has over three and a half million square feet of rentable space.

1974: A New Record. On April 8, a cold, damp evening at the Atlanta Braves stadium, Hank Aaron hits his 715th home run off Dodger pitcher Al Downing, breaking Babe Ruth's lifetime record.

1974: Lucy: Mother of Us All? In the Awash Valley of Ethiopia, anthropologist Donald Johanson discovers a hominid fossil skeleton he calls Lucy, which turns out to be the so-called missing link in human evolution.

Lucy's scientific name is *Australopithecus afarensis*. Johanson named her after the Beatles song "Lucy in the Sky With Diamonds," which was playing on his tape recorder as he perused the new find. The hominid was about three and a half feet tall, weighed about seventy-five pounds, and walked upright. The upright part is the clue. Lucy also swung from the trees. According to the bone structure, and that of others of Lucy's type which have been found in the past two years, *A. afarensis* was bipedal as well as arboreal, meaning the arm bones had a curving form for swinging and climbing trees, while the structure of the leg bones indicates a hominid that could also walk upright.

Lucy and her relatives appeared about 3.5 to 4 million years ago and were around for an amazingly long time, for almost one million years. Maybe they were just having too much fun swinging around in the trees to get down to much serious bipedal locomotion. The next generation in the evolutionary line, *Australopithecus africanus,* inherited Lucy's genes and appeared about three million years ago, and they, in turn, gave way to *Homo habilis.* Our brains were getting larger, but we no longer could swing in the trees. Darn it!

1975: The Great Uhuru Railway. The African railroad
stretches from Kapiri Mposhi in Zambia to Dar es Salaam on the coast of Tanzania, a distance of 1,162 miles. Chinese engineers and Africans labored through remote terrain to build the project, which includes three hundred bridges and twenty-three tunnels. Where there's a will, there's a way.

1976: Supersonic Airliner. Passenger service on the French-
British Concorde SST begins January 21, 1976, between London and Bahrain and between Paris and Rio de Janeiro.

The SST, which made its first test flight on March 12, 1969, can attain a speed of 1,448 miles per hour and carry up to 139 passengers. The Concorde first landed in the United States at Andrews Air Force Base outside Washington, D.C., on May 17, 1977, with French President Giscard d'Estaing aboard the inaugural flight. Daily service from Dulles International began a week later, and passenger service from JFK, in New York, began on November 22. The British and French Concordes make the transatlantic flights in just under four hours, which means you get here before you left. It cuts down on jet lag.

1977: Magnetic Resonance Imaging. The first MRI scan-
ner is tested on July 2 and becomes an important diagnostic tool.

Back in 1937, the technique for observing atoms and molecules in the radio frequency range was invented by Austrian-born American physicist Isidor Isaac Rabi. MRI machines have been used since 1984 to detect abnormalities in the nerves and brain as well as to show if treatments are working. Blood can be monitored flowing through an artery, and soft tissue such as muscles can be imaged through radio waves in a magnetic field. The images produced can distinguish between normal tissue, tumors, and cysts.

Rabi was awarded the 1944 Nobel Prize in physics for his work in this field.

1978: A Test-Tube Baby. Louise Brown is born on July 25 in England, the first baby born through in vitro fertilization.

Baby Brown is the culmination of twelve years of research by two doctors. IVF, as it is called for short, had been used for years in the world of veterinary medicine, but it was up to British physicians Robert Edwards and Patrick Steptoe to take the courageous step of applying the procedure to humans. In IVF, an egg is removed from the mother, placed in a lab dish, and fertilized with sperm from the father. The fertilized egg is then transferred to the mother's uterus, and if the egg implants, pregnancy results. The process offers new hope to infertile couples and those unable to have children because of medical complications.

In 1981 the first test-tube baby was born in the United States. It won't be long before many other children can brag about being conceived in a petri dish.

1979: Mother Teresa Awarded Nobel Peace Prize. The small, quiet, unassuming organizer of the Sisters of the Missionaries of Charity receives the Peace Prize for her selfless humanitarian efforts with the sick and poor of India.

Born in Yugoslavia in 1910, Mother Teresa, after taking her vows, left for India, where she taught geography at St. Mary's High School in Calcutta. In 1952, after serving and living among the poor for six years, she opened a Home for the Dying in a squalid section of the city, where the indigent and ill are tended with love and kindness. Mother Teresa and her devoted associates live in the slums among the people they care for and have expanded their ministries to over twenty-five cities in India and several other countries.

1981: The Humber Bridge. The 4,626-foot bridge over the Humber Estuary at Hull on England's east coast becomes the world's longest suspension bridge. Another engineering marvel.

1981: The Space Shuttle. Named the *Columbia,* the first reusable spacecraft is piloted by American astronauts John Young and Robert Crippen. The 4.58-million-pound craft is launched from

Cape Kennedy on April 14. After a fifty-four-hour flight, the *Columbia* lands at Edwards Air Force Base in California.

We now have a new means of space transportation. The *Columbia* and other shuttles to follow will be used on missions to deploy, retrieve, and repair satellites, and for space walks.

1983: First Female Astronaut. Sally Ride becomes the first female American astronaut in space when she and three other crew members are launched aboard the shuttle *Challenger* on June 18, for a six-day voyage. Hooray for Sally!

1983: Barbara McClintock, Nobelist at Last. At the age of eighty-one, Dr. Barbara McClintock finally receives her due when she is the lone recipient of the Nobel Prize for her pioneering work in plant genetics.

Dr. McClintock, born in 1902, grew up in an era when women weren't expected to be seriously educated or become employed in a field in which men predominated. Her father, however, did not feel that way and encouraged in her a sense of freedom and opportunity that laid the groundwork for her persistence in following her dream. Against the wishes of her mother, but with her father's blessing, she attended Cornell University. Since women were refused entrance to the plant-breeding department, she enrolled instead in botany, and by the time she graduated, was already doing postgraduate research work in genetics. The year was 1923, and Mendel's work with the heredity of peas had been recently rediscovered. The double helix and DNA sequences were unknown, and scientists thought genes were formed in a single line. By 1927, she had her Ph.D. and stayed on at Cornell as a botany instructor, a position far beneath her abilities, but then the department discriminated against women. McClintock had worked for seven years tracing the genetic changes in kernels of corn, and when she published her findings in 1931, she was laughed at. Many scientists couldn't even understand all she was doing. Dr. McClintock proved that the genes for physical characteristics are carried on chromosomes and that the exchange of these chromosome sections creates a biological variety. It would be years before other genetic developments proved the importance of her findings, not only for botany but in human genetics.

The Cornell faculty fervently opposed giving a permanent position to a woman, as did most universities, so Dr. McClintock left for the University of Missouri, where she was hired as an assistant professor. Again she ran up against discrimination, so again she left. She refused to leave the work she loved, however, and finally, after several temporary positions, she found her niche in Cold Spring Harbor, New York, where she spent the rest of her life at the Carnegie Institute Research Center doing biological studies of corn. Her further investigations showed that genes can move around and turn on and off during a cell's development.

In 1944 Dr. McClintock was elected to the National Academy of Sciences, and the same year was elected the first woman president of the Genetics Society of America. In 1983 she received her long overdue Nobel for what the committee said was "one of the two great discoveries of our times in genetics."

Gender discrimination seems to have gotten in the way of scientific progress, as frequently happened until recently. Those men should have paid attention to a woman who was twenty years ahead of her time.

1985: Baseball Career Record. The Houston Astros' Nolan Ryan strikes out his four thousandth batter and sets a major league career record. When he retired at the age of forty-six in September of 1993, Ryan, who had once set a speed record of 100.9 miles per hour for a pitched ball, had racked up a staggering 5,714 strikeouts. Ryan ended his career, the longest in major league history, with the Texas Rangers.

1986: The Rod Is Spared. The British Education Bill abolishes corporal punishment in state-supported schools or for students whose fees are paid by the state.

As far back as ancient Egypt and Mesopotamia and for centuries after, students had their lessons beaten into them by the cane or birch rod or other available means. It was the standard method of teaching. It didn't stop during the Middle Ages either, when children were thought of as diminutive adults and therefore physical punishment could be sanctioned by Biblical authority. Johann Comenius, a seventeenth-century Moravian pastor, questioned the validity of corporal punishment. His philosophy of education was that learning should be humane and attractive to the intellect and feelings. Rote memorization and beatings were unnecessary.

Before 1870, in England, most children went to private elementary schools or church-supported institutions. The Education Act of 1870, however, changed that by permitting elected boards of education to levy local property taxes to support schools. At the turn of the century, opponents of corporal punishment, who maintained it was brutalizing and counterproductive to learning, formed the Society for the Reform of School Discipline to gather data and print literature to further their cause. In 1901 the Education Department finally forbade corporal punishment in kindergartens and girls' schools and recommended that another form of punishment in boys' schools would be advisable. In 1911 boys in a school in South Wales went on strike in September to protest caning, and several days later, schools throughout England were struck. Most of this activity took place in the industrial areas where the students imitated the methods of the labor unions. The strike was to no avail, however, and was shortly quelled.

After World War II, progressive education came to the forefront, and its proponents recommended abolishing corporal punishment altogether. In 1982 the European Court of Human Rights, part of the Common Market to which Britain belongs, ruled that students could not be physically punished if their parents disapproved. Four years later, Great Britain abolished corporal punishment for state schools. Private school students, however, were still subject to the whims of the masters.

1989: The Human Genome Project.

The Program Advisory Committee of the National Institutes of Health meets on January 3 to administrate one of the most important and most expensive scientific research projects ever undertaken, the mapping and sequencing of the entire human genetic code. The project is expected to take at least a decade to complete at a cost of about four billion dollars.

The project is a mind-boggling intellectual challenge that, when accomplished, will pinpoint the exact location of all three billion base pairs of human DNA (deoxyribonucleic acid), the component of chromosomes that contains our genetic characteristics and makes each of us who we are.

The consequences of this biological engineering project will be enormous and revolutionary. Researchers will have the ability to manipulate genes and transplant healthy genes into abnormal cells to effect cures. Experiments with gene therapy are under way now to control or eliminate diseases such as cystic fibrosis, AIDS, and various types of cancer.

When the mapping and sequencing are complete, human beings will truly know themselves.

1989: Restitution. President Bush signs the Internment Compensation Act, awarding twenty thousand dollars each to surviving Japanese-Americans who were interned during World War II.

In an act that will live in infamy, President Roosevelt signed an executive order in February 1942 requiring all Japanese-Americans living along the Pacific coast to be interned in camps until the end of the war. However, Japanese in Hawaii and elsewhere in the United States, as well as alien Germans and Italians in the States, were not so confined. Native-born Americans of Japanese descent as well as Japanese aliens were herded into camps in the Southwest, where they lived in barracks under constant guard. Many of these citizens lost millions of dollars in property, and some renounced their citizenship.

In 1959 full citizenship was granted to those who relinquished theirs, but no compensation was accorded those who lost so much. It took another thirty years to compensate these citizens for the indignity foisted on them.

1989: Fall of the Berlin Wall. On November 9 the Berlin Wall dividing East and West Berlin is breached and there is dancing in the streets. A blow for freedom had been struck and the reverberations echoed throughout the Communist world.

After World War II, the Germans in USSR-dominated East Germany continually crossed over to the west through Berlin. To stem the tide and loss of manpower, the East German government, during the night of August 12–13, 1961, erected a barbed-wire fence cutting off access to West Berlin. On the night of August 17–18, it was replaced by a six-foot-high cement wall, topped by barbed wire. Official crossing points were established and guards patrolled the wall from turrets, shooting anyone who attempted to escape.

By 1989, the Communist regimes in Eastern Europe were in dire economic straits and crumbling. In August, Hungary opened its frontiers, enabling East Germans to enter and apply for asylum at the West German embassy. Czechoslovakia followed suit, and soon the West was deluged by people wanting to leave. Riots and demonstrations against the corrupt Communist government broke out in Berlin. The party leaders were dismissed, but the unrest

continued to grow, until, on the night of November 9, the wall
was breached, as the guards stood by and watched. The Communist East German government had been overthrown; the rest of
the wall was then demolished. It was the end of Communism and
the beginning of a reunited democratic Germany.

1989: Czechoslovakia Breaks Communist Yoke. On
December 29 Václav Havel, playwright and dissident, is elected
president of Czechoslovakia as democracy rears its resplendent
head.

Demonstrations in October and November had been crushed
by the government, but at the urging of Russia's Gorbachev, the
reins are loosened. Travel to the West is allowed and the Communist party general secretary resigns. As more people cry out for
democracy and civil rights, the president steps down and a new
cabinet is formed, with the Communists in the minority. Parliament then votes to institute a Western-type democracy, and Havel
is elected to lead it.

1990: Smoking Ban. By an act of Congress on February 25,
smoking is banned on all domestic airline flights.

Not everyone will take an optimistic view of this.

1990: A Good Act to Follow. On July 26 President George
Bush signs the Americans with Disabilities Act, which prohibits
discrimination in employment, public accommodations, and transportation against any disabled person and also protects employees
with AIDS.

1990: A Reversal of Heart. On September 26 the Supreme
Soviet ends years of religious repression when it enjoins the government from interfering in religious exercises and sanctions the
rights of its citizens to study religion in their homes and in private
schools.

After decades of silence and secrecy, one's religion can now be
openly part of one's life.

1991: Yeltsin Elected. For the first time in history, Russia
holds democratic elections on June 13, electing Boris Yeltsin to
the presidency.

1991: Population Registration Act Repealed. On June 17 the parliament of South Africa repeals the forty-one-year-old act by which every newborn child must be classified according to race: white, black, Asian, or mixed parentage.

1991: The End of an Era. Seventy-four years of Communist rule come to an end when the Communist party is suspended by Soviet President Mikhail Gorbachev on August 24.

The Union of Soviet Socialist Republics collapses as the republics strive toward individual autonomy. Russian, Ukrainian, and Belorussian leaders announce the establishment of a commonwealth of independent states, and on December 21 representatives from the eleven former Soviet republics meet to confirm the action.

It was, to say the least, a dramatic turn of events.

1993: Middle East Peace Try. On September 13 Israel and the Palestine Liberation Organization (PLO) reach an accord on Palestinian self-rule. After nearly fifty years of deep hatreds and violence on both sides, Israeli prime minister Yitzhak Rabin and PLO chairman Yasser Arafat, coaxed by United States president Bill Clinton, shook hands in Washington, D.C., before the television cameras for all the world to see.

The unrest in the Mideast began before November 1947, when the United Nations voted to divide Palestine into independent Arab and Jewish states, and Israel proclaimed itself a republic on May 14, 1948. Prior to that, Palestine had been under British mandate since World War I, during which time the British secretary of state, Arthur Balfour, promised support for the establishment of a national home for the Jews, with the understanding that the civil and religious rights of non-Jews be protected. Clashes between the Zionist Jewish settlers and Arabs began when the Zionists felt they were being undermined and the Arab residents' rights had priority over theirs, and the Arabs felt the new Jewish immigrants were jeopardizing their livelihood. In 1933 the Arabs announced a boycott of Zionist and British goods. At the same time, Jewish immigration increased due to the rise of Hitler. In 1935 Arab political parties, Christian and Muslim, demanded Jewish immigration stop, the transfer of property be prohibited, and democracy be established. The British offered to set up a legislative council to include the British, Arabs, and Jews, but the Zionists opposed it for fear it would halt their establishment of a national home. The British House of Commons attacked the legislative council idea as being anti-Zionist, which angered the Arabs, who then rebelled. In 1937 the British decided their mandate was not working and that they could not oblige both Arabs and Jews. They recommended the country be partitioned and Jewish immigration be regulated. The Arabs remained defiant. In 1939 the British assumed their pledge of a Jewish national home had been fulfilled and that indefinite Jewish immigration and transfer of Arab land should be limited. The new policy allowed seventy-five thousand Jewish immigrants within five years, after which they would be able to enter only with Arab acquiescence. Specific areas would be set aside for land transfers, and within ten years an independent Palestinian state was to be considered. The Arabs were still mistrustful of the British and disdainful of the British mandate being extended. The Zionists considered they had been betrayed and the Balfour Declaration disregarded.

During World War II, the Zionists joined with Britain against the common enemy while fighting against Arabs, and later fought the British themselves, in the underground Haganah and Irgun movements. In November 1943 Britain extended Jewish immigration for another five years. Twelve thousand Arabs, in the meantime, had enlisted in the British armed forces. The Zionist movement by this time had enlisted the help of the United States and demanded a program of unrestricted Jewish immigration, a Jewish army, and the establishment of a Jewish commonwealth in Palestine. In August 1945 U.S. president Harry Truman requested that British prime minister Clement Atlee admit one hundred thousand Jews into Palestine, and later that year the U.S. Congress asked for unlimited immigration as far as economics in Palestine would allow. In March 1945 the League of Arab States was formed, and in December they declared a boycott of Zionist commodities.

An Anglo-American commission recommended continuing Jewish immigration, continuation of the British mandate, and repeal of land restrictions, while at the same time requiring that the underground Zionist forces be disbanded. The commission also worked out a plan for provincial autonomy for both Arabs and Jews. Both sides undermined the plan, and the Palestine question was finally submitted in 1947 to the United Nations, which recommended the country be partitioned into Arab and Jewish states and that Jerusalem be an international city. At the time there were 1,269,000 Arabs and 678,000 Jews in Palestine, and the Arab nations rejected the U.N. plan of partition, arguing that it was contrary to the wishes of the majority of its people. The division also placed as many Arabs as Jews in the new Jewish state. The British mandate was to end on May 15, 1948. As the British government in Palestine wound down its administrative affairs, civil war and bloody fighting erupted as the well-equipped Zionists fought for their state and the Arabs tried to counter them. Finally, in defeat, Arab refugees flowed out of Palestine and into neighboring Arab states. The last British high commissioner left on May 14 and the state of Israel was proclaimed and recognized by President Harry Truman. The next day army units of neighboring countries Syria, Transjordan, Egypt, and Iraq crossed their frontiers to restore order, and the United Nations appointed Count Bernadotte as mediator in the settlement. Truces went unobserved, Bernadotte was assassinated, and finally agreements were reached. War between Arab countries and Israel broke out in 1967 for six days. Israel won the war, which solved nothing and created more refugees. Skirmishes and guerrilla warfare have been going on in the Middle East ever since, as Arabs and Jews continue their ongoing battle.

In 1977 Egyptian President Anwar Sadat made an unprecedented trip to Jerusalem, and in 1978 met with President Jimmy Carter and Israeli premier Menachem Begin to negotiate a peace treaty and restore relations between the two countries. Perhaps peace will now begin to reign over these tortured lands in the Middle East. Only the people there can determine that by living up to the agreement, forgetting and forgiving past inequities and hatreds, and moving forward. It won't be easy. Maybe Rabin and Arafat can pull off the miracle. It's a beginning.

1993: We Do the Impossible. In 1990 NASA launched the $1,000,600,000 Hubble Space Telescope, designed to see farther into space than ever before possible. Expectations were crushed, however, when it was found the Hubble was in big trouble: The mirror was flawed, some of the electronic systems were faulty, and two solar panels vibrated. What to do? Fix it, of course.

The crew was assembled: veteran American astronauts Richard Covey, Jeffrey Hoffman, Thomas Akers, Story Musgrave, Kathryn Thornton, Kenneth Bowersox, and the Swiss Claude Nicollier.

For ten months the spirited septet trained for the mission and spent over four hundred hours in the underwater tank practicing their routine in simulated weightlessness. Then they trained in the cold chamber where the temperature reached three hundred degrees below zero, simulating the temperature in space. All this in their clumsy space suits and gloves. Sort of like trying to thread a needle while wearing mittens during a free fall.

In December the gallant crew was launched into space on board the shuttle *Endeavor,* and on December 9 they accomplished their repairs. They had made an unprecedented five space walks, replaced the faulty electronics and solar panels, added an electronics box, placed covers over magnetic sensing units, installed a new gyroscope, and most important, positioned a new wide-field camera to compensate for the telescope's focusing errors in the primary mirror. They also corrected Hubble's vision with an apparatus containing ten small mirrors to correct the light for the important faint-object camera. On December 10 the twelve-and-a-half-ton, forty-three-foot-long telescope was released from the shuttle's cargo bay and once again floated into space in all its reconditioned glory. The astronauts had accomplished the most spectacular mission since the moon landing.

The crew returned to earth safely at the Kennedy Space Center in Florida after having circled the earth 162 times and traveled over four million miles.

On December 18 the Hubble telescope was put to the test. The results were glorious. Better than scientists had ever imagined. Astronomers may now be able to answer some of the questions that have been on the minds of humans since time began. Are there other planets out there that revolve around stars? What are the black holes in galaxies? How old is the universe? Exactly how did the galaxies form? There may be some awesome discoveries.

We will learn a lot from Hubble thanks to the magnificent seven for whom the word *impossible* doesn't exist.

1994: A Repeat Disaster Averted. On January 17 a loose barge hit a railroad bridge near Amelia, Louisiana, knocking it six inches out of alignment. The quick-thinking bridge tender immediately notified the Coast Guard, who were able to stop Amtrak's Sunset Limited train ten minutes before it would have crossed the bridge. An accident a few weeks before had resulted in forty-seven deaths when a train derailed on a similarly damaged bridge. One of our unsung heroes, the bridge tender.

1994: In a Galaxy Far, Far Away. In February Alexander Wolszczan of Penn State University confirms the existence of two planets orbiting a star in the Milky Way galaxy.

Two years ago he and a colleague discovered evidence that two planets were circling a pulsar (neutron star) about thirteen hundred light-years from the Earth. (A light-year is equal to about six trillion miles—that's a one followed by twelve zeros.) These are the first planets discovered outside our solar system. We may not be alone.

1994: A Political Phenomenon. On March 29, 1994, Congressman William Natcher, a Democrat from Kentucky, dies at Bethesda Naval Medical Center at the age of eighty-four. His terms in office spanned four decades, during which time he never missed a roll call or a vote and racked up an astounding 18,401 consecutive votes, placing him in the *Guinness Book of World Records* and earning him the Presidential Citizen's Medal.

Now, that's integrity and attention to duty!

1994: The Chunnel Connection. On May 6 Queen Elizabeth II and President François Mitterrand, along with numerous dignitaries, board the high-speed Eurostar passenger train and roll through the just-completed thirty-one-mile-long Channel Tunnel to Calais. They then return to Folkestone, England, in the queen's Rolls-Royce via one of the car-carrying trains, inaugurating the greatest engineering feat of the century, the Channel Tunnel.

The idea of a tunnel connecting the two nations had been proposed many times since the nineteenth century, but the engineering job seemed nearly impossible and relations between the two countries weren't always congenial. With modern construction methods and European unity, however, the idea became feasible, and in February 1986 the Channel Tunnel Treaty was signed by Britain and France. The construction was subcontracted to a consortium of British and French firms, and after three years of underground work, the two construction teams met in the middle, poked a hole in the dirt, and shook hands.

The Chunnel, as it is affectionately called, is built in ten-ton bomb-proof sections, 165 feet below sea level, and consists of three tunnels; two for trains and one running in between for service and repairs. Special equipment had to be built for the project, including the biggest drill in the world, which can cut through two thousand tons of rock per hour and is capable of boring out chunks of granite as large as a three-story house.

The fifteen-billion-dollar Chunnel, with main terminals at Waterloo Station in London, Gare du Nord in Paris, and Gare Centrale in Brussels, will facilitate travel between the countries. The ride through the tunnel takes but twenty-one minutes; London to Paris takes three hours. You can jump in your car and zip over to the coast of France for bread and wine, or conversely, have tea and crumpets on England's shores. Of course, it will cost you money; you have to pay for convenience.

1994: Compassionate Kids.
Friends of fifth grader Ian O'Gorman shave their heads so he won't feel out of place and be made fun of at school.

Ian decided to shave his head completely before undergoing chemotherapy treatments which would make his hair fall out in batches. His classmates at Lake Elementary School in Oceanside, California, elected to go bald, too, so Ian wouldn't stand out as different.

Just like the Three Musketeers, all for one and one for all!

1994: Black Holes Do Exist.
The Hubble telescope is paying its way. On May 25 scientists confirm the existence of black holes, those elusive areas in space in which a massive collapsing star pulls in all matter around it with such a powerful gravitational force that nothing can escape, including light.

Everything inside the black hole is trapped forever; time and space do not exist; it is invisible. We only know it is there by the detectable masses of energy surrounding it, waiting to be sucked into the maelstrom.

With the Hubble out there, who needs science fiction?

1994: Mandela Elected.
On May 9 Nelson Mandela, Nobel Peace Prize winner and leader of South Africa's African National Congress, is elected president of South Africa, defeating fellow Nobelist President F. W. de Klerk in South Africa's first all-race election. Apartheid, the rigid racial segregation policy that has wracked South Africa for so long, has ended and a new South Africa with equality for all has begun.

Mandela, born into a royal family of the Xhosa tribe in the Transkei, was brought up to rule as a future chief. He became a lawyer, however, and as a militant member of the African National Congress urged the nonviolent ANC to take up arms. The leadership refused but quietly encouraged Mandela to form a combative group which did partake in violence. In 1960 the government banned the ANC and in 1962 Mandela was arrested and later sentenced to life in prison, where he remained for twenty-seven years. As a political prisoner, Mandela became a symbol of all that was wrong with South Africa and an inspiration to black people. Apartheid slowly began to disintegrate while civil disobedience and black demonstrations gathered force. The ferociousness of the protests and the contravening police action were seen on television worldwide, leading to sanctions against the country and international outcries against apartheid.

In July 1989 President P. W. Botha met with Mandela, who had suggested a dialogue on the future of the country. The two pledged peace, and after Botha had relinquished his office to de Klerk, Mandela was released from prison and the ban on the ANC was removed. The task of abolishing apartheid completely and setting up a government of equality wasn't easy, and both sides needed to compromise. Finally it was decided that a majority-rule democratic government of national unity would be established with free elections.

The two leaders did their best for their country. It is now up to the citizens of South Africa to build a great nation of, by, and for all the people.

1994: The Washington Declaration. On July 25, a hot, sunny day in Washington, D.C., King Hussein of Jordan and Israeli prime minister Yitzhak Rabin sign an agreement ending a technical state of war between the two countries that has been in existence since 1948.

The two leaders agree to settle differences by peaceful means and to "bring an end to bloodshed and sorrow." According to King Hussein, the agreement will bring people "security from fear, which I must admit has prevailed over all the years of our lives," while Prime Minister Rabin looks forward with hope that "our children and grandchildren will know no more wars."

With the signing of the accord, a prelude to a formal peace treaty, economic development can now begin between the two

nations, border crossings will be opened, tourism will be enhanced, the police will cooperate with each other against smug-
glers and crime, and both nations agree not to allow their
respective countries to be used as bases for terrorist activities.

Another great step forward in the world of politics.

1994: A Cure for the Common Cold? Dr. Asim Dasgupta,
a University of California professor, accidentally discovers that
baker's yeast can stop the cold virus cold. At least in a lab dish.
A molecule in the genetic makeup of the yeast when intermingled
with human cells containing the virus prevents the cold virus from
reproducing itself. It also seems to prevent replication of the hepa-
titis A, and polio virus, but unfortunately doesn't affect the flu
bug. It will be a few years before human testing begins, but if it
works, and there are no or minimal side effects, at the sign of the
first sniffles we may soon be spraying our noses and throats with
a new medication and never have to advance to the coughing,
sneezing, aching, scratchy throat stage.

Don't start gulping plain old baker's yeast, though. The lab has
to perform its wizardry to purify and concentrate the little molecule before it can work its magic.

1995: More Union Members. On January 1, Austria, Finland,
and Sweden join the European Union increasing the total number
of countries in the Common Market to fifteen. They join the six
other countries that have joined the European Economic Community since its original inception in 1957: Great Britain, Spain,
Portugal, Ireland, Greece and Denmark.

2000+: Fusion in Our Future. Power plants of the future
are driven by nuclear fusion as scientists overcome the technical
difficulties involved.

In fusion, two nuclei of light atoms join together at high temperature to form the nucleus of a heavier atom plus an extra
neutron, during which tremendous energy is released. Scientists
use two isotopes of hydrogen, deuterium (containing one proton
and one neutron) and tritium (containing one proton and two
neutrons), in this process. The tritium and deuterium fuse in a
reactor under temperatures that reach four hundred million degrees Celsius and turn into a plasma or cloud of electrically charged
particles.

Eventually we will run out of coal and oil as well as uranium and plutonium, which now power nuclear plants. Fusion seems to be the answer to the world's energy problems. It produces no pollutants and only minute amounts of radioactive waste, which decays quickly. Hydrogen supplies are virtually inexhaustible.

Scientists at Princeton University are currently working with experimental reactors to create efficient and continuous power. Another giant step for humankind is in the making.

SELECTED BIBLIOGRAPHY

Botermans, Burrett, Van Delft, Van Splunteren. *The World of Games*. New York: Facts on File, 1987.

Boyer, Carl B. *A History of Mathematics*. New York: John Wiley & Sons, Inc., 1991.

Brennan, Richard P. *Dictionary of Scientific Literacy*. New York: John Wiley & Sons Inc., 1992

Cook, S. A., ed. *The Cambridge Ancient History*. *Vol. IX*. Cambridge: Cambridge University Press, 1951.

Cubberley, Ellwood P. *The History of Education*. Boston: Houghton Mifflin Co., 1920, Rev. 1948.

Cumston, C. G. *An Introduction to the History of Medicine*. New York: Dorset Press, 1987.

Daniel, Clifton, ed. *Chronicle of the Twentieth Century*. Mt. Kisco: Chronicle Publications, Inc. 1987.

De Bono, Edward, ed. *Eureka! An Illustrated History of Inventions from the Wheel to the Computer*. New York: Holt, Rinehart and Winston, 1974.

Encyclopedia Britannica. Various volumes. Chicago: Encyclopedia Britannica, Inc., Wm. Benton, Pub., 1970.

Evening Standard. London: May 5, 1994 edition.

Flexner, Stuart Berg. *I Hear America Talking*. New York: Van Nostrand Reinhold, 1976.

Flexner, Stuart Berg. *Listening to America*. New York: Simon and Schuster, 1982.

Gibney, Frank, ed. *Britannica Book of Music*. Garden City: Doubleday & Company, 1980.

Giscard d'Estaing, Valérie-Anne. *The World Almanac Book of Inventions*. New York: World Almanac Publications, 1985.

Goulding, Phil G. *Classical Music*. New York: Fawcett Columbine, 1992.

Greenfield, Jeff. *Television: The First Fifty Years*. New York: Harry N. Abrams, Inc., 1977.

Gurko, Miriam. *The Ladies of Seneca Falls*. New York: Schocken Books, 1974.

Larsen, Egon. *A History of Invention*. New York: Roy Publishers, 1961.

Magill, Frank N., ed. *Great Lives from History*. Various Series. Englewood Cliffs: Salem Press, Inc., 1987–1990.

MacGowan, Kenneth, and Melnitz, William. *The Living Stage. A History of the World Theater*. Englewood Cliffs: Prentice Hall, Inc., 1955.

Mount, Ellis, and List, Barbara A. *Milestones in Science and Technology*. Phoenix: Oryx Press, 1987.

Nuland, Sherwin B. *Doctors—The Biography of Medicine*. New York: Vintage Books, 1988.

Ohles, John N., ed. *Biographical Dictionary of American Educators*. Westport: Greenwood Press, 1978.

Panati, Charles. *Panati's Browser's Book of Beginnings*. Boston: Houghton Mifflin Co., 1984.

Panati, Charles. *Panati's Extraordinary Origins of Everyday Things*. New York: Harper & Row, 1987.

Robbin, Irving, and Nisenson, Samuel. *Giants of Medicine*. New York: Grosset & Dunlap, 1962.

Ronan, Colin A. *Science—Its History and Development Among World Cultures*. New York: The Hamlyn Pub. Group Ltd., 1982.

Strayer, Joseph, ed. *Dictionary of the Middle Ages*. New York: Charles Scribner's Sons, 1982–4.

Toll, Robert C. *On With the Show*. New York: Oxford University Press, 1976.

Trager, James. *The People's Chronology*. New York: Henry Holt & Co., 1992.

Waldman, Carl. *Who Was Who in Native American History*. New York: Facts on File, 1990.

Wetterau, Bruce. *The New York Public Library Book of Chronologies*. New York: The Stonesong Press and The New York Public Library, 1990.

World Book Encyclopedia. Chicago: Field Enterprises, 1952.

TIMELINE OF EVENTS

Architecture and Engineering Feats

Ca. 2600 B.C. The Pyramids of Giza, 20

Ca. 772 B.C. Temple of Artemis, 26

6th Century B.C. Hanging Gardens of Babylon, 26–27

438 B.C. The Parthenon Completed, 30–31

280 B.C. The Colossus of Rhodes, 32

214 B.C. Great Wall of China Begins, 32

19 B.C. The Pont du Gard, 34

121 The Pantheon, 37

Ca. 766 Baghdad on the Tigris, 41

1065 Westminster Abbey Consecrated, 45–46

12th Century Beginnings of Gothic Architecture, 47

1150 Angkor Wat, 48

1174 Leaning Tower of Pisa, 51

1260 Chartres Cathedral Consecrated, 56

1345 Notre Dame Completed, 58

1354 The Alhambra, 58

1436 The Duomo is Consecrated, 60

1446 Blarney Castle Completed, 61

1525 Low-Rent Housing, 72–73

1561 St. Basil's Cathedral Completed, 75

1574 Uffizi Palace Completed, 76

1587 Isfahan, 80

1624 Louvre Palace Completed, 92–93

1627 The Forbidden City, 93–94

264

1654 The Taj Mahal, 98

1675 The New St. Paul's Cathedral Begins, 99–100

1725 The Spanish Steps, 103

1790 Washington, D.C. Planned, 121

1826 Menai Strait Bridge Completed, 136–37

1833 The Balloon Frame House, 138

1851 London's Crystal Palace, 149–50

1852 Mr. Otis's Elevator, 150

1853 Private Baths, 151

1855 The Parker House, 153

1855 Niagara Bridge, 153

1863 The London Underground, 157

1873 Cable Cars, 166

1874 We Bridge the Mississippi, 167

1877 Low-Rent Housing, 170

1880 Cologne Cathedral Completed, 171

1882 St. Gothard Tunnel, 172

1883 The Brooklyn Bridge, 172

1885 The First Skyscraper, 172–73

1889 The Eiffel Tower, 175

1889 The Savoy Hotel, 176

1913 Higher and Larger, 195

1916 The Imperial Hotel, 198

1925 The Motel, 207

1931 New Delhi, 211

1931 The Empire State Building, 211–12

1937 Fallingwater, 214–15

1943 The Pentagon, 218

1947 Levittowns, 223

1950 Automatic Elevator Doors, 227

1959 The Guggenheim Museum, 234–35

1960 Brasilia, 235

1964 Verrazano Narrows Bridge, 240

1967 Habitat Apartments, 240

1971 Aswan High Dam Completed, 243

1973 The Sears Tower, 245

1975 The Great Uhuru Railway, 246

1981 The Humber Bridge, 247

1994 The Chunnel Connection, 257–58

The Arts

50 Thousand Years Ago The Theater Begins?, 7–9

Ca. 850 B.C. The *Iliad* and the *Odyssey*, 24–25

5th Century B.C. Herodotus, 29

Ca. 518–438 B.C. Pindar, 29

Ca. 460–404 B.C. Thucydides, 29

458 B.C. The Oresteia Trilogy, 30

Ca. 430 B.C. Statue of Zeus, 31

411 B.C. Aristophanes Presents Lysistrata, 31

70 B.C. to A.D. 18 Three Giants of Poetry, 33–34

Ca. 500 Grammar, 39

731 English Chronicles, 40–41

Ca. 1000 Beowulf, 43

11th to 16th Centuries Miracles, Mysteries & Moralities, 43–45

1010 The Book of Kings, 45

1123 Omar Khayyam Dies, 47–48

Ca. 1170 Arthurian Romances, 50

1307 The Divine Comedy, 57

1384 The Flourishing of No Theater, 59

1400 The Canterbury Tales, 59–60

Ca. 1507 La Gioconda, 69–70

1508 Michelangelo Tackles the Sistine Chapel, 70

Ca. 1550 The Theater Stages a Comeback, 75

1576 England's First Theater, 76

1581 Ballet Comique de la Reyne, 76–78

1586 Kabuki Theater, 79–80

1587 Tamburlaine, 80–81

Ca. 1591 Shakespeare Treads the Boards, 81–82

1597 A New Art Form Begins, 85

1599 The Globe Theater Built, 85–86

1621–1665 King Philip IV, the Ultimate Angel, 92

1623 Shakespeare's First Folio, 92

1642 Rembrandt Paints *Night Watch*, 96

1658 Molière Turns Defeat into Triumph, 98

1660 It's Comedy Tonight!, 98–99

1660s Revising Shakespeare, 99

1685 Bach is Born, 100

1762 Mozart Mesmerizes Maria, 107–108

1795 Beethoven's Vienna Debut, 125

1822 Franz Liszt Debuts in Vienna, 135–36

1830 Chopin's Concert, 137–38

1843 *A Christmas Carol*, 141–42

1845 Juba's Jig, 143

1860 *The Woman in White*, 155

1866 Musical Comedy Germinates, 160–61

1871 *Thespis* Opens in London, 166

1885 Marie Lloyd Debuts, 174

1896 We Put Motion in Pictures, 180

1903 The Great Train Robbery, 187

1904 The Yankee Doodle Boy, 188

1911 Keystone Company Founded, 191–92

1913 The Little Tramp, 196

1916 Griffith's Masterpiece, 198

Ca. 1918 The Jazz Age Begins, 199–200

1927 *Showboat* Opens, 207–208

1928 Bojangles on Broadway, 208

1928 Mickey Mouse is Born, 208

1932 "The Jack Benny Show," 212

1933 Movies Outdoors, 214

1938 Bob Hope on the Air, 215–16

1948 The Dawn of a New Entertainment Age, 225

1950 "Your Show of Shows" Debuts, 227–28

1951 "I Love Lucy," 228

1954 The Birthday Present, 229–30

1960 John, Paul, Ringo & George Debut, 235–36

Discoveries

1845 Ancient Nineveh Discovered, 142

1856 Neanderthal Man Discovered, 153

1868 Cro-Magnon Man Discovered, 161

1870 Schliemann's Dig, 162–63

1900 Knossos Revealed, 182

1912 The Piltdown Man, 193

1922 Ur Uncovered, 203

1922 Tut's Tomb, 203–204

1974 Lucy: Mother of Us All?, 245–45

Education

3000 B.C. Early Schools, 18–19

2500 B.C. Higher Learning, 21

Ca. 11th Century Medical School, 42

11th Century Law School, 42–43

1249 Universities Begin in England, 53–54

1253 The Sorbonne Founded, 54–55

16th Century Native Tongues Begin to Babble, 65–66

1636 Four Hundred Pounds for a Colledge, 94–95

1642 Compulsory Education, 96

1760 School for the Deaf, 106

1769 Dartmouth College; Private Means Private, 113

1781 Pestalozzi Publishes, 116–17

1784 School for the Blind, 118

1789 University of North Carolina Chartered, 120

1796–1859 Horace Mann, the Father of American Public Education, 126

1800 Library of Congress Established, 128

1811 Special Education, 131–32

1819 Plan for Improving Female Education, 133–34

1821 High School, 135

1829 Braille, 137

1837 Kindergartens, 140

1859–1952 John Dewey, 154–55

1881 Booker T. Washington Heads Tuskegee Institute, 171–72

Everyday Things

40 Million Years Ago Cats, 4

Ca. 12,000 B.C. Man's Best Friend, 9

Ca. 6 Thousand Years Ago Cosmetics, 11–12

Ca. 3000 B.C. On Pins and Needles, 17–18

11th Century Forks Introduced in Tuscany, 43

Ca. 1280–1286 Eyeglasses Invented, 56–57

13th Century The Buttonhole Devised, 52

1498 Chinese Invent the Toothbrush, 64–65

16th Century Pencils and Pens, 66–67

1596 The Water Closet, 83–84

1681 Matches Invented, 100–101

1762 The Safety Razor, 106–107

1857 Toilet Paper Packaged, 153–54

1874 The Typewriter, 166–67

1876 Rules of Order, 168

1876 The Dewey Decimal System, 168

1883 Time Zones Adopted, 172

Ca. 1900 The Paper Clip, 182

1901 Fingerprint Classification Introduced, 182–93

1905 A Permanent Wave, 189

1908 Portable Vacuum Cleaners, 190–91

1909 The Toaster, 191

1913 The Refrigerator, 194–95

1914 Traffic Signals, 197

1914 Air-Conditioning Arrives, 197

1916 The Supermarket, 198

1921 Band-Aids, 201–202

1923 Work Hours Reduced, 206

1924 Disposable Tissues Marketed, 206

1939 Automatic Washers & Dryers, 216

1947 Microwave Oven Invented, 222

Explorations and Discoveries

Ca. 800 B.C. Phoenicians, the Great Traders, 25

Ca. 600 B.C. Africa Circumnavigated, 26

Ca. 500 B.C. Carthaginians Explore West Coast of Africa, 28

Ca. 300 B.C. Tales of India, 31

Ca. 300 B.C. Explorations of Pytheas, 31–32

Ca. 200 Ptolemy's Geography, 38

8th Century Scandinavians Explore and Settle, 40

Ca. 1245–Ca. 1324 The Adventures of Marco Polo, 55–56

Ca. 1394–1460 Prince Henry of Portugal, 59

1492 Columbus Discovers the New World, 62–63

1497–99 Vasco da Gama Rounds Africa, 64

1500 Amazon River Discovered, 68–69

1513 Ponce de León Discovers Florida, 70–71

1513 Balboa Discovers the Pacific Ocean, 71

1519–21 First Circumnavigation of the Globe, 71–72

1540–42 Coronado Explores the Southwest, 73

1541 De Soto Discovers the Mississippi, 73–74

1570 First World Atlas Published, 76

1577–80 Sir Francis Drake Sails Around the World, 76

1607 Jamestown Settled, 88–89

1609 Hudson Explores River, 89

1678–82 La Salle Claims Louisiana Territory, 100

1741 Alaska Discovered, 104

1768–79 Captain Cook's Voyages, 109–10

1770 British Claim Australia, 113–14

1793 MacKenzie Explores Canada, 124–25

1804–06 Lewis and Clark Expedition, 131

1821 Antarctica at Last, 134

1871 Stanley and Livingstone, 163–65

1871–88 Central Asia Explored, 165–66

1898–1923 Rocket Pioneers, 181–82

1909 Peary Reaches the North Pole, 191

1911 The Race for the South Pole, 193

1957 The Space Age Begins, 234

1958 The North Pole via Submarine, 234

1960 The Sky Above, the Sea Below, 235

1961 First Man in Space, 238

1961 First American in Space, 238

1962 Outward Bound, 238

1963 Spacewoman, 239

1968 The Impossible Dream, 241

1969 The *Eagle* Has Landed, 241–42

1971 First Space Station, 244

1981 The Space Shuttle, 247–48

1983 First Female Astronaut, 248

Food, Drink, and Clothing

1 Million Years Ago Clothing, 5–7

Ca. 10 Thousand Years Ago Our Daily Bread, 9–10

4000 B.C. Beer is Brewed, 13–14

4000 B.C. Wine Making Established, 14–15

Ca. 2000 B.C. Ice Cream, 21–22

Ca. 200 B.C. No More Two Left Feet, 32

16th Century High Heels, 67

16th Century Doughnuts, 67–68

17th Century Pockets, 86

Ca. 1690 Bustles and Hoops, 101

18th Century Off-the-Rack, 102

1819 Chocolate Bar Invented, 133

1850 Jeans, Levi's, Overalls and Dungarees, 148–49

1853 Potato Chips, 151

1854 The Mortarboard, 152

1886 Soda Pop, 174–175

Ca. 1896 Fudge, 179

Ca. 1904 Hamburger on a Bun, 187–88

1904 Banana Split Created, 188

1906 Hot Dog! 189–90

1921 Chanel No. 5 Introduced, 202

1925 Frozen Foods, 206–207

Ca. 1930 Chocolate Chip Cookies, 210–11

1940 Nylon Stockings, 216–17

1946 The Bikini, 222

1959 Panty Hose Introduced, 235

1965 Miniskirt Madness, 240

Inventions and Technology

2 Million Years Ago We Make Tools, 5

1.5 Million–500 Thousand Years Ago Homo Erectus, 5

100 Thousand Years Ago Homo Sapiens, 7

Ca. 8000 B.C. We Learn to Weave, 10–11

Ca. 4000 B.C. The Solar Calendar, 12–13

4000 B.C. We Develop Writing, 15–16

Ca. 3500 B.C. The Wheel, 16–17

3500 B.C. Bronze Discovered, 17

Ca. 3000 B.C. The Abacus, 20

Ca. 2600 B.C. Weights and Balances, 21

Ca. 2500 B.C. Egyptians Produce Papyrus, 21

Ca. 2000 B.C. Glass Discovered, 22–23

Ca. 1400 B.C. Time Drips By, 23

105 The Art of Paper Making, 36–37

Ca. 1440 The Gutenberg Press, 60–61

1600 We Discover Electricity, 86–87

1642 The Adding Machine, 97

1769 The Steam Engine, 111–13

1787 Fitch's Folly, 119

1804 The Steam Locomotive, 129–30

1866 Transatlantic Cable, 160

1876 The Telephone, 168–69

1879 We Light Up the World, 170–71

1885 The Automobile, 173–74

1889 The Birth of the Movies, 175–76

1903 The Airplane, 186–87

1947 The Transistor, 224

1949 The Computer Age, 226–27

1973 UPC, 245

1976 Supersonic Airliner, 246

Just Plain Fun

Ca. 4 Million Years Ago This Thing Called Love, 4–5

Ca. 10th Century Fireworks, 41–42

1769 The Circus, 110–11

1825 Carousels & Merry-go-Rounds, 136

1893 First Ferris Wheel Rides, 178

1919 Two National Parks, 200

1955 Disneyland Opens, 231

Laws and Human Rights

Ca. 1750 B.C. Code of Hammurabi, 23

Ca. 590 B.C. The Reforms of Solon, 27

313 Edict of Milan, 38

1086 The Domesday Book, 47

1215 Magna Carta, 52–53

1517 Ninety-five Theses, 71

1534 Act of Supremacy, 73

1598 The Edict of Nantes, 85

1620 Mayflower Compact, 92

1628 Petition of Right, 94

1776 Declaration of Independence, 115

1787 The Constitution, 118–19

1789 The Rights of Man, 120–21

1791 The Bill of Rights, 122

1789–91 First Constitutional Amendment, 122–23

1789–91 Amendments II and III to the Constitution, 124

1804 Napoleonic Code, 130

1848 The Convention at Seneca Falls, 146–47

1860 Married Women's Property Acts, 155

1862 The Homestead Act, 157

1862 Emancipation Proclamation, 157

1865 Thirteenth Amendment Ratified, 159–60

1869 Wyoming Women Vote, 161

1870 The Fifteenth Amendment, 162

1906 Equal Suffrage in Finland, 190

1913 The Sixteenth Constitutional Amendment, 196

1920 Prohibition, 200–201

1920 Nineteenth Amendment Ratified, 201

1921 Sweden Abolishes Capital Punishment, 203

1924 Native Americans Declared Citizens, 206

1931 Statute of Westminster, 211

1934 Indian Reorganization Act, 214

1935 Social Security Act, 214

1938 Fair Labor Standards Act, 215

1942 Ethiopia Abolishes Slavery, 217

1944 The GI Bill of Rights, 220

1948 Armed Forces Desegregated, 225

1948 Universal Declaration of Human Rights, 225–26

1954 Brown v. Board of Education, 230–31

1960 The Sit-In, 237

1964 The Civil Rights Act, 239

1986 The Rod is Spared, 249–50

1989 Restitution, 251

1989 Fall of the Berlin Wall, 251–52

1990 Smoking Ban, 252

1990 A Good Act to Follow, 252

1990 A Reversal of Heart, 252

1991 Population Registration Act Repealed, 253

Medicine

Ca. 460–377 B.C. Hippocrates, 29–30

1st Century A.D. Celsus, 34–35

Ca. 50 De Materia Medica, 35

130–200 Galen, 37–38

1493–1541 Paracelsus, 64

Ca. 1545 Artificial Limbs Designed, 74

1590 The Microscope, 81

1596 Thermometer Invented, 83

1597 Plastic Surgery Textbook, 84

1619 Harvey's Discoveries, 91–92

1789 Dentures, 119–20

1796 Smallpox Vaccination, 126–27

1816 The Stethoscope, 132

1820 Quinine Isolated, 134

1846 Anesthesia, 144–45

1849 First Medical Degree to a Woman, 148

1851 Ophthalmoscope, 150

1853 Take Two Aspirin . . . , 150–51

1861 Pasteur's Germ Theory, 156–57

1865 Antiseptic Surgery, 159

1869 DNA Discovered, 161

1890 Tetanus Vaccine, 176

1895 X Rays Developed, 178–79

1901 Blood Types Discovered, 183–84

1903 Electrocardiograph Invented, 184–85

1904 Novocain, 188

1911 *Vitamines* Introduced, 192–93

1912 Tying Up Loose Ends, 194

1922 Insulin, 205

1926 Morgan's Gene Theory, 207

1928 Iron Lung Invented, 208

1928 Penicillin Discovered, 208–209

1932 Cardiac Pacemaker, 212–13

1932 Sulfa Drugs Discovered, 213

1933 The Incubator, 213–14

1937 Antihistamine Discovered, 215

1944 Kidney Dialysis Machine, 218–19

1944 Blue-Baby Surgery, 220–21

1944 Streptomycin Developed, 221

1952 Transistorized Hearing Aids, 228

1953 Heart–Lung Machine, 228

1953 The Double Helix, 228–29

1954 A Successful Kidney Transplant, 230

1955 Chlorothiazide Discovered, 232

1955 Polio Vaccine, 232–33

1960s Laser Surgery, 236–37

1960 The Pill, 237–38

1967 Heart Transplants Pioneered, 240–41

1971 CAT Scan, 243–44

1972 Artificial Hip Designed, 244–45

1977 Magnetic Resonance Imaging, 246–47

1978 A Test-Tube Baby, 247

1983 Barbara McClintock, Nobelist at Last, 248–49

1989 The Human Genome Project, 250–51

1994 A Cure for the Common Cold?, 260

People, Heroes, Legends and Just Plain Folks

Ca. 1372 B.C. The Exquisite Nefertiti, 23

551–479 B.C. Confucius, 27

5th Century B.C. Aspasia, 28

52 B.C. Vercingetorix, 34

60 Queen Boudica Strikes, 36

Ca. 1057 Godiva's Guileless Gallop, 45

1152 The Magnificent Eleanor, 48–50

Ca. 1378 Robin Hood, 58–59

Ca. 1483 A Shropshire Lad, 61–62

1835–1919 Andrew Carnegie, a Self-Made Man, 138–39

1841 Westward Ho!, 140–41

1845 Narrative of the Life of Frederick Douglass, an American Slave, 142–43

1849 A Modern-Day Moses, 147–48

1861 Mary Walker Volunteers, 155–56

1864 Dunant's Good Deeds, 158

1903 Emmeline Pankhurst and the WSPU, 185–86

1913 A Hospital in Lambaréné, 195–96

1916 Margaret Sanger Opens Clinic, 199

1922 Nansen Awarded Nobel Peace Prize, 205

1928 Volunteer Rescue Squads, 209

1929 The Seeing Eye, Inc., 210

1942 Super Secret Code, 217–18

1944 Wallenberg's Mission, 219–20

1953 Mt. Everest Conquered, 229

1955 Rosa Parks Sits and Stays, 233

1963 Martin Luther King Jr., Has a Dream, 239

1970 Hale House Founded, 243

1971 Doctors Without Borders, 244

1979 Mother Teresa Awarded Nobel Peace Prize, 247

1994 A Repeat Disaster Averted, 256–57

1994 A Political Phenomenon, 257

1994 Compassionate Kids, 258

Politics, Wars, and Treaties

510 B.C. The Roman Republic, 27–28

458 B.C. Cincinnatus, 30

43 Londinium Founded, 35

1066 The Battle of Hastings, 46–47

Ca. 1500 The Iroquois League, 68

1626 Manhattan Island Purchased, 93

1648 Treaty of Westphalia, 97

1713 Treaty of Utrecht, 103

1776 Common Sense, 115

1783 Treaty of Paris, 118

1791 The Whiskey Rebellion, 121–22

1803 The Louisiana Purchase, 129

1817 Rush-Bagot Treaty, 133

1821 Mexican Independence, 134

1846 The Oregon Treaty, 145–46

1848 Treaty of Guadalupe Hidalgo, 146

1918 Wilson's Fourteen Points, 200

1925 Locarno Pact, 207

1929 Kellogg-Briand Pact Proclaimed, 210

1941 Atlantic Charter, 217

1945 Germany Surrenders, 221–22

1945 The United Nations, 222

1947 The Truman Doctrine, 222–23

1948–52 The Marshall Plan, 224

1948–49 Berlin Airlift, 224–25

1957 European Common Market, 233–34

1959 We Become Fifty, 234

1963 Nuclear Test-Ban Treaty, 239

1989 Czechoslovakia Breaks Communist Yoke, 252

1991 Yeltsin Elected, 252

1991 The End of an Era, 253

1993 Middle East Peace Try, 253–55

1994 Mandela Elected, 258–59

1994 The Washington Declaration, 259–60

1995 More Union Members, 260

Science, Math, and Astronomy

15 Billion Years Ago, More or Less The Beginning, 1–2

Ca. 4.5 Billion Years Ago The Earth, 2

Ca. 4.5 Billion Years Ago The Moon, 2–3

Ca. 3.5 Billion Years Ago Life, 3

Ca. 228 Million Years Ago Dionsaurs, 3–4

Ca. 3500 B.C. The First Numbers, 17

Ca. 5 Thousand Years Ago Egyptian numbers, 20

6th Century B.C. Greek Numbers, 26

Ca. 400 B.C. Atomic Theory of Democritus, 31

Ca. 250 Algebraic Notation, 38

Ca. 680–750 Al-Khwarizmi, Mathematician, 40

1202 Zero, 52

1489 Plus or Minus, 63

1543 A Revolutionary Idea, 74

1546–1601 Tycho Brahe, Astronomer, 75

1557 The Equal Sign, 75

1582 The Gregorian Calendar, 78–79

1585 The Decimal System, 79

1596–1650 René Descartes, 82–83

1609 Astronomical Theories, 89

1610 Galileo's Universe, 89–91

1614 Logarithms, 91

1642–1727 Sir Isaac Newton, 95–96

1642 The Adding Machine, 97

1705 A Comet Named Halley, 102–103

1737 Mathematical Pi, 103–104

1768 Spontaneous Generation Debunked, 108–109

1774 Priestly Discovers Oxygen, 114–15

1781 Uranus Discovered, 115–16

1783 Lavoisier's Chemistry, 117–18

1799 The Metric System Fixed, 127–28

1846 The Smithsonian Founded, 144

1849 Speed of Light, 147

1858 A New Theory, 154

1858 The Basic Cell, 154

1859 The Origin of Species, 155

1863 National Academy of Sciences, 158

1865 Mendel's Law, 159

1890 Java Man, 176

1897 Electrons Discovered, 180

1898 Radium Discovered, 180–81

1900 The Quantum Theory, 182

1915 Einstein's Theory of Relativity, 197–98

1930 Pluto Discovered, 211

1940 The Electron Microscope, 216

1947 Carbon Dating, 223

1967 Pulsars Discovered, 240

1993 We Do the Impossible, 255–56

1994 In a Galaxy Far, Far Away, 257

1994 Black Holes Do Exist, 258

2000+ Fusion in Our Future, 260–61

Sports, Games, and Toys

Ca. 4000 B.C. Fun and Games, 15

Ca. 4 Thousand Years Ago Dice Games, 21

Ca. 3000 B.C. Dolls, Dolls, Dolls, 19

Ca. 3 Thousand Years Ago Marbles, 24

776 B.C. The Olympic Games, 25

Ca. 2,500 Years Ago Spinning Tops, 28

Ca. 2 Thousand Years Ago Hopscotch, 33

6th Century The Noble Game of Chess, 38–39

7th Century Playing Cards, 39–40

1174 The Sport of Kings, 50–51

13th Century Checkers, 51–52

Ca. 1457 The Game of Golf, 61

1603 Football, 87–88

18th Century Dominoes, 101–102

1744 Baseball, 104–105

1759 Roller Skates, 105–106

Ca. 1855 Ice Hockey, 152

1863 Soccer, 157–58

Ca. 1874 Lawn Tennis, 167–68

1891 Basketball, 177–78

1896 The Modern Olympics, 179–80

1903 The Teddy Bear, 184

1906 The Forward Pass, 190

1913 The Crossword Puzzle, 195

1915 The Babe, 198

1921 Basketball Is On the Air, 203

1921 World Series Broadcast, 203

1931 Scrabble Invented, 212

1933 The Game of Monopoly, 213

1947 Jackie Robinson Signed by Dodgers, 223–24

1956 Perfect Pitch, 233

1957 Frisbees, More or Less, 233

1958 Baseball on the Move, 234

1958 The Barbie Doll, 234

1961 A Record Season, 238

1974 A New Record, 245

1985 Baseball Career Record, 249

About the Author

DORIS FLEXNER is a native New Yorker, was a California advertising executive, a Connecticut wife, mother and part-time editor, and is now, much to her amazement, a writer in North Carolina. She has always been an optimist.